MAHE & MANO

Mahe & Mano

Challenges, Resilience, and Triumphs

MANOHAR DEVADOSS

ALEPH

ALEPH

ALEPH BOOK COMPANY
An independent publishing firm
promoted by *Rupa Publications India*

First published in India in 2021
by Aleph Book Company
7/16 Ansari Road, Daryaganj
New Delhi 110 002

ISBN: 978-81-949372-4-1

1 3 5 7 9 10 8 6 4 2

To,
My grandsons,
Aniketan Raphael Pelletier
and
Ethan Masilamani Pelletier

CONTENTS

FOREWORD

Creation shields within its coffers, not only the rarest of stones like diamonds, but precious gems of human beings. Among those rarest of gems are Mahe and Mano and the story of their eventful life amidst ordeals is sure to enter into the annals of Chennai. If one desires to learn the art of living, loving, and giving with grace, a reference to the lives of Mahe–Mano is mandatory. In this millennium, when marriage has descended to a mere coexistence of convenience, this special couple could teach all humanity how to live, savouring every shade and hue of the manifold strands of pleasure and pain, and converting the chance of being together as husband and wife at home into an artistic experience rather than a mechanical coexistence.

Even today, Mano teaches everyone whom he meets, how to translate pain into joy and convert even the physical labour of nursing an immobile companion into one of joyous sharing. Their indomitable will helped them metamorphose the twin challenges—the failing vision of Mano and the quadriplegia of Mahe—into a life of ebullience, fellowship, benevolence, and creativity.

From their book of life, there are lessons to cherish about what it means to treasure the kinship with all those whom we meet in our lives, besides our blood relations. Fellowship yields unceasing reverberations of great experiences, and this noble couple related with everyone, irrespective of age, gender, caste, or class. Since there was perfect harmony in their being, they have always been able to strike a friendly chord even with strangers.

Living means sharing, and Mano is proud to announce that the latent benevolence in him was kindled by a similar spark in Mahema. Besides their unquestioning acceptance of each other with their limitations, they were ever willing to walk an extra mile in extending their time, warmth, delicious food, and even their hard-earned money, to those who needed them most. Mano's various trusts in the schools and colleges he studied and two important eye hospitals, Sankara Nethralaya (Chennai) and Aravind (Madurai) are extraordinary gestures, by any standards. They gave what they needed most, and in donating her eyes, Mahema continued to give, even after her death.

Their harmonious togetherness unleashed the artistic and creative writing skills dormant in Manohar Devadoss. The collection of Mano's paintings in Indian ink is awe-inspiring, and equally astounding is the prolific writing that has flowed from his pen. In this book, Mano enters the being of Mahe and presents in his vivid, lucid, dramatic, conversational, and humorous way how the spirit of Mahe made him what he has been when she was with him and what he has become, continuing his journey with her in his memory, still giving wherever and whenever possible.

Let us delve into this rich treasure trove to feast our senses, sharpen our wit, sober our spirits, and ennoble our inner selves.

Dr Geetha Ravi[*]

---

[*]Dr Geetha Ravi completed her doctoral work on African-American Literature. Her inter-genre study on the impact of African-American music on literature fetched her the prestigious National Award for the Best Doctoral Thesis from ASRC, Hyderabad, in 1994.

1

Mahema looked like an early morning, serene pond. She wore an elegant cotton sari with a profusion of jasmine in her hair. It was the morning of our ninth wedding anniversary—just two days after Christmas in 1972. Our gleaming, slender-stemmed, five-wick kuthu-vilakku, stood patiently on the dining table. After saying a brief prayer thanking God for all the blessings that were being showered upon our family, she lit the five wicks of the lamp with a small lit candle—I symbolically kept my fingers on the candle.

We then went back into our room. She read to me a beautiful anniversary note that she had written for me and gave me her surprise gift—a leather purse that she had bought in Madrid. I had given her the pale olive-green Kanjeevaram sari with a blue shot and a delicate jarigai that we had chosen together a week earlier, so that there was sufficient time for her to stitch a blouse. I also gave her a single sheet of paper in which I had drawn a few bold ink drawings of some European sculptures and architecture with just one sentence: 'Dreams came true, dear.'

She then gave me a passionate kiss. I was not surprised. Nine years of married life had not in the least diminished her passion for me.

We returned to the dining room for breakfast. Just then I saw the helper placing the kuthu-vilakku on a windowsill and walking away. I told her to take away the lamp from the sill as the curtain might catch fire. But before she did, a sudden gust of wind billowed out the curtain like a sail and the slender kuthu-vilakku fell and broke into two. But amazingly, all the five flames continued to burn. The viscous coconut oil of the winter morning had more or less held the wicks in position.

Our common cousin Satya was getting married two days later on the 29th. While she was pursuing a PhD at Purdue University in the US, she fell in love with a fellow-researcher, a Swede named Lars. Their wedding was to be solemnized at Wesley Church in Madras. Mahe decided to wear the anniversary sari along with some of her own simple wedding jewels for the wedding reception.

After breakfast, Mahe, my mother, my daughter, Sujatha, and I went to the bride's house. Mahema stayed overnight with the bride, while the rest of us returned home in the evening.

On Satya's wedding day, Mahema drew a small rangoli inside our room, took an oil bath and went to the wedding house where she drew an elaborate rangoli, much to the joy of the Swedish family members of the bridegroom.

After we returned home, I pushed our double cot to one side, spread a jamakaalam with a pair of pillows on the floor and strategically placed half-a-dozen lit candles on small brass dishes. I placed Debu Chaudhuri's sitar recital in the cassette player, switched it on and waited for Mahe. After handing over our sleeping daughter to my mother, Mahema entered our room, bolted the door and stood quietly on the little rangoli. In the soft golden light shed by the candles, her sari appeared more gorgeous and her jewels, more exquisite. I thought that she looked lovelier than ever before—the beautiful girl I married had blossomed into a lovely woman. I untied her kondai and her hair tumbled loose. The jasmine charam that she wore in her hair fell on the rangoli. I untied her sari and undressed her completely and led her to the jamakaalam and laid her down. She took off her dollaks, let them roll down on the floor like a pair of dice and closed her eyes. The oil bath made her hair fragrant and luxurious. Her skin was more smooth and supple. She was thirty-two but she appeared more like she was twenty-three—her age when she became my bride.

After about an hour she fell asleep, exhausted. I lay silently looking at my dear sleeping wife. The cassette player had become quiet by then. I could hear the rustle of the neem leaves. Her flawless skin shone like gold in the yellow candlelight. The mangalyam pendant rose and fell, rose and fell. Hypnotized by the gentle movements of her bosom, I too fell asleep.

I woke up to the sound of Mahe's tinkling laughter. It was four in the morning and the candles had all burnt out but she had switched on the night lamp.

She said, 'I felt cold and I put on my nightgown. I wanted to get a bedsheet to cover myself. So, I switched on the light. When I looked around, I couldn't help but laugh.'

I saw what she meant. The wilted jasmine charam lay on the now smeared rangoli. Her necklace, dollaks, and bangles shimmered softly across the floor.

The six yards of the gorgeous sari lay coiled in a pile at the foot of the jamakaalam and her undergarments, all hooks and laces, were scattered all over.

I laughed and said, 'One would think, Mahe, that an orgy had taken place here.'

She countered happily, 'It did, didn't it?'

We had set the alarm at 4.30 a.m. Now it was 4.10. We might as well start getting ready for the journey to Madurai.

It was pitch dark at 5.45 in the morning, when my mother, my daughter, Sujatha, Mahema, and I gathered by our new Herald car. My elder brother, Divakar, was a professor of chemistry at American College in Madurai. Divakar went to the US in 1962. He had married Mary, an American woman, fifteen years younger than him, and had settled down in Madurai. From the time he was a boy, Divakar had had a soft corner for the old world Hollywood heroines. I often teased my brother saying that he had fallen for Mary because she vaguely resembled Ginger Rogers.

I was looking forward to visit my home town. My family could spend time with my brother and his wife and also meet many relatives and friends, including an Oberlin friend, Charlie Mehl. More importantly, Mahe and I were to meet Professor Richard Reiz—a meeting that could very likely change our lives.

Mahema's aged parents came to the car. Her mother said a brief prayer, asking God for travelling mercies. It was still dark on this winter morning as the car sped past Tambaram, the southern outer limit of greater Madras. Sujatha, after celebrating the birthday of her doll, Raggedy Ann, possibly for the seventy-eighth time, went back to sleep while the rest of us remained silent, absorbed in our own thoughts. My mother had reasons to enjoy a complete sense of security and happiness because all her three sons were doing well.

Fifteen years earlier, in 1957, my father, a municipal doctor of Madurai had died suddenly. He was only fifty-two years old. My mother had become a widow when she was only forty-three. Since then it was I, her middle son, Manohar, who took care of her and Chinnah, my younger brother. But the best thing that happened to her was when Mahema became her daughter-in-law.

Mahema made my mother feel special. For instance, when she said one day that only Manohar and Mahe supported her and not Divakar, Mahema at once said, 'We are not supporting you, Aunty. You are supporting us.'

I went to the US in 1969. Mahema and our daughter, Suja, joined me in 1970. During the one-year gap, Mahema often visited the tiny house where my mother moved in. Neighbours would ask her teasingly, 'Amma, you look very happy today. Are we to assume that your daughter-in-law and your granddaughter are visiting you?' Or they would say, 'Such appetizing smells are wafting from your kitchen. We are sure your "daughter" would be arriving soon.' And, they were right, because, more often than not, she thought of Mahema as her own daughter.

When Mahema and I along with with Suja returned from the US in August 1972, my mother had at once moved into the more spacious apartment above Mahema's parents' house. Chinnah soon left for the US for further studies. After our return to India, Mahema seemed to her even more lovable and me more likeable. Why, at Satya's wedding reception the previous evening, she felt so proud of her 'children' and granddaughter. Had she been 'casting an evil eye' on her own children? She wondered whether other guests were 'casting their eyes' on them. When she thought about our kuthu-vilakku, she became visibly worried. At our wedding, Mahema's father had arranged a simple lamp-lighting ceremony with readings from the Bible and the Upanishads. In 1963, this was somewhat unusual at a Christian wedding.

Since then, Mahema had been lighting the lamp on our wedding anniversary. This year the lamp had broken into two. My mother was not a superstitious woman. All the same, this had seemed a bad omen, like what is shown in Tamil movies.

'Why does this have to happen, of all days on your wedding anniversary?' she had lamented.

But I had scoffed at the idea of a bad omen. 'The vilakku is handled by many, washed with tamarind, wiped, and moved from one place to another, only on our wedding anniversary. So, it is more likely to break on this day than on other days, when it remains safely inside the cupboard.' There was much truth in what I had said. At any rate even after it broke, the lamp continued to burn almost defiantly, she noted with some relief. Her daughter-in-law seemed to have taken the incident calmly. The only observation Mahema had made was that the lamp should be brassed together at the earliest to which I had replied, 'Yes, we should get it done, at any rate before our next wedding anniversary.'

~

Now, as she drove the car, Mahema kept her eyes glued to the road, lit by the headlights, but her thoughts were on a 7,000-mile camping tour that she, Mano, and Suja undertook across the US, in the company of a newly-married Brahmin couple, Gayathri and Hari. Every morning, as they drove from one campsite or another, Mano and Hari would play a tape of M. S. Subbulakshmi's 'Meera Bhajans'. After that Suja would be busy celebrating Raggedy Ann's birthday, with Gayathri's help. Suja was a very good travelling companion. She was a bright-eyed, highly active child and yet could sit in the confines of a car for long stretches without being troublesome.

She thought of the spectacular photographs that Mano had taken during the tour. Some of his photographs were like oil paintings. 'He's so intelligent and talented,' she thought proudly. Above all, he was a loving husband. He channelized his creative skills in ever so many ways to express his deep abiding love for her. And his physical desire for her seemed to increase with every passing year. Their love life played a crucial role in their matrimonial harmony.

And he made love in imaginative and artistic ways. Every celebration was followed by an extra special event in bed. The previous night was an example. He kept her high for a little over an hour and finally had his crescendo while she had many in-between.

~

To be sure, they were at a crossroads and at an interesting juncture in their lives. Professor Jeswant and Dr Reiz, who were on the Board of Trustees of the International School in Kodaikanal, were very keen that Manohar and Mahema should teach Science and English respectively in this school. Mano was excited about taking up this proposal. Both of them loved teaching and enjoyed the company of youngsters. If they did join the school, they would have the joy of living in Kodaikanal. Mano wanted to accumulate portfolios of his ink drawings, paintings, and photographs of Kodaikanal during their stay. Eventually, they wished to publish a book entitled *A Jewel in the Hills* for which she would write the text. Mano assured her that they could retain the apartment and visit Madras often....

~

As Mahe drove the car absorbed in her thoughts, I looked blankly at the road, thinking about this and that. I could see a bit of the road illuminated by the headlights of the car, but I knew that Mahe saw the road farther than I did. Inside the car, I could see nothing but the tiny jewel-like lamps of the dials on the dashboard. However, last night, I could so enjoy visually the beauty of Mahe's female form, her beauty enhanced by the light of a dozen candles. Now as I looked at the highway, I began seeing light on the east, very uncertainly at first, but more certainly as minutes ticked by. As the inky grey of the sky was slowly washed away by the spreading liquid gold of the eastern light, I began discerning the silhouettes of palmyra trees rushing by. This was flat country and soon I saw the sun peering out from the horizon, as the bushes vainly tried to hide it. Mahema switched off the headlights. I noticed the beauty of the winter sunrise and the colours of the early morning sky. The rains had carpeted the barren landscape with lush greenery. There were countless puddles of water, and the kammais were full of silvery or pale brown water, depending upon whether the kammai was to my left or right. I heard the steady drone of the car engine and the variations in the chirping of birds and enjoyed the pleasant smell of the upholstery inside the new car and that of the vegetation outside.

But my thoughts were all with Mahema. I turned to look at her. She wore a pale brick-coloured cotton sari pleated neatly at her shoulder. The only chain that she had around her neck was the mangalyam. She wore a pair of small earrings. Her hair was swept up into a big kondai above the nape of her neck. As we had left our house very early in the morning, she could not wear flowers in her hair. The soft, morning rays of the sun fell directly on her clear profile, stirring in the depths of my mind, memories of another image—like something seen in a previous incarnation.

~

Suja was born in 1966. By 1967, I decided to go to the US for higher studies and went there in 1969. Mahema and Suja joined

me in 1970. We returned to India in 1972. Only now we were free
to think of a second child. From very early December 1972, we
stopped 'family planning'. This became an even more active period
in our love life. Mahema's passion for me remained unabated. But
surprisingly, she did not conceive. It was a bit disappointing for us,
especially because her periods ended just on our wedding anniversary
day. So, I could make 'special love' only the previous night and not on
our ninth wedding anniversary. But then Mahema smiled and said
'Mano, we can have a higher level of activity for one more month.'
Yes, that was also true.

I looked at her again. Mahema's face looked peaceful, like a
placid lake concealing mysteries in its depths. It was this calmness that
others saw and admired in her. But I knew only too well, that with
me, in complete privacy, she could be a different sort of person...a
very different sort. I thought that perhaps the unrevealing, serene,
seemingly dignified, Devi-type of women were in reality, far sexier
than the revealing, flirtatious, seemingly lascivious, Mohini-type.

Before I met Mahe, our common cousin Satya once told me
humorously that to cart all the prizes, awards, and medals that Mahema
had won in college, one would need a wheelbarrow. Later I wrote
two stanzas of an ongoing verse on Mahema that I entitled 'A Woman
of Serenity'.

When Mahema was a Stella girl
To her peers she was a precious pearl
To the nuns all dedicated and prudent
She was the epitome of an ideal student.
The prizes she won I'll show you tomorrow,
To cart them all, you know, I need a wheelbarrow.

Soon, Mahema became my devoted wife:
Together we had a joyous life.
When I came to know her closer than before
I liked her even more—and some more
The picture of her that they all drew,

I happily agreed, was completely true.
I had been working on the third stanza.
I remembered it now:
But wait, now wait…just wait,
I noticed in her a certain trait
Which was not in line with what
Everybody else had always thought.
Serene she remained to all those who knew her
With me, oft' times, she wasn't even sober.

'What's so funny?' Mahe asked all of a sudden, which abruptly ended my stream of thoughts.

'How did you know that I had an amusing thought?' I asked her.

'Well,' she replied, 'you kept looking at me with an expression that I can't complain about! You looked very, very pleased with yourself, except for a brief while when you had a sour expression, though.'

So she had noticed that I was studying her face. But were not my thoughts pleasant all along?

Suddenly I remembered that when I had thought of Mahema not conceiving that second child in December I was mildly disappointed. Though she had not taken her eyes off the road, she had detected every flicker of my face, every smile or scowl. Was I so transparent?

'My gosh, Mahema,' I observed, 'I ought to be very careful if I want to cheat on you.'

She said, 'You have tunnel vision. To compensate for this, God in His mercy has blessed me with extra-wide angular vision.'

I smiled and replied, 'All the same, it seems to me that I can't do something behind your back and assume you wouldn't find out.'

I heard her 'silver bell' laughter. The laughter at this particular juncture was to take on a special significance, as I was to realize later that this was the last time I would ever hear her laugh in this ebullient manner.

~

We had breakfast at Villupuram. I was to have taken over driving from then on, but when we came out of the eatery, Mahema happened to be on the right side of the car. She said that she would drive down to Ulundurpet, hand over the wheel to me and go to sleep. Poor Mahema had not had a moment's break the previous day and had hardly slept four hours that night. She had to somehow catch up with her sleep.

Before the car picked up speed, while it was still in the third gear, a fully loaded lorry overtook it. In the left rear-view mirror, I saw four or five young men inside the driver's cabin—boys probably in their late teens. One boy sat to the right of the driver, between the driver and the door. This boy noticed that an attractive young woman was driving the car they had just overtaken. His eyes flashed with excitement.

Smiling broadly, he peered out of the cabin, craning his neck and waving his hand. I was amused. India was at that time ruled by a woman—a widow at that—and this was taken for granted. And yet, a woman driving a car, especially on the highway, was still a novelty, which often provoked macho feelings in many men. The boy opened the cabin door and stood on the short footboard. He hung out, waved his free hand more vigorously now and grinned, showing all his even white teeth.

As Mahema was caught behind the laden lorry which was moving slowly, she could drive only as fast as the lorry. I advised her to maintain a safe speed of 55 kilometres an hour. So, Mahema made an attempt to overtake the slow-moving lorry. The boy who was standing on the footboard communicated something to the driver, who moved the vehicle to the left as if allowing her to overtake it. The boy even waved his hand to indicate that Mahema could pass the lorry. But when she came to the middle of the road to pass, he said something again to the driver who at once swung inward, blocking the way. The lorry kept spewing smoke, perhaps not as much as some of its less illustrious cousins, but all the same, enough to pollute the immediate atmosphere.

I then remembered that while I was in the US, Ralph Nader's

crusade for safer automobiles had received much media attention. I had become quite aware of the fact that an automobile was no plaything. But the boys in the lorry—like the hero in the Tamil film *Penn* (Woman)—regarded it as one. In the movie, I remembered that particular scene—which was lapped up by the audience—Balachandar, the hero, driving a car in the highways, teases Vyjayanthimala, the heroine, driving another car. As Vyjayanthimala gets angrier, Balachandar becomes more boisterous.

Soon, a straight stretch of the road presented itself, with no vehicles coming from the opposite side. The road was on a higher level with a clear view all around. I told Mahe, 'This is your chance. Overtake the lorry now.' She shifted to the third gear, accelerated and swiftly shifted back to the top gear. Miscalculating the speed of the car, the boy signalled to the lorry driver to block it. This he did but just a little too late. By the time the lorry began to swing to the right, the car's front wheels were in line with the lorry's rear wheels and it was running faster. Mahema at once slowed down. To avoid the lorry, she moved more and more to the right, till the two right wheels went off the road. The earlier rains had eroded the shoulder of the road into countless little gullies. While the left wheels of the car ran smoothly, the right wheels bumped violently. I saw Mahe straining to hold the steering wheel from going out of control as the car began to slow down. It was at this moment that the rear of the lorry touched the front of the car making an ugly noise. Mahe at once lost control and the car began to roll off the road. I caught a fleeting glance of the worried expression on the boy's face. And then there was a clang of crushing metal which went on and on, echoing in my ears. Along with this, there was a rushing sound like that of a roaring waterfall. Everything became a blur in which the predominant colour was pale olive green. 'Why isn't the car coming to a stop?' was the only thought in my mind. The gentle downward gradient prevented the car from coming to a halt sooner. After two or three somersaults the vehicle eventually came to a halt in a large puddle of knee-deep water.

'Is Suja all right?' I asked anxiously.
'Suja, are you hurt?' my mother asked.
'I'm not hurt. I'm okay.'
'I am all right too.'
'What about Mahe?'
She was not to be seen anywhere.
'Where's Mahe?' I asked with alarm.

2

It was a wedding reception towards the end of May 1963. A whole lot of my relatives and I were there. We knew that Mahema's family too attended the reception. As we walked towards the reception hall after tea, I saw a girl whom I did not know. I wondered whether it was Mahema. 'Ah, she is a beauty,' I thought. Actually that was why I noticed her. The girl saw me, and almost at once recognized who I was. Her face brightened. She detached herself from her family, rushed towards me and asked, 'You are Manohar, aren't you?' But before I could answer she continued, 'I want to tell you that you suffer from an inferiority complex.'

Verily, verily, these were the first words uttered to me by the girl I was destined to marry.

It was not customary for a young woman to tell a young man such a thing, especially when she was meeting him for the first time ever. And yet, 'You suffer from an inferiority complex,' was precisely what she told me. From all accounts I had gathered the clear impression that she was a quiet, calm girl who did not make strong statements to any one, least of all to a stranger.

I was totally taken aback, as were some of my relatives, including my mother, who were within earshot. Was this girl Mahema at all?

Indeed she was. She had said what she did with her eyes twinkling with mirth, her voice brimming with good humour and with an artless trust that I would never, ever take her comment amiss. Almost the first thing I noticed at close range was her gently pouting, well-defined, rounded full lips. I fell for her that very moment and actually have never recovered fully since then.

But why did she make such a comment? Further, she had never seen me or my photographs before. How did she recognize me in the first place? In order to explain why she made this unilateral declaration to me and how she knew who I was, let me briefly narrate a few incidents from the time I was a little boy.

I have been drawing pictures ever since I could remember. When I was in primary school, I mostly drew pictures of animals—elephants, tigers, and lions. Then in middle school, my topics of interest shifted to steam engine trains, road rollers, and World War II aeroplanes. When I went to high school, the main topic of my interest was girls. I drew mostly sari-clad women, but frequently did women in bathing suits too...and some without bathing suits.

Around this time, my school friends Gabriel and Jayaraj, the artistically gifted Fernando brothers, went away from Madurai (where I lived then) to Champion Reefs. We began exchanging letters sprinkled with illustrations, mostly of women. While I was in college I wrote letters with drawings in conversational Tamil to my cousin and childhood friend Prema, who went to college in Madras.

After moving to Madras, I started exchanging letters with our (Mahema's and my) common cousin Satya. Now, Satya's paternal grandmother and Mahe's maternal grandmother were sisters, while Satya's and my maternal grandmothers were sisters. So Satya is a second cousin of both Mahema and me. But Mahema and I are not related. Mahema and Satya were close to each other from childhood. I came to know him more closely only after I moved to Madras as a young man. Though Satya is eight years younger than me, we became good friends. When she was a hostel student in Women's Christian College, I met her once in a while and took her out sometimes. I sent her letters with illustrations narrating one humorous incident or another, much to the envy of her hostel mates.

Satya often talked about her favourite cousin Mahema, who was four years older than her. 'Mahema is a brilliant girl, like me,' she would declare proudly. When Mahema was in PUC, the Christian Medical College in Vellore offered her a scholarship. But Mahema was more interested in the arts and literature. So she chose her B.A. in Fine Arts at the Stella Maris College in Madras. During her college years Mahema had won many prizes and awards. Mahema was the student's union president of the college in her final year. The faculty admired her and the students adored her. She was a rank holder and a gold-medallist in fine arts, Satya boasted. 'But with all the achievements, she is a quiet and a very unassuming person. She listens more than she talks. If you meet her, I am sure you would like her,' Satya said. She had a hunch that Mahema would like me too.

One early summer evening in 1963, Satya told me, 'Our whole family is making our annual summer stay in Kodaikanal. Mahema too is going with us. Mano, will you promise to write a letter to me?'

I felt that perhaps Satya wanted to show off to Mahema my illustrated letter. I did write to her, but did not oblige her with illustrations, as I did not want to seem too eager to impress Mahema.

Satya reproached me in her reply. She wrote that she had hoped to receive a letter with nice drawings. She wanted to impress her cousin. But I had chosen to send a particularly drab one. So, Satya wanted to show off my letter to Mahema after all. Now I wrote my second letter to her, taking extra care with the drawings and the text. By way of explanation as to why I had not included any drawings in my previous letter, I wrote that I felt diffident, what with her having a qualified artist around. I concluded the letter with a soft caricature of my face instead of my signature, something I did now and then.

Mahema was very impressed with my drawings and thoroughly enjoyed reading the text in the letter and carefully noted the caricature. She decided that if she met me—which was likely as I was a common cousin of Satya—she would deliver a proper rejoinder. She never expected to confront me ever so soon.

In later years, I kept remembering with great relish Mahema's very first encounter with me. I felt happy that I did not oblige Satya with drawings in my first letter to Kodaikanal, which made her chide me. I was glad that I wrote my second letter with illustrations, with humour in the text, made an oblique tongue-in-cheek comment about her cousin and also did a caricature of myself. These four aspects in my letter had prompted Mahema to express her 'admiration' for me in her own unique way.

~

Now, let me go to the wedding reception where Mahema met me.

Responding to her unilateral declaration, I said teasingly, 'Surely, you are not the same, sober, sane, soft-spoken, serene, quietly dignified girl named Mahema that Satya keeps talking about.'

Mahema laughed. Her laughter sounded like a cluster of silver bells tinkling in the breeze.

'Yes, indeed, I am Mahema,' she replied adding, 'if Satya had given you the impression that I am a staid person, I am not responsible for that.'

'But why do you accuse me of suffering from an inferiority complex?'

'In your first letter to Satya in Kodai, you wouldn't include any artwork because, I, a qualified artist, was with her. But the artwork in your second letter was of such high quality that many trained artists, including my teachers and myself, could not match it. And yet you were so diffident. That's why I said what I did.'

'Well, Satya told me that you hold the state rank in fine arts. Isn't that right? Then how do you expect me not to be diffident?' I asked her.

'I was the state rank holder,' she said giggling, 'because Stella Maris is the only college in the whole state that offers a BA degree course in fine arts. We were just three girls in my class. Just one, two, three. I scored more marks than the other two. That was all.'

'But Satya had not revealed such finer details.'

'I know you were pulling my leg when you wrote about "a qualified artist". So I decided to pull your leg in return.'

I could guess that she recognized me by the caricature in my letter. To affirm this, I asked her, 'How did you recognize me as Manohar?'

'Because I saw your self-portrait in your letter, I knew who you were when I saw you.'

As I had used only subtle exaggeration, the cartoon could easily be mistaken for a portrait. Nevertheless, I said, 'Hey, you qualified artist.... It is not a portrait. It is a caricature.'

'Yes, I agree. But I must say that you look more like yourself in the caricature, than you would have in a portrait!'

I laughed. There was a strong element of truth in what she said, as some of the defining features—in my case, small forehead, unruly thick black mop of hair, deep set eyes—are a bit exaggerated in a caricature.

I was impressed by her insight. Yes, the minimal exaggerations would have more strongly displayed my facial features. So, I said, 'What you said is quite true. Ah, you are an artistic person after all.'

She flashed a smile and said, 'You look a bit better in real life than you do in the caricature you drew.'

It was now my turn to laugh.

Then she said, 'Really, Mano, I have heard so much about you from Satya, I think that I wouldn't mind having you as my cousin.'

I thought to myself, 'Why just a cousin? I could become your fiancé and later your husband.'

But, of course, I did not say it.

I asked her about her 'art tour' with her professors, Mother Greta and Mother Edith and classmates to Ajanta, Ellora, and other places. She talked eloquently about the places that she had visited and strongly recommended that I visit the art and architectural treasures in our country. Then she asked me about my Parisian and Roman holiday. I briefly narrated some of my humorous experiences. Then I heard the same silver bells ringing.

So we talked on and on, much to the amazement and amusement of our relatives and of even some other guests. Her mother told mine, 'Well, they seem to know a lot about each other. Perhaps, we should think of a meeting at a common relative's house to talk about a possible marriage alliance.'

Mahema drove back home in the Morris Minor car her family owned, with her mother and aunt in it. Her aunt gently told her that their family was thinking of me as a possible life partner and sought Mahe's thoughts on it. Mahe, by then, had the hope that her family had that very thought. Her face glowed in the dark interior of the car. But as she was driving the car, she kept her emotions under control. After a long pause, she calmly expressed her acceptance without any reservations.

On our way back home from the wedding reception, my relatives relentlessly teased me, but with joy. Their teasing was for me like water on a duck's back. Emotionally I was on a different plane altogether.

That night, I lay awake in bed well after the others had slept. My thoughts were all on the enchanted evening. From the time I was in ninth standard in school, I had been terribly and overwhelmingly interested in girls. But Mahema moved me in a way no other girl had. With her broad forehead, liquid eyes, prominent nose, rounded cheeks, well-defined, slightly pouting lips, small chin, and the high kondai that she wore, this Christian girl resembled statues of Hindu Goddesses. There was lakshanam in her countenance. She appeared like a very traditional Tamil woman, but spoke in impeccable English with a pleasing, natural accent. She appeared mature and dignified, but had a vibrant lovely voice with a girlish tinge to it. And what a repartee she and I had had, oblivious of the relatives who were watching us. It was magical.

That night, Mahema's mother told her that before they left the wedding reception, my aunt Punitha had told her I would be very happy about the marriage alliance and that she was relieved 'the search' was over. Then Mahema's mother said a prayer thanking God and beseeching His continued guidance and blessings.

That night like me, Mahe too could not sleep for a while. Her mind kept spinning, her heart kept singing and her thoughts kept going in circles around me. She recollected the wonderful conversation that she and I had. Her face was all aglow yet again.

She also recollected some of the things that Satya had said about me: A couple of years earlier, I was virtually assured of an assistantship for higher studies at a small college in the US by a chemistry professor, who taught briefly at the Women's Christian College in Madras. But because my elder brother already had a confirmed assistantship at another college in the US, I had given up my plan in order to support my widowed mother and put my younger brother through college.

Mahe smiled. Destiny seemed to have prevented me from going to the US so that I could meet her. She was also glad that the British company that I worked for had sent me to England for a special training. With all the knowledge and all the experience that I had gained, in her mind, I had become a more interesting person.

The following morning, my mother received a letter from Satya's mother who was still in Kodaikanal. In a plain inland form, she wrote that she was aware that my mother was on the lookout for a suitable girl for me. Mahe's parents were also looking for a match for their daughter. She felt that a marriage alliance could be considered by both sides.

She wrote that Mahema was a talented, academically brilliant girl. And yet she was a very unassuming, happy, serene person. She was full of goodness and dignity, and also blessed with a keen sense of humour. She was beautiful and very attractive.

In her reply, my mother wrote that when Mahe and I met, our relatives watched us in stunned silence—stunned in a nice sort of way. The wedding seemed to my mother to be a foregone conclusion and she was very happy about it.

Three days later, on 27 May 1963, after our first long chat, Mahema's family and mine with relatives had an informal tea in the garden of Satya's grandmother's house. On this evening, it was agreed by all concerned that Satya's very attractive, serenely quiet, yet brilliant and talented cousin with a sense of humour, and I, should get married.

Mahema's mother invited me to visit her daughter in their house. Way back in 1963, 'the boy' visiting 'the girl' before an engagement, was rather unusual in Tamil Nadu. So, the invitation delighted me.

On the last day of May, I entered the bungalow—that was to become my home for more than half a century—that Mahe's father had built in the late 1930s. The bungalow had an understated elegance, a friendly ambience and some unusual features. But it did need maintenance and repair work. Why, on this very first day of my visit, I had to climb a wall to fix the overhead tank which began spouting water, trying to empty itself.

On this day, Mahema wore a Pochampalli sari and a jasmine charam in her hair. She said that her father had planted a mullai creeper and a Rangoon creeper in the southeastern and southwestern sides of the house at the time of her birth.

She and I settled down on the sofa. She told me, 'At the wedding reception, where we met, had I known that my parents were thinking of you as a possible match for me, I would have felt so self-conscious I would never have said what I uttered. I would have kept quiet and waited for you to talk to me first. Besides, I would not have taken the liberty of addressing you by your name.'

I observed, 'Ah, I am most thankful to your family for choosing not to tell you about my "special status". So you opened the gambit. And what a gambit it was. Please do continue to call me Mano.'

Later, during our engaging conversation, she told me, 'Ever since I went on an art tour with the teachers and two classmates, I had had a dream. The dream is that I should visit the heritage sites with my partner in life. My hope was that the man that I marry would be a person who would enjoy such a tour. Then, at the reception, when I advised you to visit our country's art treasures, a thought flashed across my mind that it would be wonderful to visit the treasures with you as my life partner.'

I was touched by what she said. I stretched my hand towards her and sang spontaneously, '*Take my hand and see our land with me....And see our lovely land with me.*' These were two lines with minor changes from Pat Boone's song 'The Exodus Song (This Land is Mine)' which he had composed after reading Leon Uris's novel, *The Exodus.*

After a fleeting hesitation she took my hand in hers. I looked up and said, 'Thank you, Leon Uris.'

She smiled and said, 'Ah, Mano, Satya didn't tell me that you can sing well.'

I replied. 'How could she have? She had never heard me sing. Anyway, even now, I sang only two lines. How could you say, I sing well?'

'The two lines were a good enough sample,' she replied and added, 'Besides, I hear Pat Boone's 'The Exodus Song' on the radio. So, I am familiar with the melody.'

There was a small, old radiogram in their house. So I said, 'I shall play the record for you when I visit you next.'

We talked on and on about music, paintings, sculpture, literature, movies, and plays, but not about chemistry.

Later that evening, Mahema said, 'Tomorrow is the first of June. Oh, already half a year has gone by.'

I laughed and said, 'Ah, Mahe, I see you are not strong at maths. We have to wait till the end of June for half a year to be over.'

Our relatives, who were staying with us throughout the summer vacation, had returned to Madurai only a day earlier. That night, in the silence of my room, my thoughts went revolving around Mahema. My heart brimmed with feelings that I had never, ever experienced before. My emotions were tranquil and yet sparkling, like a pristine mountain stream. They were full of gentle beauty and yet had emotional power—like Debussy's 'Clair de Lune'. Yes, 'Clair de Lune' epitomized what I felt. So I played the 45 rpm record that my friend John Bairstow had sent from England. Listening to the moving piano piece again and again, while thinking more and more about Mahema, further enriched the beauty of my sentiments.

Happily, this moving piece was to become my very first 'Mahema song'. After a long gap, later in life, whenever I played the record of this piano piece, nostalgic memories of this beautiful period would flood my mind. It still does.

Many years later, Anil Srinivasan, the extraordinarily talented pianist, who has grown very fond of me, came to know about my association of this piece with Mahe. He chose to play this piece in some of his public performances, if I happened to be in the audience, as a special favour.

3

Three days after our ninth wedding anniversary, it happened…the accident.

Why was Mahema not to be seen? Had she fallen out of the car as it rolled down? My eyes swiftly swept the wayward path of the car after it rolled off the road, but there was no sign of her. All I had was a fleeting glimpse of the lorry on the road, at a distance on a higher plain. The image of the young fellows peering out of the window and the lorry shuddering, spewing smoke and speeding away—all in a matter of seconds—were to remain engraved in my mind for as long as I lived.

I felt desperate. Suddenly it occurred to me that Mahema could have been knocked unconscious and that she could asphyxiate in the water. What if she was caught under the car?

'My beloved wife,' I screamed, 'might drown in the shallow water.' I asked my mother and Sujatha to wade quickly through the water and raise Mahema's head above it. I lay down in the water, stretched my legs under the car and swung them sideways to ensure that she was not underneath.

'We must find her fast,' I yelled.

I feared that if she remained under water for more than five minutes, her brain could be permanently damaged.

As we searched silently and desperately, we heard an eerie, drumming sound from the car, which looked like a squashed cabbage leaf. The front windscreen had become detached and fallen unbroken beyond the puddle of water. One windscreen wiper was vigorously sweeping the hollow air, its blade dangling clumsily like a broken arm.

Someone shouted, 'A lady is lying over there.' I turned and saw a group of villagers running down a slope. I rushed to the spot with my heart pounding wildly. Sujatha and my mother ran behind me as fast as they could.

Mahema lay there as if she had actually chosen that spot. She lay partly sideways, her legs gently folded together, one arm resting on her hip and the other stretched out on a thick mat of grass. Her kondai had moved to one side. This is how Dushyanthan might have seen Sakunthalai from a distance. When I came close, I noticed that Mahema was in great pain. I knelt down beside her and asked, gently, 'Are you all right?'

'Mano, Mano,' she said, sobbing, 'my neck…pain…Mano. I'm not able to move my hands.' Her reply shocked me. I pinched her hand. 'Do you feel pain in…your arm?'

She replied feebly, 'No, no…It's my neck…excruciating pain.'

My throat went dry. 'Please, Mahe try hard and move your hand.'

'Oh Mano, I'm not able to move my hands or legs at all,' she said in a feeble voice.

~

Many years ago, when I was in the sixth standard in school, my father, a doctor, had described an accident to me. A chiththaal (woman helper on a building construction site) had fallen from the scaffolding. He had told me, 'She sustained a spinal injury in her neck and is now a quadriplegic—a person who has no control over or sensation in all four limbs. She, in short, is a prisoner in her own body.'

I had been rattled to hear of such a terrible possibility. It had been the first time I had heard of quadriplegia. 'How long will she be a quadriplegic, a prisoner in her own body?' I had asked.

My father had replied, 'Perhaps till she dies.' He then added hesitantly, 'She'll degenerate and probably die within a year or two.' One of my pastimes during those days was climbing trees...or buildings...or anything at all. My father had advised me, 'Remember son, if you are careless or take undue risks, while climbing trees, you might end up like this woman.'

I had thought then that something as frightening and as horrible must never happen to me, my kith and kin. Now, it seemed that my precious wife was in that same dreaded condition.

The first book that I had read when I came back from the US was *Take My Hands*, the true story of Dr Mary Verghese who had become paralysed below her waist because of a spinal injury in her lumbar region. I remembered her many ordeals only too well. But her hands had been spared. Mahema's situation could be far worse.

~

The villagers surrounded Mahema in no time. An old villager, probably a masseur, took the liberty of turning her this way and that. He announced with some satisfaction, 'No broken bones. No blood.'

Another villager told Mahema, 'Amma, you are all right. You can get up.'

'Oh, aunty,' Mahema called my mother, 'I can't bear the pain in my neck.'

The old villager gently pressed her neck.

'Please don't press her neck,' I shouted, 'she might have sustained a spinal injury and it's not....'

'No injury in the neck, only a superficial sprain with pain. That's for sure,' pronounced the 'expert'.

I felt crushed. I turned my head with tears streaming down my cheeks.

'Don't cry,' admonished a villager. 'After all, her bones aren't broken.'

'She gonna die?' asked Suja in English. While in the US, Suja had spoken English like the American children of her age. When she returned to India, her new classmates at Rosary Matric School had teased her about her accent. So, Suja had put in a lot of effort to drop it and to speak English like the other convent girls. However, when she was jubilant or anxious, she unconsciously reverted to her old American way of speaking.

'No, Sujamma, she'll be okay.'

My mother stood there dazed. 'Merciful God, spare my daughter's life,' she prayed.

The villagers lifted Mahema gently. I knew that it was not wise to move her but what other option was there? She might be bleeding internally and could even die if she was not taken to a hospital in time.

As they carried her up towards the road, I saw a middle-aged couple rushing towards us. The villagers laid Mahema down, not far from the car.

'I'm Dr Ramamurthy,' he said, 'Why are they carrying her? What's the problem?'

I explained briefly what had happened. 'I'm afraid she might have become a quadriplegic,' I said.

The doctor examined her. I desperately hoped that the doctor would say that she was in a state of shock and would recover soon. Alas, instead he said gravely, 'Yes, it's probably traumatic quadriplegia.'

When the doctor reaffirmed my worst fears, I shed tears again.

'If she's not gonna die, then why are ya crying?' asked Suja.

'It's sad,' said the doctor, 'but who knows? Her condition could partly be due to pressure caused by fluid collection. If the fluid is drained she might recover partially.'

The battered car standing in the puddle continued to make the rhythmic drumming sound as if it was beating its chest in despair. Suddenly, the doctor folded his dhoti, walked into the water, in his Duckback sandals, inserted his hand through the gaping hole where the windscreen had been and fiddled with the controls. The windscreen wiper which was sweeping the air with a dangling arm stopped dancing and fell silent. 'Otherwise, the battery will unnecessarily run down.' he said.

The Good Samaritan told his wife, 'Stay here with the child and her grandmother, I'll take the couple to Ulundurpet, drop them in the hospital there and come back for the three of you.'

'No, no, no,' protested Sujatha. 'I don' wanna stay here, I wanna be with my mom.'

Later in Ulundurpet, the doctor told me, 'My wife and I are continuing with our journey. I have done the little I could. Please don't give the police my name or my car number. I don't want endless court summons.'

When he took leave of us, the good doctor told me, 'You know, with her huge kondai on one side, your wife reminds me of the goddess of Madurai. I shall say a special prayer to Meenakshi Amman for her.'

When I met Mahema for the first time, I had thought of her as Goddess Parvathi. And now, nine years later, here was the doctor telling me that she reminded him of an incarnation of Parvathi.

The old doctor in charge of the small Ulundurpet hospital was helpful but was unable to do much. 'This hospital is really nothing more than a glorified first aid centre. She needs special attention. Her blood pressure is low. Take her to JIPMER Hospital in Pondicherry as soon as you can. You'll be stretching your luck, if you try to take her all the way back to Madras, to admit her in the General Hospital.' (JIPMER is the Jawaharlal Institute of Post Graduate Medical Education and Research in Pondicherry.)

I thought about the logistic problems of admitting her in a hospital in Pondicherry, a hundred miles away from our home.

The doctor could see my dilemma. 'If you decide to take her to the General Hospital in Madras, then please keep two hundred rupees ready, in one and two rupee notes, to grease the palms of stretcher bearers, ward boys, ayahs and the like.'

I thought that my first cousin Chithra, who was an intern at JIPMER, would be of help. All things considered, I decided it was best to transport Mahe to Pondicherry. The journey I now took with my family from Ulundurpet to Pondicherry in a hired car was the unhappiest one of my life.

At JIPMER, two young male doctors wheeled Mahema into an operation theatre, while the family members stood vigil outside. After a while, one of the young doctors came out and gave me Mahema's mangalyam, bangles, earrings, and her clothes.

He told me, 'We have examined her body thoroughly. Excepting for the fracture dislocation of her neck, she has no other injury.'

I felt no sense of jealousy when I heard that the male doctors had examined her body. Perhaps, a tragic situation of such magnitude elevates a person above pedestrian levels of jealousy. Indeed, a certain thought crossed my mind, making a flicker—just a flicker—of a smile alight upon my countenance, for the very first time after the accident. The thought that crossed my mind was that I, Mano, had undressed her fully, just the previous night. At that time, would I have, ever, ever guessed that within fifteen hours from then, two young men—two utter strangers—would take the liberty of not only removing all her clothes but also closely examining her body.

My cousin Chithra came running up to us, looking distressed. She had a pair of men's sandals wrapped up in a newspaper.

'Here, wear these, Annan. I've borrowed them from a fellow doctor. They told me that you were barefoot,' she said.

Later, she and another woman doctor removed twenty-two thorns from the soles of my feet. 'The back of your shirt and trousers are caked with mud,' Chithra said.

'Yes, I lay down in a puddle of muddy water when I searched for Mahe,' I replied and added, 'That's where I lost my slippers too.'

She told me, 'I couldn't get you a pair of trousers and a shirt from my male colleagues because their clothes just wouldn't fit you.' She said this with a puckish expression.

I smiled for the first time after the accident and asked, 'Yes, I have become a bit hefty, have I not?'

In the meantime, the young doctors put Mahema on halter traction. A padded cloth belt was passed around her chin and above her head to a pulley mounted on the bedstead from which a weight of 4 kilograms was hung. This made her lockjawed. Now, she could talk only in whispers through her teeth. As she could not open her mouth, she could not eat. A tube was inserted through her nose for nasal feeding. A catheter, an intravenous drip, an oxygen line, a blood pressure apparatus, and a heart monitor were connected to her body. I feared that Mahe's aged parents, who were expected to reach JIPMER late that evening, might collapse on seeing their only child in this state. But they were, I learnt later, made of sterner stuff. Indeed, I could personally see why her father had a reputation for bravery during his years of service.

The following morning, Mahe's friends, three Brahmin sisters, Meera, Hyma, and Shashi came to see her. They sang Christian hymns with tears rolling down their cheeks. I found this so intensely poignant that I shed tears.

Mahe called me near her and pacified me, 'Don't cry, Mano, it hurts me to see a strong bear like you cry,' she whispered through her teeth in a weak hoarse voice.

Her blood pressure kept falling and it was constantly boosted by closely monitored medication, through yet another intravenous line. At one stage, three young doctors thought that she was heading towards a coma. They peeped above Mahe's head and asked her, 'Akka, what do you see?'

Mahe at once whispered, 'I see three bright, young stars,' and smiled.

With tears, I thought, 'Her spirit and her beautiful personality are indomitable. It is only her neck that is vulnerable.'

My brother Divakar and my college friend Ramu and his wife, Rajam, rushed to Pondicherry. My school friends, Gabriel and Thiagarajan, came from Madurai. Through the following week, Mahe's and my relatives, my school and college friends, my colleagues, many with their spouses, came and went. It all seemed like a blur to me.

Dr Makhani, chief of the orthopaedics department, who had been away, returned to Pondicherry two days later and came straight to Mahema's room. After making a thorough examination he declared,

'Tomorrow, first thing in the morning, I'll remove the halter traction and put her on cervical traction.'

He taught the junior doctors and me how to turn Mahe in bed with the traction. 'She must be turned every three hours or so, day and night,' he said.

The next morning Mahe's head was is only used in a religious context. Chithra began to cry when she saw Mahe's hair being shaven off. Dr Makhani admonished her, but not unkindly, 'Chithra, you mustn't cry for her hair. After all, her hair will grow again. It is her severed spinal cord which will not rejoin.'

Dr Makhani peeled away a part of Mahe's scalp on either side above her ears, drilled two holes in her skull and inserted the two pegs of a steel 'C' clamp. A steel wire was attached to the 'C' clamp and the wire was passed through the same pulley mounted on the headstead. A weight of 6 kilograms was hung at the other end. The halter traction strap that had been passed under her lower jaw for three days had caused heavy blisters along her chin. The doctors applied liberal quantities of gentian violet to aid the healing process.

It was just three nights earlier that I had thought that Mahe looked her loveliest. But now, with innumerable tubes and wires attached to her, a steel clamp sprouting out of her bandaged, shaven head and with the gentian violet staining her chin, she looked like a bearded Sufi trapped by an octopus.

Mahe smiled and told me, 'At least, the halter traction is out and I can talk freely now.'

I did not know whether to laugh or cry at her cheerfulness.

Charlie Mehl had been a student at Oberlin College and had lived in Asia House when Mahema was the programme director and housemother of this coeducational dormitory. His friendship with my family had reawakened in him an interest in India and he had won a grant for studies in Madurai, and he was in the city at the time of our misfortune. As soon as he heard of the accident, Charlie rushed to Pondicherry. Mahema was asleep when he entered her room. He had one look at her, and began crying without saying a word, blowing his nose as silently as possible. When Mahema woke up and saw Charlie, her face brightened. 'Hello Curly,' she said, smiling.

From then on, Charlie spent nearly all his time with us. He kept Suja entertained and made her giggle with his capers. He went to Madras with me. Thanks to Charlie, I did not feel too lonely in my empty house. One night, Charlie said, 'Hey, Mano, I have a bottle of French wine. If you buy some cheese and bread, we can have a fondue dinner with wine.'

He must have noticed the uncertainty in my face. So he said, 'Life has to go on, Mano.'

Yes, life had to go on. Logistics had to be worked out. I applied for leave from work, stating that I would attend the office for three-and-a-half days each week of five working days so that I could divide my time between Madras and Pondicherry. The managing director of the company, an enlightened man, at once granted me leave. In the meantime, Charlie went to Madurai to tie up his project work and returned to Pondicherry.

Telegrams and letters started pouring in from Oberlin and other places around the world. It was Charlie who read those moving letters to Mahema. I read them only when I was all alone, because my heart ached with emotion when I read them. Yet, I read them again and again, almost compulsively.

Charlie helped my family in many small ways. He classified my entire collection of LP records, typed the titles according to classification and made a beautiful folder. He transferred Mahema's favourite songs onto cassette tapes. He taped Suja singing, 'We Shall Overcome', along with Pete Seeger's recording of the same song. I dared not play this tape to Mahe as the recording was sure to be too poignantly painful for her. Mahema's favourite song at that time was 'Who Knows Where the Time Goes' by Judy Collins. Charlie recorded it consecutively four times on a tape so that she could hear the song repeatedly to her heart's content.

Who knows where the time goes?
Who knows where the time goes?

Sad deserted shores
Your fickle friends are leaving
Ah, but then you know
It's time for them to go.

Soon, it was time for Charlie to leave. His eyes all wet, he said to me, 'Mano, your fickle friend—that's I—shall be leaving soon.'

I replied, 'Ah, but then, Charlie, I know it's time for you to go back to the US and that can't be stopped.'

Charlie bid us goodbye and left. After he left, Mahe cried a lot. I played Mahe's favourite song again.

Ah, but then you know
It's time for them to go. But I will still be here.
I have no thought of leaving
I do not count the time
Who knows where the time goes?
Who knows where the time goes?

'Mano,' Mahe called. I turned to look at her. She was crying and smiling at the same time.

'Yes?'

'You know Mano, I'll not be lonely as long as you are with me.'

And I'm not alone
While my love is near me,
And I know, it'll be so....

continued Judy Collins.

'I hope to be always with you, Mahe,' I replied.

'I know it'll be so, Mano, and that gives me the strength to fight my battle,' declared Mahe. The last three lines of the song are:

I do not feel the time.
Who knows how my love grows?
Who knows where the time goes?

4

When Mahe was brought to JIPMER, she could make no bodily movements whatsoever, nor had she any sensation below her neck. But after the cervical traction operation, she could use her shoulder muscles, feebly at first, but with increasing power as the days went by. This was fortunate, because she could now control the complex—if gross—movements of the ball-and-socket joints of her arms. So, she could now be described, not as a person paralysed below her neck, but rather as one paralysed below the shoulder level. Soon she could flex her forearms.

One early morning, Mahe was in a chatty mood. I lay next to her carefully avoiding the traction prongs—so that we could talk softly. Dr Makhani and his team suddenly invaded the room, unusually early this morning. I jumped out of the bed in a hurry as I was sure that Makhani would frown upon the relative of a patient lying down on the hospital bed. But to my surprise, Makhani smiled and asked Mahe, 'So, is this how you cast your "pillow magic" over him and keep him under your spell?'

She replied smiling, 'Yes, I try.'

'Lying down next to you is all right. But don't allow him to go a step further.'

'If you say such naughty things, Doctor,' said Mahe, 'I'll give you a punch on your tummy.'

The young doctors silently listening to this verbal exchange were stunned. Normally, their chief did not crack indulgent jokes with his patients, but Mahema seemed an exception. No patient talked to him the way Mahema did. To add to their surprise, Makhani replied, 'If you can move your arm sufficiently to give me a punch, you'll make me a very happy man.'

'Is that so?' asked Mahema, her eyes gleaming. She requested him to move a little closer to her and swung her right arm saying, 'Here take this, I'll make you happy,' and gave him a wallop on his stomach.

'Ouch,' cried out Makhani, but he soon laughed and said, 'Bravo, Mahema,' in a ringing voice.

Word spread throughout the hospital like wildfire that a patient had dared to hit the much revered Dr Makhani on his tummy, and that he had only laughed approvingly.

In general, her adductor (flexing and contracting) movements recovered to a greater extent than her abductor (stretching and extending) movements. To her relief, Mahe could now wipe her face or scratch her head, if the need arose, without having to depend on others. Then the recovery of her muscular movements abruptly stopped.

'Would she get a spurt of recovery again after a gap?' I wondered. A few days later, suddenly, Mahe moved one leg, flexing it rather substantially at her knee. I jumped with joy. But it turned out that this leg movement was totally involuntary, caused by a spasm—a real bane for quadriplegics—something that was to hound Mahema in later years. Below her neck, Mahema could move only her shoulder muscles, biceps, and the adductor muscles of her wrists. She could not voluntarily move her triceps or finger muscles. She could make no voluntary movements at all below her arms. These were depressing realities. But before I could dwell at length upon the dismal situation, the Shinns arrived at Madras.

Dr Larry Shinn, a professor of religion at Oberlin College, Ohio, USA and an ordained Christian priest, had an abiding academic interest in Hinduism. Larry Shinn joined Oberlin College in 1970, the same year as Mahema. His family grew very fond of ours. A few months after our return to India, the Shinns undertook a mammoth tour of the Indian subcontinent, visiting temples' and religious sites.

During the last lap of their journey, the family had planned to spend a couple of days with us and then go to Madurai and other temple towns in the deep south. The day he arrived in Madras, Dr Shinn telephoned me ebulliently from the Central Station.

'Mano, we have arrived in Madras and our children have taken it all quite well. Please tell Mahema that....'

'Larry, at the moment, I am all alone in an empty house. Mahema is admitted at the JIPMER Hospital in Pondicherry and....'

'What?'

'We had a car accident and she is paralysed below her neck and will be under traction for another two months and more.... Larry, Larry, are you still there?'

Larry was there, but he was too stunned to respond. Finally he groaned, 'Oh no.'

The Shinns rearranged the last lap of their journey to spend the greater part of their remaining days in Pondicherry and Madras, so that, in turn, they could spend more time with Mahema and me. This worked out quite satisfactorily from Larry's professional point of view too. While in Pondicherry he became so interested in Auroville that he decided to return alone to India, a year or two later, during the vacation time at Oberlin College, to make an in-depth study of Auroville, its ideals and problems. The Shinns spent many evenings with Mahema. Larry travelled to Madras with me. We talked a great deal about the past, present, and the future.

'During Mahema's tenure, Asia House throbbed with life and there was magic in the air,' observed Larry. He added, 'I'm sure, Mano, that you and Mahema can recall many, many incidents that would bring you both much happiness. And these memories, I am sure, would strengthen and sustain you to face difficulties in your life ahead.'

I became thoughtful. 'I'm sure that such happy memories would strengthen us,' I agreed. 'Yes, Larry, I love reminiscing...all the same, I don't want to live only in the past. We're too young for that. So I hope that in the future too there will be many events, the memories of which we will treasure. In other words, I hope that Mahema and I will somehow collect a new portfolio of rich memories of events in the years to come, whatever difficulties lie ahead.'

Now Larry became thoughtful. 'You know, Mano,' he said, 'if a person in Mahe's or your situation does not go into depression, that in itself could be considered a worthy achievement. I wish you the best.'

~

In the meantime, JIPMER continued to give Mahema the best treatment that it could. The way Makhani and his team handled the 'periodic turning' of Mahema, was a case in point: If a normal person remains without movement in one position, messages of discomfort travel to the brain from those portions of the body experiencing higher pressures. Then, the person will, by reflex, shift the position to relieve the pressure on those portions of the body. This is true of persons standing, sitting or lying down. Normal persons change their position even while sleeping.

But a quadriplegic like Mahema does not feel this conventional discomfort, caused by pressure points, because the sensory messages do not reach the brain. A quadriplegic cannot consciously move from one position to another because the motor commands from the brain do not reach the muscles. Therefore, they may lie in one position for long stretches of time without complaining, as they neither sense the discomfort nor can they shift their position. So they are very susceptible to pressure sores—also called bedsores.

Bedsores are terrible. The body tissues at the pressure points are starved for blood and oxygen and they begin to die due to lack of nourishment. Often the decay can be extensive under the skin. The natural course of healing is long and tedious. In bad cases, the dead putrefying tissues may have to be surgically scooped out before the healing process starts. Throughout the period of recovery, the patient cannot lie down in those natural positions where the affected regions would come under pressure again, thus limiting the options of positions that can be taken.

As long as the cervical traction was on, changing Mahema's position was complicated, needing the coordinated teamwork of a minimum of four persons. Dr Makhani insisted that at least three of them should be doctors. One day, when Makhani came on his usual morning round with the junior doctors, he asked Mahema, 'So, the lazy young doctors did not turn you at two in the night, did they?'

The young doctors had, for the first time, missed turning Mahema, once, during the night. I wondered how Makhani knew this. I was even worried that the young interns might wrongly conclude that I had complained to Makhani. Later I asked them, 'How did he know that you missed turning her?'

The young men sheepishly replied, 'He has instructed us to telephone him in his residence every time we turn her during the nights. We did not make the 2 a.m. call and that's how he found out.'

I was amazed at Dr Makhani's dedication to work. After a hard day's work, if the chief orthopaedic surgeon wanted to be woken up twice at home, night after night, merely to be told that Mahema had been turned in bed, I realized that there was more to bedsores than I knew. I must learn all that I could about this treacherous scourge. I requested the young doctors to loan me a good physiology book.

'But, Annan,' observed one intern, 'surely, you won't be able to understand much of what is written in a medical book.'

'Oh, come on,' I replied, 'I am qualified to teach quantum mechanics and thermodynamics to university students. A person who understands such heavy stuff, can understand almost anything. As for the medical terminology, the courses I did in biology will help.'

That evening, a young intern named Rajayee lent me the book. This was most fortunate because I read the gory details in characteristically flat medical prose and saw some horrible photographs of bedsores in vivid colours. That day I vowed to myself, 'My wife

will not have bedsores for as long as I live.' Brave words, those. Would
I be able to keep my promise to myself?

When Mahema was turned in bed to the left, she could
comfortably see the room, the visitors, my oil painting that I had
hung on the opposite wall, and much more. When she was turned
to the right, she was confronted by a plain wall for the next three to
four hours. To relieve the monotony, I stuck on this wall at Mahe's eye
level, the poems and limericks that she liked, her favourite passages
from the Bible, and cartoons that I specially drew for her, with
appropriate comments. Soon the doctors caught the spirit behind the
cartoons and began asking me, 'When is the next change?'

But when Mahema lay flat on her back, with the cervical traction
firmly holding her head, she could only stare at the blank ceiling.

And she lay supine longer than she did on her left or right.
Suddenly a thought flashed across my mind. Why not project my
photographic slides, using the ceiling as the screen? I was quite excited
by this idea. I knew Mahe loved our collection of slides.

I was fast gaining a reputation as an artistic photographer. While
we were in the United States, I had presented many slide shows on
India and America, with Mahema's narration. Soon after our return
to India, my photographs were exhibited and my slides presented
at the US consulate, followed by successful shows at the Madras
Photographic Society and other institutions. Now, before presenting
my slides exclusively for Mahema, I first tried projecting them on the
ceiling of my own house. I kept a small mirror at 45 degrees near the
projector lens. I fed a slide into the projector with lateral inversion so
that the image reflected by the mirror corrected itself. The picture was
projected successfully on the ceiling. The only minor deficiency was a
weak, stray image caused by the external glass surface of the mirror. I
solved this problem by using a polished, small, rectangular ABS plastic
plaque which had been vacuum deposited with aluminium. This
highly reflective surface gave a crisp, brilliant image on the ceiling.

When I returned to Pondicherry from Madras this time, I carried
with me a little bonanza-box for Mahema. Fortunately, she was

sleeping when I entered her room at half past four in the evening. I at once opened the bonanza-box and set the slide projector on the floor, so that the image falling on the ceiling would be large. I then fed the slide-dispenser into the projector, plugged a record player and waited.

Mahema was on sedation. When she eventually woke up and saw me, her face brightened. 'Mano, why didn't you wake me up?' she chided.

I did not answer. Instead, I asked, 'Mahe, would you like to see our slides, sometime?'

'Wouldn't I love to?' she replied. 'But Dr Makhani tells me that it will take at least a month before I can sit up. The bed cannot be cranked up because of the traction, you know.'

'Dr Makhani may allow you to sit up only after a month. But you are going to see the slides right now,' I told her expansively.

I promptly turned off the lights, switched on the music, lay down on the couch and started the slide show using the remote control. Mahe gasped when she saw the first brilliant image on the ceiling. I had chosen a set of pictures I had taken in Kodaikanal, the beautiful mountain resort near Madurai. The first slide was of the imposing Pillar Rocks. Clouds partly hid and partly revealed the stunning gigantic, pillar-like rocks and the primordial jungle slopes right below. The second slide was a shot of the boat house in the morning with the lake so still that I had difficulty distinguishing the boathouse from its reflection in the water. Mahe told me, 'You used to play "Songs of Praise" all the time while we were in Kodaikanal. Now, when I see the images and hear the music, I am transported to Kodaikanal.'

The next slide was of a mountain stream. Mahe and I had climbed to the top of Bear Shola Falls and from there continued to climb upstream, a difficult task for Mahe. The picture on the ceiling now was of the stream tumbling down its rocky path, making countless mini-waterfalls. Bushes with wild flowers could be seen at the edges.

'Do you remember,' I asked, 'that the stream was covered high above by a canopy of tree branches, through which shafts of light streamed in here and there? We had the company of only birds and bees.'

'And you became preoccupied with the birds and the bees, didn't you?' she asked, giggling. She savoured the memory of those moments near the brook. How, like a mountain goat, I jumped from one rock to another and then helped Mahe climb up. The chirping of birds and the buzzing of bees had been in harmony with the music of the mountain brook. It had been intoxicating. I had led her to a dark corner, surrounded by big boulders and covered by wild boughs. 'It's risky,' she had half-heartedly warned me.

'Nonsense,' I had countered, 'No one will ever come here. Even if someone does, we'll spot the person well on time.'

I had made her lie down on a somewhat flat rock with an incline. She had begun to blush. I had told her, 'You know, when you glow with anticipation, you are irresistible.'

She had looked at my bare torso, my unruly hair, and my burning eyes.

'You are a caveman,' she had whispered, 'And I can't…resist…a… caveman.' As she spoke, her voice had trailed off and she closed her eyes….

Her eyes were wide open now. 'Oh, thank you, Mano, for this rare treat…I mean, for these spectacular images on the ceiling, the evocative music, and the wonderful memories they bring,' Mahe declared as she lay limply on the JIPMER hospital bed, her body immobile. Though she could move her eyes, they stayed riveted to the ceiling, immobile like her body.

The next slide was a view of Dolphin's Nose. At this stage, Bach's 'Jesu, Joy of Man's Desiring' rendered on the harpsichord filled the room. In this slide, Dolphin's Nose, a narrow ledge-like rock resembling a dolphin's beak amidst lemon grass and rhododendrons, could be seen perched atop a near-vertical slope, jutting into the precipice. And Mahe stood on the rock.

'Will I ever stand on Dolphin's Nose and enjoy the magnificent view again, Mano?' asked Mahe.

'The chances are,' thought I, sadly to myself, 'that you won't stand up at all, let alone stand on Dolphin's Nose.' But I only replied, 'Well, let's hope for the best.' The next slide was of the lake, taken from Levinge Road. The picture had captured the placid mood before sunset. The lake itself was in deep shadow, but the evening sun had lit Perumal Hill with an orange-purple glow. The peak dominated the view. At that moment in Kodaikanal, six years earlier, Mahema had been so filled with contentment that she had spontaneously said a prayer of thankfulness. Now at JIPMER, looking at the skyline of the image, I observed, 'What Meenakshi Amman Temple is to Madurai, I'd say, Perumal Hill is to Kodaikanal.'

Mahe did not reply. I could hear Mahe crying quietly in the darkness as the recording of 'Jesu, Joy of Man's Desiring' ended. My heart ached. Suddenly my eyes became wet, completely blurring the beautiful image on the ceiling.

The following week I took with me to Pondicherry my slides of Grand Teton Mountains and the Yellowstone National Park, which I had captured in my Canon FTQL camera during the 7,000-mile camping trip across the US, a year-and-a-half earlier. But when I was about to start the slide show, Larry Shinn, his wife, Nancy, and their two daughters dropped in. 'Perhaps, we should see the slides later,' suggested Mahe to me.

'But Mahe,' protested Nancy, 'We'd love to see the slides, especially as they are Mano's.' Larry added, 'Particularly since they are of the Wyoming area.'

I told my American friends, 'But there are practical difficulties. You can see the slides comfortably only if you lie down. My mother takes the couch, and Suja and I lie down on the floor to see the slides.'

Larry replied, 'If you can lie down on the floor, so can we.'

Before I could respond, Larry plonked himself on the floor and Nancy followed suit. Their daughter, Christie, who was seven, lay down next to Sujatha and their toddler, Robyn, lay down with her head on Larry's arm. I began the show. The first slide was that of a geyser, shooting dazzling white steam and hot water high into the azure sky.

'Old Faithful,' declared Sujatha, matter of factly.

I then showed a slide of back-lit elks with silver-lined antlers, standing majestically in a lush meadow with a backdrop of nearby snow-capped mountains, followed by a close shot of a bison with a luxuriant mane and a huge hump, peacefully grazing near a clump of trees beside a tranquil stream.

'Though I used a 135mm telelens, I had to go fairly close to the animal,' said I.

'It's a serene picture. But look at the bull's eye. Isn't it fierce?' Mahe chipped in and added, 'The following day on our way to Montana, Hari bought a small town newspaper. On the front page was a news item about how an unsuspecting photographer was gored to death by an annoyed buffalo. I thanked God that Mano's buffalo had not got angry with him.'

Meanwhile, Dr Makhani was on one of his unscheduled evening rounds with his retinue. As the doctors approached Mahe's room, they saw that the doors were shut. The frosted glass panes of the doors indicated that all the lights inside had been turned off.

'Perhaps, she is sleeping. Shall we skip her room?' asked a senior doctor.

'You mustn't find excuses to shorten the rounds,' Dr Makhani admonished him. 'If she is sleeping at 7.30 in the evening she may be unwell. So, let's find out, shall we?'

The doctors opened the doors, switched on the lights and gasped. They had not anticipated the strange sight that met their eyes. Sprawled on the floor was a giant of a white man in Bermuda shorts, a shapely white woman in T-shirt and jeans, a little girl with flaxen hair and a toddler along with me and Sujatha. All of us were lying on the bare floor, for heaven's sake.

'What happened, what happened?' asked Makhani with concern.

Before the doctors had entered and disturbed the peace that reigned over the entire group in the room—except Robyn who was sleeping—had been fully engrossed in the slide show. Now, suddenly, in the harsh brightness of the tube lights, we looked rather stupefied. Dr Makhani's first impression was that we lay in a random, haphazard manner but he then noticed that without exception, the entire group lay supine and that everybody's head, like Mahema's, was oriented towards the east.

'My God,' said Makhani. 'I hope this is not some sort of a macabre, ritualistic mass-suicide pact.'

He then shouted, 'Alert the Emergency, bring all the oxygen cylinders.'

One of the doctors dashed out at once. Realizing that things were getting out of control, I came out of my stupor and sprang into action.

'Oh, Doctor, Doctor, we are fine. Don't worry, I'll explain it all in a minute.'

I sent someone flying to call the doctor who had gone to alert the Emergency. By now Larry and the others sat up. Having been rudely awakened, Robyn started screaming at the top of her voice. His voice shaking with anger, Makhani asked, 'Why the devil are you all lying down on the hospital floor at 7.30 in the evening?'

'We were all looking at slides,' I explained, calmly.

'Slides?' asked Makhani, his anger unabated. No one had noticed the innocuous, compact, grey-coloured Kodak carousel slide projector on the floor which was, anyway hidden by Shinn who was now seated on the floor, watching the proceedings with a bemused smile. The tube lights, which were burning brightly, had almost completely faded out the image on the ceiling. At any rate, none of the doctors had any reason to look up at the ceiling.

'Slides?' asked one of the doctors, 'we don't see any slides.'

I switched off all the lights and asked the doctors to look up. They gasped again, but now on seeing an imposing image before them.

'This is Yellowstone River,' I said proudly. 'I am projecting the slides on the ceiling because this is the only way Mahema can see the slides. The rest of us are forced to lie down to look at the pictures,'

I added laughing.

Then I switched on the lights, switched off the projector and began to introduce my friends to the doctors. Dr Makhani looked at me with an expression bordering on admiration. This guy seemed not only devoted to his wife, but full of innovative ideas to keep his wife's morale high. Nevertheless, characteristically, he wanted to have the last word.

'There is a ward here full of patients in casts,' he admonished me with mock anger, 'who are bored stiff and would enjoy a slide show on America. But our friend here is so very selfish that he'll show the slides only to his precious wife and foreign friends.'

In early 1973, there was no television in South India. The following weekend, in the orthopaedic general ward, a wall was cleared to project my slides. A motley group of patients, young and old, male and female, some with crutches, some in wheelchairs and two or three in cranked up beds, all of them in plaster casts, waited impatiently to see the slides. Almost all the patients were simple, village folk. A few doctors, nurses, and orderlies were also in the audience. The first slide was that of a 'clover leaf' road intersection of 'free ways', taken from a descending aircraft. I explained how this helped the free flow of vehicles at road junctions. The next slide was that of a behemoth multi-wheeled truck. I had taken a shot of this parked vehicle with my four-year-old daughter Sujatha sitting on the front bumper. The next slide showed an elephant with a sparrow sitting on one of its tusks.

'Doesn't the sparrow resemble my daughter, sitting on the bumper in the earlier picture?' I asked the group. The patients momentarily forgot their pain and sorrow and laughed with total abandon.

5

I often found myself in a semi-dazed state, despite the helpful, friendly attitude of the JIPMER staff. Sometimes, I found the hospital atmosphere stifling. At such times—especially when Mahema was on a long spell of sedation—I would wander to the back of the hospital premises where there was a small cashew grove devoid of cashewnuts. I would sit on one of the low-flung, sprawling, strangely beautiful branches, with my feet nearly touching the ground, to reflect and contemplate.

As an undergraduate student at American College in Madurai in the late 1950s, all I wanted was to do my MSc in Chemistry and, after a break, become a lecturer, preferably at my alma mater and then work on my PhD, to become a professor.

Unfortunately, my father, a Madurai municipal doctor, suddenly died of a heart attack when he was only fifty. The duty of supporting my widowed mother and my two brothers fell upon my shoulders. In those days, jobs were hard to come by. Just then, my college principal received a request from a British factory in Madras to recommend a bright young chemistry graduate for the post of a chemist. The principal thought that it was 'Godsent'. So, I joined this company.

I was not jumping with joy. In my professional life, I had hope of walking between noble edifices in a college campus, through paths shaded by stately trees. Now, in reality, I was walking from one asbestos roof shed to another through acid mist and oxide dust. I had hoped to listen to lectures, the laughter of young boys and girls and the chirping of birds. Instead, I heard the pounding and screeching sounds of machines. Then I told myself that if this was my lot, at least for then, I would do my best and try to shine. So, I worked innovatively, going beyond a chemist's job. My British bosses liked me. Within a span of three months, I introduced an electro polishing process which improved the quality of a component and reduced its cost. My basic salary was virtually doubled. With my BSc degree, I was getting as much as a lecturer would get with an MSc degree.

Soon I began enjoying my work. There were opportunities for being creative. The company introduced into India, in a big way, miners' electric safety cap lamps, which began replacing Davy's safety lamps in collieries. The electric lamp is far brighter, more efficient and much safer than Davy's lamp. This improved the lot of the miners and helped the vital coal sector a bit. And I was happy that I had a small part in this.

However, my heart was in teaching. So, when my elder brother completed his higher studies and became a lecturer, I resigned from my job to do my master's degree at my alma mater. My British bosses were reluctant to let me go. I was given a good increment and a promise to send me on a three months special training to England in some style. I was even offered a holiday in Paris and Rome, at the company's expense. This was rather unusual in those days. In the meantime, my principal—who recommended me to the company in the first place—also thought that I should stick to the job. So I withdrew my resignation.

There were procedural delays in sending me abroad but the company did keep its promise. I had wonderful enriching experiences in England, Paris, and Rome in 1962. In those days, someone going abroad was so uncommon that a person is likely to introduce his friend saying: 'Meet my friend Ramu, "foreign returned".' I was ready for marriage and I realized with great joy that my new qualification of a 'foreign returnee' greatly enhanced my value in the matrimonial market.

Just at the right time, Mahema's parents were looking for a suitable boy. The fact that I was a foreign-returned chap helped them to accept the proposal for the alliance readily. During the time when I was Mahema's fiancé, almost everyday I used to think without a shadow of doubt that it was most fortunate that I was stopped from resigning my job to go for higher studies. Had I done it, I would not have even met Mahema, leave alone becoming her fiancé. I smiled and swung my legs, thinking about the period of our courtship.

When Mahe's mother invited me—that is, soon after Mahe's and my marriage alliance was agreed upon by all concerned—to visit her daughter in her house, I felt jubilant. As I wrote earlier, I visited Mahe's house for the first time on 31 May 1963, seven months before our wedding. The process of falling in love, even if ours was a 'partially' arranged one, was a wonderful thing. My first visit to Mahe's house was a memorable one for me as well as for her.

From then on I began visiting Mahema's house twice or thrice a week. And we began exchanging letters in between my visits. Naturally, I took a great deal of trouble to make the illustrations in my letters to my fiancée better than those I had done for mere cousins. I wanted my fiancée to fall head over heels in love with me. So, I did what I could do well. Needless to say that she loved the illustrations.

At this stage, naturally, I found the time I spent with Mahema, heavenly. One evening I told her, 'You have beauty, an innate good nature and poise. You are religious. I must say that you are a little angel.'

'Am I, really?' she asked me with an angelic smile.

'Yes, you are,' I affirmed.

'And by contrast,' I added, 'I am a ruffian sometimes and look like one too. I'm irreverent and not very religious.'

'You are a Kutty Chathan, then,' she observed. (Kutty Chathan means 'mischievous little devil').

I laughed and asked her, 'How are you going to put up with a little devil?'

'Once in a while, Mano, a little angel finds a little devil so irresistible that she'll willingly follow him!' she said and then her tinkling silver bell laughter cascaded over me.

Our delightful conversation inspired me to send her a letter with a cartoon of a little devil leading a little angel.

'Thunder Cloud' was the high sounding name that Mahema affectionately gave, to my low-powered, second-hand scooter. I drove this vehicle to her house on the evening of the very day I had bought it, though the scooter badly needed tuning up. It produced such a racket and spewed out so much blue-grey smoke that Mahema teased me saying that she thought that I had arrived there on a thunder cloud. By the time I visited her again after three days, the scooter had been fully tuned up.

It had become quiet and had stopped smoking. But its name remained. Later, when Mahema wrote a verse for me, 'Thunder Cloud' had a place in it.

'TIs TWILIGHT
Soon IT'LL BE NIGHT'
SHADOWS CREEP
STARS BEGIN TO PEEP
BUT
you ARE NOT HERE
MY EYES GLISTEN WITH TEARS
My HEART FILLS WITH FEARS

WHEN... OH ...WHEN
WILL you COME ?
MY BELOVED ...
RIDE FAST
TIME'S PAST
RIDE TO ME
ON your PRANCING STEED
THE THUNDER CLOUD
RIDE - RIDE - RIDE WITH SPEED
COME ... OH ... COME
FASTER ~ NEARER · CLOSER
TO ME

As both Mahema and I were interested in art, we talked a great deal about art and architecture—Indian, Chinese, and Western, but especially about Renaissance art and architecture. We had already decided on an Indian art tour. Going on a European tour to see its art treasures was a far-fetched dream in those days, for young middle-class Indians.

For our engagement, I wished to present Mahe an ink drawing by me, as a part of my 'engagement letter'. So, two weeks before our engagement, I started working on a fine, detailed ink drawing of the handsome head of *David*, Michelangelo's famous marble sculpture, which I completed on time. Later, one of Mahe's Irish friends teased her saying that by presenting my drawing, without spending any money, I escaped from presenting her a diamond ring. Mahe told her friend that any man could buy a diamond ring from a shop. Not everybody could present his own original artwork. For her, my drawing was more precious than a diamond ring. It occurred to me that a person's action could be looked at in a negative or a positive way. Fortunately for me, Mahe looked at my action positively.

After our engagement, Mahema's parents allowed me to take her out, which was quite unusual in those days. However, they didn't want me to take her on my scooter, till we were married. Now, they allowed me to take her to church, restaurants, and cinemas, nowhere else of course. Actually, it wasn't I who took her out. Rather, it was Mahema who took me around in the old Morris Minor her family owned. I couldn't drive a car then and so I sat primly—sometimes not so primly—by her side, as my fiancée drove the jalopy that was a decade or so older than her.

About two months before our marriage, we went to the movie, *To Kill a Mockingbird*. In a restful scene, the child goes to sleep with a teddy bear by her side. I asked Mahema, 'As a child, did you take a teddy bear with you when you went to sleep?'

She at once replied, 'No, Mano, I didn't,' and after a brief pause added, 'But two months from now, I will be taking a big teddy bear with me to bed.'

I laughed so boisterously that the quietude of the movie house was briefly disturbed. In my next letter to her, I drew a cartoon of a pretty doll resting her hand gently upon the arm of a teddy bear, for the salutation. Mahema noticed the greed and great expectations in the facial expression of the bear. She was delighted.

Many years later, our conversation and this drawing had far-reaching beautiful consequences.

The next film we saw was *My Geisha* starring Shirley MacLaine. The light-hearted story is about filming Puccini's *Madama Butterfly*. It was shot in Japan, in order to capture the flavour of the country. The aria 'Un Bel dì, Vedremo' from this opera was used as the theme song and Mahema loved it. She borrowed a record of *Madama Butterfly* from an Irish friend, Amy. Mahema and I played this aria again and again whenever I visited her house. We talked a great deal about Japan's scenic beauty, its people and their aesthetic traditions.

During this period, one evening when I visited Mahema's house, her mother told me that Mahema was upstairs on the open terrace admiring the moonlit night. She wanted me to join Mahe there. I was delighted.

'Aha,' I told myself, 'I can now be alone with her without periodic scrutiny.'

When I went up to the open terrace, I was simply floored. There she stood shyly, clad in a genuine kimono, with a matching hairstyle, a fan in hand. She even wore traditional Japanese wooden sandals. There was a small, low wooden board with a tablecloth and an ikebana-like flower arrangement on it. Two silk grass mats lay on the floor for us to sit on. A print of a Japanese watercolour hung close by, on the outer wall of the staircase room. All this was set near the Rangoon creeper, which was now in full bloom.

Mahema called herself Miss Foofutsin, knelt down beside me to serve me tea in a small Japanese tea cup. I asked her whether Foofutsin meant anything. She replied that it meant 'Maiden Butterfly'.

One can imagine what a boost all this gave to my already inflated ego!

In the soft moonlight, it all appeared unreal and dreamlike. When I tried to kiss her on her lips, she moved away from me and stood under the Rangoon creeper. Mahema, like the blossoms above her head, seemed to glow in the slanting rays of the moon. I walked to where she stood. Perfunctorily, she held her fan in front of her lips and said, 'No, no, no, Foofutsin won't,' but anyway allowed me to lower her fan and give her a long, intense kiss. So, it came to pass that when I kissed her for the first time ever on her lips, she was in a beautiful kimono, bathed in moonlight, blushing deeply and under a bower of clusters of flowers. That night when I went home, I felt that I was riding on clouds. So, I made an appropriate drawing in my next letter to her.

Our wedding day drew near. Two weeks before the wedding, as it sometimes happens before weddings, there was a difference of opinion between one of Mahema's uncles and me. I thought he was pompous and he thought I was boorish. He declared that I was a jungli…a kaattaan…(loosely a savage).

I wondered how I should react. Actually, I had nothing against kaattaans. They had certain virtues which more civilized persons often lacked. Indeed, in those days, I was a bit of a bumpkin. Now, what with our international outlook, what with Mahema and I listening to arias from *Madama Butterfly*, with her serving me tea in Japanese style and what with I being called a kaattaan, I was given on a golden platter an idea for my next letter to Mahema. I did a cartoon of a kaattaan with a jolly expression holding a shield and a lance in one hand, and the hand of a cute woman in a kimono in his other hand.

To complete this drawing, I had to race against time. I had to work on it in my office too. While I was giving the final touches, an old man who worked in my department chanced to look at this drawing. With a horrified expression, he asked me to destroy the drawing at once. I asked him, 'What? I've spent many hours developing the drawing. Why should I destroy it now?'

But he was insistent. 'Saar,' he said hesitantly, 'I'll give you the reason if you promise not to get angry with me. I want nobody else to see the drawing because…well, because the savage has a rather striking resemblance to YOU!'

When Mahema received my letter with this cartoon, her delight and relief were immeasurable. She showed the drawing to her uncle who burst out laughing and even said, 'Mahema, what an imaginative, talented guy you are marrying.' Since then he became an affable uncle to me too.

Later in life, Mahema often used to narrate this incident to her friends and in public speeches. She would say: 'For every adversarial event one has many options to react. Mano had a way of winning without hurting the opponent.'

My extra reward was my wife's words of admiration!

On 27 December 1963, our wedding day, early in the morning, I was busy gift-wrapping Jack London's classic *The Call of the Wild* to give Mahe in the bridal chamber. A whole lot of relatives were around. My aunt Kiruba asked me which book I was wrapping to give to Mahema in the night. At once, my eight-year-old cousin Nirmala observed, 'What else? It ought to be a book on kudumba kattu-pattu thittam.' ('Family planning' euphemism for 'birth control'). Everyone burst out laughing. Her father, Thambu, said that he did not know whether to laugh or cry, but laughed anyway.

We were married. For the wedding, Mahema wore a sari of simple elegance, a charam of fragrant Madurai jasmine on her kondai, and a garland of fresh tuberoses. She did not go to a hairdresser or a beautician, nor did she wear lipstick, not even face powder. But they all decreed that she was a lovely, lovely bride and I, of course, readily agreed.

Friends and relatives talked approvingly of the tilt of her head towards mine in the formal wedding portrait. An uncle of mine, Muthaiah, became the butt of much teasing now, as he had tilted his head towards the uninclined, upright head of my aunt Doris. A girl cousin tried to give a Mahemaesque tilt of her head towards her groom for her wedding picture. But the unimaginative, unromantic photographer kept telling her, 'Oh, Amma, your head has sagged to one side yet again.'

After our wedding reception, there was an informal dinner for a group of relatives and friends. At the dinner table, as her bridegroom, I commented about her sari and what I was looking forward to do with it. She blushed and then had a dream-like expression. I had never before seen her face like this. I shared my thoughts with her about her appearance. Her face now had almost a trance-like quality and she subconsciously tilted her head towards me yet again. Then there was a flash. Fortunately, the official photographer had recorded her facial expression as I shared my thoughts with her.

The food arrived, but her plate remained empty. So, I served her food, when she came out of the trance. At that time would I have guessed that in later years, it would be my destiny to serve her for the rest of her life?

Now, nine years later, as I sat on the cashew branch at the back of the JIPMER hospital complex, I told myself, 'The time had come for the acid test.' Would I have the moral fibre and the mental stamina or even the willingness to serve her for years on end? Yes, I believed I would.

There were many good reasons for my resolve. At the solemn wedding service, in the reverent atmosphere of the church, witnessed by many dear ones, I made the pledge: 'To have and to hold, for better, for worse, for richer, for poorer, in sickness and in health, to love, cherish and honour, till death us do part.' I have known some religious Christians who made this pledge and did not keep the promise later. I am not even a very religious Christian but I intended to keep the promise solemnly made. This was not the only reason. I adored Mahe and I would do my best to keep her morale up. My mother would be a great support. So I had every hope of passing the acid test. Time would tell whether I would succeed.

My feet was touching the ground as the cashew branch that I sat on had slowly sagged under my weight. Earlier, as I sat on the branch, swinging my legs, revelling in happy memories, my head had been briefly in the clouds. Now my feet were on earth, bringing me back to the hard reality of the present. I looked at my watch.

'Whether it is time for the acid test or not,' I told myself, 'it is time I went back to Mahe's room.'

In the gathering darkness, I walked briskly toward the hospital's main door, squaring my shoulders, fortified anew after the brief respite, to meet the difficult situation ahead...at least for the present... hopefully always.

6

I used to sit close to Mahema's bed and pinch her hard on different parts of her body, below her shoulders while earnestly talking with her. She never protested as she did not realize that she was being pinched. One day, while standing at the foot of her bed, I pinched her toe and she screamed, 'Mano, something is hurting my toe!' I was jubilant. Obviously she had regained sensation, at least in one spot. Messages of pain had travelled from one end of her body to the other, from her toe to her brain. From that time, Mahe began regaining sensation in patches here and there. The area of recovery began to increase too.

When I went to Madras, I drew two abstract female figures in outline—the front and the rear views, along with drawings of the palms and soles, all on A4-size tracing paper. From this original, I took many ammonia prints, Xerox machines not being available in India then. Back in Pondicherry, on every third or fourth day, I would put down the date on a fresh print, take an 'inventory' of Mahe's areas of touch perception and shade appropriately those regions in the ammonia print with a blue pencil, the depth of the colour indicating the extent of recovery. I mounted these date-marked drawings in series on the wall in her hospital room. When Dr Makhani came to her room with his retinue, he would ask, 'What is the writing on the wall today?' Such a marked extent of recovery was apparent between the first and the fifth prints that I wrote on the fifth print in bold letters, 'You've come a long way, baby.' But after that, to my disappointment, the pace of Mahe's recovery of touch perception began slowing down. There was hardly any difference between the eighth and ninth prints and to my utter dismay, none at all between the tenth, eleventh, and twelfth. Really, there were only patches of recovery here and there, much of which was only partial.

On the day I shaded the thirteenth sheet, I had a foreboding sense of finality. The recovery of her muscular movements seemed to have already ended. Now the recovery of her touch perception too had stopped. That afternoon I walked slowly with a heavy heart, my head downcast, to my peaceful cashew grove for solitude and introspection.

When we returned to Madras from Oberlin, I had every reason to hope for a bright future. We had new dreams. It seemed that I had the means to make the dreams come true. Now, it seemed that my dreams had been all but wiped out. When I thought of my earlier high hopes and the utter hopelessness that I felt in my bones now, new lines for the ongoing verse came to my mind:

'We've only just begun,' Mahe and I swore
But cruel Fate had some other plan for us in store
For, it was misfortune that smote
And my hopes vanished in clouds of smoke
My dreams, my dreams, those highway bandits stole
And took away with them, a part of my soul.

I felt very low. I repeated the last two lines and tears filled my eyes.

My dreams, oh my dreams, those highway bandits stole
And took away with them, a part of my soul.

I began chanting the two lines in a slow, sorrowful, singsong way. During the following two or three months, whenever I felt low, I chanted the two lines in privacy.

Now, sitting on the cashew branch, I suddenly thought about the chiththaal who had fallen from a scaffolding many, many years ago. When my father talked about this woman, I was a schoolboy. I had been quite rattled to learn about the possibility of people living without sensation and bodily movements. That seemed terrible enough. But now after reading all that I could about spinal injuries, I had come to realize that quadriplegia was a far worse monster. I knew now, that apart from being prisoners in their own sensationless bodies, quadriplegics were susceptible to bedsores, and that avoiding this scourge was an endless battle. As quadriplegics did not have bladder control, they lived under the constant threat of acute urinary infection, stones in the bladder and more. Bowel movements were undignified and could be a source of social embarrassment. Quadriplegics who did not sweat below their shoulders found the summer heat unbearable. Spasms could be debilitating. While the muscles began to waste away, a quadriplegic tended to put on weight due to the build-up of adipose tissues resulting from total lack of physical activity. On the other hand, drastic reduction in the intake of food could cause dietary imbalance and acidity. The situation of the quadriplegic only worsened with advancing age.

I felt that Mahema herself might have the fortitude to bear the ordeals and indignities that were in store for her in the years to come. But how was I going to watch her suffer year after year? I was just an ordinary human being with human frailties. How long could I sacrifice my own legitimate human needs and suppress normal human youthful desires? How would I stand the endless trial?

To add to our troubles, I myself was slowly but irrevocably moving towards blindness. I suffered from retinitis pigmentosa, for which there is no known cure. How were we going to cope? How could I withstand the constant economic drain? What kind of a wife was Mahe going to be? What kind of a home could we provide for our daughter? When I thought about Sujatha, I felt a wrenching sensation in my heart.

But wait, I thought. After all, Sujatha's mother is still alive. While there is life, there is always room for hope. I knew that I was a creative, artistic, scientific person, a problem-solver by nature. I could surely channelize these talents into rebuilding a home based on our altered situation.

Besides, from the time I met Mahe, I had realized that people were extraordinarily warm to her....

~

A year after India's Independence, Mahema's father accepted a position as an attaché in the Indian embassy in Singapore. At that time, Malcolm MacDonald, the British Governor General for Southeast Asia, was then the most well-known and popular man in Singapore. He built excellent rapport with the then Third World leaders—including Jawaharlal Nehru, Sukarno, and Jomo Kenyatta—and favoured the end of the colonial era. Actually, his Tory blimps later called him the man who made the sun set on the British empire.

One day, Mahema's family went to see a ship docked at Singapore, where the family happened to meet Malcolm MacDonald, who struck up a lively conversation with Mahe. Later, Malcolm sent Mahe an autographed picture of him chatting animatedly with her. And she wrote him a letter thanking him for the photograph. A regular correspondence between them ensued, which flowered into a long-lasting friendship. When Malcolm met Mahe for the first time in the ship, he was forty-nine and she was a child of nine.

Many years later, after Malcolm had retired from active service, when Mahe was the programme director in Asia House at Oberlin College, she invited him to talk about the end of the British colonial era. In a dinner hosted by the president of the college in Malcolm's honour, a professor asked him, 'Mahema was only a child and you were a statesman, what did you two talk about?'

Malcolm promptly replied, 'Oh, she talked about the problems in school and I talked about the problems in the world.'

When Malcolm MacDonald heard about Mahe's spinal injury,

he sent her a cable from England saying that he received the saddest news in his life and that he would like to visit her at JIPMER, if his visit would not cause her inconvenience. Mahe dictated a letter to him saying that she would rather have him visit her after she returned home, when she would be in a better state to receive him. He did visit her after she returned home.

From statesmen to clergymen, from storekeepers to floor sweepers, both men and women, trusted Mahe and tended to be warm, friendly and helpful to her. I attributed this to her good looks, dignity, and poise. But now, after the ravages of the accident, confined to a bed in JIPMER, as she was, she could hardly be described as traditionally attractive. Even then, I realized with amazement, that everybody in the hospital was virtually 'turned on' by her. Divakar wrote, 'If she can stir a hospital, clamped down to a bed, what can't she do when she begins moving about in a wheelchair?'

I concluded that it was the beauty of her personality rather than her patrician good looks or accomplishments that made people rally round her. She won the trust of the young doctors and some of them—especially the women doctors—confided their heartthrobs and heartaches to her. Soon Mahe's room became a meeting place after work hours for many young doctors of both sexes. Their presence in turn helped Mahe to be in good cheer. Dr Rajayee even held an informal party with cakes, savoury dishes, and coffee, in Mahe's room. Other doctors followed suit and threw parties in her room under one pretext or another.

However, a doctor named Paragon Chellamuthu, a regular visitor to Mahe's room, was not a part of this group. He was a well-groomed young man who dressed with care and wore a large badge with the logo 'JESUS SAVES'. He would visit Mahe's room only when other young doctors were not there.

When I returned to Mahe's room from the cashew grove, brooding on the difficult future, I found Dr Chellamuthu sitting there with an air of self-importance. Mahe's mother Sundaramma told me, 'Paragon was telling Mahe about God's mysterious ways. I wish you too had been here to listen to him. Anyway, you're right on time, Manohar, for the prayer he's just going to begin. Do join us.'

Though I had agnostic tendencies, I liked the comforting aspect of prayers, the goodwill they generated and the fellowship they fostered. I had often felt good hearing Mahe's heartwarming prayers for others. But Paragon's prayer was very disappointing. His prayer was long, repetitive and interspersed with too many 'sweet Jesuses' and 'beloved Christs'. Actually Paragon's prayer was a constant reminder to God about what a wonderful Christian Paragon was.

When Paragon Chellamuthu was eventually ready to depart, I told him, 'Saying a prayer for Mahema is fine. But helping her concretely is even better. Why don't you join the midnight doctors who turn her in bed every three hours? You can occasionally relieve one of the doctors from his nightly chore.'

'But, brother, I'm now in paediatrics. Dr Makhani would not like me to interfere....'

'That's no problem. I'll get Makhani's clearance. He would in fact....'

'I'm sorry, brother. If I join the group that turns her at night, it will interrupt my sleep. I am preparing to appear for the entrance exam for M.S., you see.'

'But, so is Tikki.... His sleep is interrupted every night.... After all, I am requesting you to come only once in a....'

Before I could finish the sentence, Paragon hastily said, 'If you'll excuse me, I have to go now to study,' and hurriedly left the room.

The following evening, when I talked about Paragon Chellamuthu to the other young doctors, Tikki told me, 'We stay away from him. If we give him half a chance, he'll preach to us for the next half hour.'

'Yes, the fellow wants only to preach to my wife and say his long-winded self-promoting prayers,' I said, 'but he'll not lend a helping hand. He thinks that'll be too much bother.'

'Being very religious, perhaps he thinks prayers are more important.'

'How could he think that?' I asked. 'After all, Christ's most important parable clearly says that the Good Samaritan did not merely say his prayers for the injured man and push off. Had he done so, he'd not have been called the "Good Samaritan". Instead, he'd have been called the "Paragon of Prayers".'

Everybody laughed so uproariously that Mahema woke up. 'Let me also hear the joke,' she begged.

A week or so later, Paragon held Mahema's sensationless hand in his and prayed. 'Lord, I am not bothered about her physical state....Yes, sweet Jesus, I do not care about her physical cure, beloved Christ.... But, merciful Father, I am deeply concerned about her soul, sweet Jesus.... Oh yes, I am greatly worried about her soul. Make her a true believer like me, precious Saviour. Thank you, thank you, thank you Lord for making me your torchbearer.... Save her soul, beloved Christ...Save her soul.... Save her soul.... Save her. Save her. Save hersavehersavehersave her.... Amen.'

After the prayer was done, I called him aside and demanded, 'What do you mean, you do not care about her physical condition or cure? Who are you to care or not to care? Why the hell should you care anyway? After all, she isn't your wife, is she? You'll say your prayer, get your kicks and go away. The burden isn't with you. It's with her, with me...my family.'

'But, brother, the body is transient and the soul is eternal. Should I not be more concerned about her soul? As of now she remains condemned. I want our precious Christ to save her, spiritually. I want our sweet Jesus to save her. I want....'

'Why save her spiritually? Go save yourself.'

'Brother, I am already saved.'

'Then go save your mother.'

Mahema's mother, who had quietly come up to us intervened. 'Manohar.' don't be rude to the nice boy, he's genuinely concerned about Mahema.'

Before I could answer her, Chellamuthu said, 'No, aunty, I'll answer him. He's under stress and is getting agitated because he is not God's child. Satan has a way of entering the minds of those who are vulnerable and who do not have God's protective arms around them. So, I'll answer him, aunty.'

He then turned to me and said with smug satisfaction, 'Brother, I must tell you with humility that my mother, father, their children and grandchildren are ALL saved, praise be to sweet Jesus.'

When Paragon went away, Sundaramma asked me in a reprimanding tone, 'What do you have against this very nice boy?'

I replied, 'I don't like him because he reminds me of the self-righteous Pharisees in the synagogue. According to Christ's parable, God Himself did not think much of him.'

'I do not appreciate your derisive way of talking about those who are truly religious,' she said.

'Allowing Mahema to pursue her religion does not mean stepping aside and allowing a self-centred, mind-manipulating, dandy-godman to use my wife's misfortune as a vehicle for his ego trips,' I replied.

My mother-in-law did not even try to understand what I was saying. Instead, she replied angrily, 'What you say doesn't make any sense,' and walked away.

For the next two weeks, Paragon Chellamuthu did not turn up in Mahema's room. Mahema's mother grumbled that Paragon had stopped visiting them because I was nasty to him. But I felt that the preachy types are usually thick-skinned and not easily put off. I was right. Paragon had not come because he was preoccupied with his mother.

One Wednesday evening, I returned to Pondicherry from Madras earlier than usual. When I entered Mahema's room, I heard Mahema and not Paragon, saying a prayer. I was surprised to see Paragon kneeling down on the floor with his head bent in a supplicant's posture, not his usual one of the dispenser of grace. I saw tears running down Mahema's cheeks and heard Chellamuthu whimpering. From Mahema's beseeching prayer, I gathered that Paragon's mother had some serious health problem. I marvelled that Mahema, despite her tragedy, had tears to shed for others.

After Mahema ended the prayer, Paragon lowered his head even further and sobbed. When he eventually opened his eyes, he saw me standing quietly in the room. Paragon got up, rushed to me, held my hand and said, 'Brother, brother, my mother has a fibroid in the uterus and they have sent a sample of it for biopsy. Please, please pray for her. Please pray that the tumour is benign.'

Earlier on, when the fellow was in his self-assured pompous mode, he had the smugness to declare that I was not God's child and that Satan had a way of entering the minds of those who were vulnerable and did not have God's protective arms around them. I realized that the truth was diametrically opposite. It was that self-proclaimed spokespersons of God had a way of entering and controlling the minds of those who were vulnerable due to misfortunes. So, I decided then and there to protect my dear wife from godmen and godwomen of all shades by holding my family at an intellectual distance from them.

7

There were activities in Mahema's room during the forenoons. Early every morning, she was given a sponge bath, made to lie sideways in order to brush her teeth, and her breakfast was fed to her, mostly by my mother. Then the team of doctors would spend a good deal of time with her. They would go through my bulletins on the wall. After a brief gap, the physiotherapist would come and would keep her entertained with his own preposterous stories of movies, even as he gave her the exercise. Then it would be time for lunch. In the evenings, young doctors—both men and women—would come to socialize.

What about the afternoons, especially during weekdays while I was at my work place in Madras? My mother (or her mother) who looked after her would doze off. Her head firmly held by the traction weights, Mahe could only stare at the ceiling, if she was awake. However, time did not hang heavily around her neck because she would entertain herself by thinking in great detail about many happy events in her life before the accident. She especially relished thinking about her early wedded life. I wish to present her thoughts now in her own voice....

~

For the church wedding ceremony, following the Tamil Protestant tradition, I wore a pale cream sari. Mano and I had chosen this simple but delicate Benarasi silk sari without excessive jarigai. Later, in my house, I changed into a gorgeous Kanjeevaram sari with non-flashy, muted colours for the reception dinner. It was the most beautiful sari I had worn ever since I began wearing saris. As I draped the sari, I had a happy thought that I would be entering the bridal chamber with my bridegroom in this sari. I wondered whether my groom would carry me through the threshold in the Western style.

Meanwhile, Mano went with my cousin Daya to the suite where we would be staying, to deposit my small suitcase, his shoulder bag, the two wedding garlands, an HMV record player, a 1936 Philips radio, a long-playing record with Tchaikovsky's *The Sleeping Beauty* on one side and *Swan Lake* on the other, a dozen candles, and a matchbox. He connected the player to the radio and hung the two garlands on the bedstead.

I returned to the reception hall where there was an informal dinner for close relatives and friends. Mano was already there. I could see that he liked me in this sari. Later, at the dining table he whispered to me, 'I eagerly look forward to untying this sari in the bridal chamber.' I blushed and soon slipped into a dream-like trance, full of contentment. Mano whispered again, 'During our early courtship, I told you that you are an angel. Now, with the facial expression that you have, you look almost celestial.' Just then there was a flash. The 'official photographer' had taken a shot, which soon brought me back to earth. This photograph was to become one of my favourite pictures of us. I had unconsciously tilted my head yet again towards my hero.

That night, Mano carried me across the threshold into the bedroom in the bridal suite. He gently laid me on the bed. After a couple of minutes I sat up. He gave me a gift-wrapped book. When I opened the packet I smiled and said, 'You know, Mano, *The Call of the Wild* is not at all inappropriate for a man to give his bride on the first night after the wedding.' He laughed and told me that, this naughty thought had not occurred to him. He also said that, I looked very pretty when I had an impish expression. He took a quick shower. I waited in great anticipation. Then I thought about the stream of letters Mano and I wrote to each other—around seventy of them each—during our seven-month courtship. All his letters had many illustrations. Now, would not moving in together stem the flow of letters?

'Oh, I'll miss his letters,' I thought.

Just then, he came out of the bathroom in his pyjamas, switched off the fan, lit the twelve candles, placed them strategically, then turned on the fan, gradually increasing its speed; in a way the flames of the candles just danced. He then pulled out a beautiful envelope and wanted me to read his 'wedding letter' in the candlelight. He said he could keep looking at his bride in the candlelight while she read his letter.

Just moments earlier I had thought that I would be missing his letters. I was delighted that I already received one. I sat up on the bed to 'absorb' the letter. The salutation drawing was of a doll in a Kimono with a fan in hand standing near an elegant pot with a bonsai tree. He had addressed me as his beloved Foofutsin. To give his letter an extra Japanese touch, Mano had stapled in the front a pale buff-coloured, translucent, net-like latticed sheet, which enhanced the beauty of the artwork. I so enjoyed reading it in the candlelight as Mano kept looking at my face.

Later, I freshened myself, retied the sari and went and sat quietly at the edge of the bed.

That night he told me, 'From now on, you will hear *The Sleeping Beauty* and *Swan Lake* again and again, night after night, when we go to bed. I promise you that, in later years whenever you hear *The Sleeping Beauty* and *Swan Lake*, memories of our early love life will flood your mind. But tonight, when you eventually doze off, I shall sit quietly and watch my Sleeping Beauty.'

But when the time came for the next step, I was very reluctant to allow him to undress me. I requested him with pleading eyes to put out the candles. He told me that the soft golden light shed by all the candles would enhance the beauty of my curves and contours, which would in turn heighten his visual pleasure.

'Always an artist, aren't you?' I told him, smiling shyly. He allowed me to take my own time to shed my bashfulness before I allowed him to take my clothes off. He told me that the side-lighting arranged by him did enhance the beauty of my youthful figure and added that sight was a wonderful thing. Neither poor Mano nor I knew at that time that he would be slowly losing his eyesight.

After an hour or so, it was Mano who dozed off first, even though he said that he would be watching his Sleeping Beauty. I was still wide awake. Irving Stone's popular book, *The Agony and the Ecstasy*, came to my mind. I smiled to myself. That was precisely what I had experienced tonight, first some agony, mental and physical, and then great ecstasy. How reluctant I had been to allow Mano to undress me during the early part of the night. But now? Now, the only thing I wore was the mangalyam as I lay beside him with total abandon. Rich flute trills alternated with complex violin runs to match my mood. But the music was not consistently soft. Every now and then, it rose to a crescendo.... Only, the crescendos of *The Sleeping Beauty* did not always coincide with my own. When we entered the room I had been his bride...now...now, I was his wife and the transition had been...wonderful.

The clusters of candles that he had strategically placed continued to burn, but had become short and stumpy, marking the passage of time...the most intense moments of my life, till then.

I turned to look at Mano. In the soft candlelight, he looked like a sleeping bear, a fully satisfied one. I looked at him again. He had told me that he would watch his Sleeping Beauty. Instead, now, I was looking at the sleeping bear...my own sleeping bear. And what a lot of hair my bear had on his chest. Perhaps I should comb all that unruly hair. This silly thought made me laugh. The 'tinkling bell' woke him up.

'You're still awake?' he asked me.

'Now that I know you intimately, I like you even more,' he declared and went to sleep again. I too went to sleep only to be woken up by him. Not that I minded. I was ready for him yet again. My bashfulness and apprehensions vanished once the barrier was broken. From then on, in the days, months, and years to come, I was ever ready for him, anywhere, any time of the day or night. I was ready for him, for instance, in a casuarina grove of a lonely seashore, at twilight as the crashing sounds of the relentless waves filled the air. I was ready for him under a large pungai tree, one tempestuous night, on a bed of tiny pink flowers strewn by the obliging tree, as unseasonal dark clouds from afar made rumbling sounds.... Again, I was ready for him at nightfall, near a jasmine creeper, on an open terrace of a large house, guarded by sentinels of coconut trees, their leaves rustling in the caressing breeze, while the moon hid behind a cloud and the stars winked...and on a primeval rock, hidden under a canopy of foliage, one afternoon, in the wilderness, by the side of a pristine mountain brook, intoxicated by the sensuous sounds of buzzing honey bees, warbling birds on trees and gurgling waters of the rushing stream. But more often, I was ready for him in the more conventional venue of bolted bedrooms on comfortable beds, as music from the record player set the mood and drowned out other sounds within the room.

On 28 December 1963, the day after my wedding, early in the morning, Mano took me on his scooter—for the first time ever from the bridal suite to my parent's house, where we received a tumultuous welcome. My father had arranged a beautiful lamp-lighting ceremony when passages of light were read from the Bible and Upanishads. Then Mano and I lit the five wicks of the lamp, while recorded veena music could be heard softly. This was rather unusual then in a Christian wedding house.

I may or may not be angelic but surely, I felt that I was in heaven during our honeymoon. I so immensely enjoyed our imaginative love-making, the beautiful sights we saw together, the lovely music we heard together, the book that we read together—*The Call of the Wild*—and the periodic feasts and fellowship with dear ones.

There was a touch of heritage too in our agenda. We spent a couple of days in Mahabalipuram, stayed for three days in Cubbon House, a colonial heritage mansion built around the mid-nineteenth century on the top of Nandi Hill, and a day in Mysore. Mano readily agreed to take a long, tedious journey in a ramshackle bus to Belur to see the exquisite Chennakeshava Temple, built around the twelfth century by the Hoysala dynasty. In the traveller's bungalow at Belur, just before taking me to bed, sitting opposite me, Mano held my hands in his and sang with feeling, Bharathiyar's 'Chinnan-chiru Kiliyea'. Just before he sang the line 'Kannathil mutham ittaal ullam thaan kalveri kolluthadi' (loosely translated as: A kiss on the cheek makes my heart go wild with drunkenness.) he planted a sumptuous kiss on my cheek. Apparently Mano's heart did not go all that wild, because he continued with the song. But my heart went wild. I felt intoxicated. I had always liked the song rendered by M. L. Vasanthakumari. That night, in the little town of Belur, the song took on a new dimension in my heart. That night became extra special when I received far more than a kiss on the cheek.

The following morning, we spent a good deal of time at the temple. Mano was happy that I knew a lot about it. He made two on the spot ink drawings of two apsaras, one of which was that of *Darpana Sundari* (Woman with a Mirror).

We returned to Madras. Mano went back to his technical job at Oldham and I, to my teaching job at the Stella Matutina College of Education. I felt that the honeymoon was not over. Mano felt the same way too, though for some reason, he would not use the word honeymoon.

Mano dropped me on his scooter in the mornings at my parent's house—which was fortunately just next door to my place of work— and then drove to Oldham and picked me up in the evenings from my parent's house.

He was allotted a JAWA motorcycle, which he had booked a year earlier, even before he met me. He promptly sold Thunder Cloud. When the new owner of the old scooter drove it away, I had tears in my eyes. This scooter had a prominent place in our letters during our courtship. My very first ride with Mano as his wife was on this scooter. During the three months as newly-weds, this scooter took us everywhere. But when the shiny, sleek and brand new JAWA came, I fell for it. Mano studied the manual and learnt about maintenance and repair of the JAWA motorcycle from an ace mechanic. He was able to do all the maintenance and repair work of this motorcycle with the help of a smart, young Anglo-Indian, who was keen on learning about the repair work. So, after the free services by the supplier, his JAWA never saw a mechanic's repair shop. The vehicle was in great condition, saving money and time. With confidence we went everywhere on his JAWA. Why, it even took us all the way to Kodaikanal. And what a joy it was to see from the pillion all the beautiful views of the hill road!

In Kodaikanal together, Mano took stunning photographs of the 'Princess of Hill Stations'. We went to Madurai to see the architectural heritage and the beauty of the surrounding countryside. I also enjoyed roaming around a jasmine garden with Mano. When the jasmine pickers gifted me, the pattanam ponnu (the city girl), a bunch of freshly plucked jasmine, I felt very happy. I realized time and again that one can derive great joy from simple things in life.

Moving in together, fortunately, did not stop us from writing to each other. Brief separations and special occasions always called for letters, handcrafted cards, artwork, and imaginatively created, not-so-expensive gifts.

About nine months after our marriage, Mano had to spend three weeks in Ranchi, in Bihar. He went there to train personnel in a new service branch that Oldham had opened. I missed Mano, but thoroughly enjoyed his colourful, illustrated, descriptive letters. The branch manager of the Ranchi unit was amused to find that often Mano received more letters than the office did, although not all of them were from me.

By the time Mano returned from Ranchi, my father had finished the flat that he built upstairs in his bungalow. My parents were old and I was their only child. They desperately wanted us to move into the flat. They agreed to the conditions Mano had set. Mano's mother, his younger brother, Mano and I moved into the flat, which gave us the opportunity to furnish the house tastefully. This move saved us one hour of each working day because my workplace was just next door.

When we decided to print our own Christmas cards, our very first card in December 1964, I used Mano's on the spot drawing of the statue of the 'Woman with the Mirror' at the Belur Temple. I used handmade paper for this, which was both tasteful and inexpensive. So, our greeting card project started with a romantic touch, as I used the drawing Mano did during our honeymoon.

In 1965, we went on our 'Indian art tour,' that we had often talked about during our courtship. We soaked ourselves in the rich, historic heritage of Hyderabad, Golconda, Aurangabad, Ajanta, Ellora, Daulatabad, and other places. We ended our tour in Bombay.

In Bombay, we stayed in the retiring room of Victoria Railway Terminus, that magnificent Indo–Saracenic heritage edifice. The official who allotted the room thought that we were newly-weds. He gave us the best room, normally reserved for high railway officials. He winked with good humour and said, 'Happy honeymoon at Victoria Terminus.' The spacious room lacked style. Its great asset was that water poured in profusion from the shower like a mini waterfall. I was glad I had a shower cap with me.

The night before our departure from Bombay, we went to the late show at Eros Cinema to see the movie, *My Fair Lady*. Mano and I were enthralled by this picture. He said it was the best movie that he had ever seen and I agreed. Matching the Edwardian ethos of the film, we went back to Victoria Terminus in a horsedrawn coach (appropriately called Victoria). I knew that we would be taking a shower together and the best was yet to come.... Oh, how I cherish these memories....

I had a set of Dutch oil paint tubes and brushes. In 1966, I verbally described oil painting techniques to Mano. His very first attempt was to paint an extra long country raft with a shapely, large sail that glided along Buckingham Canal, adjacent to Pulicat Lake, north of Madras. I was deeply impressed. I framed and proudly hung it in our drawing room, till an art lover picked it up, making Mano a professional artist.

Mano and I wanted a girl child and, in 1966, we were blessed with a daughter.

Mano made a detailed, large ink drawing based on his oil painting of the boat. He and I went to the Madras University Library. With the help of a librarian, we read many references—especially Henry Davison Love's *Vestiges of Old Madras*—about the canal and the boats. I took notes and then wrote a crisp text on this subject. So, we came out with a large size greeting card with the reproduction of Mano's ink drawing in front and my text inside. This card virtually became a sensation.

So in 1966, Mano was born as a professional artist, our daughter, Suja, was born, and so did this new genre of heritage collectors' cards too.

Stereophonic, long-playing records and record players were becoming available in India around this time. But the imported compact record players were expensive. Mano's brother Divakar sent from the US a set of brand new 'Phase 4' records which were then considered the ultimate in stereophony. So, Mano decided to build a high quality, powerful system at a lesser cost. He read all he could about stereophonic systems and gathered 'local information' about the market. He procured a custom-built amplifier from an electronic wizard, bought a UK-made Garrard record player from the Burma Bazaar pavement shop and two 12-inch twin cone Dutch Philips loudspeakers. He built two huge identical cabinets for the speakers, based on Goodmans design. Thus our apartment was filled with high quality music. For our fourth wedding anniversary, Mano presented me with a note which had a colourful cartoon, and a beautiful text, comparing our wedded life with stereo music.

He drew a cartoon of an old crank gramaphone but with two brass horn loudspeakers. An old-fashioned couple with their little daughter listening to the stereo music.

I HAPPY MARRIED LIFE IS LIKE A GOOD STEREO RECORD

There are two tracks within the same groove. Both are generally in unison, but they are often individualistic. Thus one track may have sweet melody while the other has rhythmic beats Again, one channel may have thundering percussion while the other has a silent pause But the combination is always harmonious, pleasing and impressive.

Anniversary 1967.

A couple of years earlier, Mano's classmate Secy encouraged him to take the AIC (Associate of Institution of Chemists) examination. Mano studied hard, took special laboratory training, appeared for the exam and came out in flying colours. Amidst all these, he also presented quality scientific and technical papers at Central Electrochemical Research Institute, at battery conventions and other institutions.

He spent long hours at the factory, studied hard for the AIC examination and built a music system. And yet he and I spent quality time together. How did we manage this? For one thing there were 104 weekend holidays plus many festival holidays, earned leave and casual leave, which gave us plenty of time. My working hours were less than Mano's, and my workplace was just next door. I had the time to spare. So, I polished Mano's shoes and cleaned his motorcycle each morning. If he worked on his oil painting in the morning, Mano would leave everything and rush to get ready. I would lay his clothes on the bedstead and keep his wallet, the motorcycle key, glare glasses, a handkerchief, and the like at the breakfast table. After he left, I would clean up the easel, wash the brushes and put everything in order. Mano's mother ran the kitchen efficiently. And I was involved in whatever he did and he in whatever I did. So, we spent plenty of time together sharing ideas and teasing each other. Oh, how wonderful it was!

It was a week before our fourth wedding anniversary of stereo music that Mano first realized that he could not see things well after nightfall. I was concerned and took him to an ophthalmologist who, after a thorough examination, advised Mano to eat carrots and take vitamin A pills.

'Then your night vision would become normal,' he assured Mano. 'Your angular perception is below average, but your equity and colour perceptions are excellent. You don't need glasses. Actually there is nothing seriously wrong with your eyes,' he declared. Alas, he was wrong. We were to learn later that Mano suffered from retinitis pigmentosa. Partial night blindness was actually the beginning of the end of his eyesight, so to speak.

I resigned from my job in 1968 to pursue my MA in English literature—after a gap of eight years—at my beloved alma mater, Stella Maris. Meanwhile, the AIC examination gave Mano the confidence and the impetus to pursue his master's degree in chemistry in the US. He chose Oberlin College. His brother too had done his master's degree at Oberlin. The college was well known for its excellence. The chemistry department was strong. The college was so enlightened that when it began in 1833, it adopted a policy of non-discrimination against blacks and women, which was extraordinary for that time. It had an exchange programme with the American College in Madurai, where Mano had studied and knew some Oberlin students.

A couple of days before his departure, we vacated the flat. Mano's mother and brother shifted to a small independent house. Suja and I moved downstairs to live with my parents. I was to join him a year later, after I completed my master's degree in 1970.

The night before Mano's departure to the US, we went to bed on a humble grass mat, lay on the floor in a very small bedroom bereft of any furniture. Both of us were acutely aware that, after this night, we would not be sleeping together for a year. Not surprisingly, the night turned out to be a rather wild one It was so wild that I could not help but repeat, in that den-like room, 'You are a primitive man...a primitive man...a primitive man.'

Now, as I lay supine on the bed at JIPMER that afternoon, I wished I could go back to that wild night with my primitive man in the den. Then I smiled. 'No,' I said to myself, 'that would not be a good thing, because my primitive man would go away the very next day to the US.'

Just as I was revelling in such thoughts at the JIPMER Hospital, three young doctors entered the room to turn me in bed. So the evening had arrived.

8

Dr Makhani assured Mahema, more than once, that someday soon, she would be able to walk out of JIPMER. Mahema implicitly believed this dynamic doctor's pronouncements. However, I thought it was exceedingly unlikely that she would ever walk again. Over the years, Mahema had learned to respect my objective, dispassionate assessments. And if I revealed my grave apprehensions about her recovery, her fighting spirit could be shattered. On the other hand, if I did not warn her about the high probability of her being a quadriplegic for the rest of her life, then, when the reality of her situation hit her hard, she could go into deep depression or worse.

What was I to do? Truly, I did not believe in hiding my genuine fears from Mahema. I wished to share all my thoughts with her, gently and sensitively, but I could not. Whenever I spoke, my voice shook and quivered like a dry twig in a storm. She listened and cried quietly.

Then one day, Makhani called me for a long private talk.

'Now Mahema is able to sit up without a stiff collar to support her neck, I think she can take a car journey safely. Perhaps it's time we thought of sending her home.'

I told him that my friend, Dr Mani M. Mani, had introduced

77

me to Dr Mary Verghese, head of the Rehabilitation Centre at the Christian Medical College Hospital,Vellore. I planned to take her there for rehabilitation so that she could learn to cope with her new way of life at home. The doctor agreed that perhaps it was not a bad idea.

I said, 'Doctor, I was touched by the way you took care of Mahema. A busy doctor like you needs undisturbed sleep. And yet you took the extraordinary measure of instructing your assistants to wake you up at least twice night after night, every time they turned her in bed. Do you do this for all the other quadriplegic patients too?'

Dr Makhani smiled. 'No, I'm afraid not. Actually, Mahema has been the only patient, at least so far, to be treated thus. Not that many quadriplegics turn up here.'

'May I know why you bestowed this special honour upon my wife?'

'Well, it's difficult to give reasons. The moment I met her I could see that she was a bright person who had the fortitude and the serenity to take this challenge. I have seen too many husbands walk out on their wives, even in less tragic situations. I had a gut feeling that you'd stick by your wife. Above all, I could see the concern and love your mother has for Mahema. Most quadriplegics don't live long. I thought this woman had a sporting chance of survival.... She may even thrive, despite her serious problems. So I decided to enhance her chances of survival. Now, JIPMER's gift to her is that she leaves this place without even a suggestion of a bedsore.'

I expressed my gratitude. Makhani was pleased. He smiled and said, 'Thank you. Most relatives of patients only complain and take special acts of kindness for granted.'

On the eve of Mahema's departure, her room was filled with young doctors. I had posted my last bulletin on the wall. I had drawn a picture of a chain of misaligned cervical vertebrae and a picture of a heart with misaligned auricles and ventricles. Underneath I had written a caption, on behalf of Mahema, 'I came here with a kink in my neck. I am leaving with a kink in my heart.'

Mahema said: 'I came here with a kink in my neck. Alas, the

kink remains. But, you have made this difficult period a little less difficult. So much so that, as Mano says in the bulletin, I am going away with a kink in my heart too, for I love you all.'

Some doctors smiled broadly, while a few had tears in their eyes. Tikki, who I thought had perhaps fallen in love with Mahema, became so emotionally overwrought that he left the room and did not come back.

The following morning, as the car took Mahema away from JIPMER, she waved her hand to the extent her quadriplegia permitted, to bid her well-wishers goodbye. Dr Rajayee came along with Mahema and me just in case Mahema needed medical attention during the 100-mile journey.

It was twilight by the time the car rolled into the Rehabilitation Centre in Bagayam, near Vellore. A wheeled stretcher was hurriedly brought out for Mahema. Many patients came out to see the newcomer and to find out what her fate had been. Two patients came out on crutches, one in a crude wheelchair and the rest sat on low wooden boards with tiny caster wheels, propelling themselves by pushing hand-pieces on the ground. They moved hither and thither, to gain better vantage points to watch the unfolding scene.

It seemed to me that Mahema was like a doe with a broken neck and the strange welcome that she received—from pairs of unblinking, staring, stabbing eyes—was from a posse of maimed rabbits, possums, sparrows, and squirrels in their pathetic mobility contraptions. One of the two on crutches was a bare-bodied, six-year-old boy in an oversized loin cloth. He stared at Mahema with such knitted eyebrows that his expression bordered on sullenness. As she was wheeled in, Mahema said to the little boy in English, 'Hullo, there.'

The little sparrow had not in the least expected the big doe to talk to him. He grinned shyly, swung around on his baby-crutches and hobbled away, wreathed in smiles.

The Rehabilitation Centre (Rehab, for short) was a few miles away from the main hospital at Vellore. It was a small, quadrangular unit with a spacious central courtyard. The land at the back of the quadrangular structure was dotted with small bushes, leading to a mango grove and thence to the slopes of a small hillock. It was a serene place, away from the madding crowd of Vellore township. The Rehab was the only one of its kind in the whole of India at that time, exclusively specializing in physical medicine and rehabilitation. And yet, during Mahema's stay, there were hardly twenty patients in all, most of them from poor families. This was not really surprising, as the poor are more susceptible to spinal injuries and malfunctions.

Murugamma, an eighteen-year-old girl, had become paralysed below her hip, when she fell into a well which was being dug. She had been on her way to work in a farm before dawn and did not see the gaping hole in the earth. Velu used to work at loading bullock-carts. When he saw a group of toddy-tappers struggling to raise a fallen palmyra tree trunk, Velu had spontaneously offered a helping hand—in this case, a helping back. The other men had decided that it was a hopeless exercise and abandoned their effort without warning Velu. The tree trunk had floored the lone man and broke his back.

Baby Gopal's parents knew about polio drops. But when they went for the drops to the neighbouring small town, the hospital there had run out of stock. Fresh stocks arrived, but Gopal's parents had not gone back to the hospital. Now, Gopal was six years old and afflicted with polio.

Biswas was a goods train guard. Somewhere in Madhya Pradesh, in a wayside station, he had spotted a group of dacoits approaching the train. He had whistled furiously and waved the green flag for the engine driver to start moving. This had angered the dacoits and one of them had shot him with a country musket. The shot had hurt only the man's knee. But when he fell from the now moving train, he had sustained a spinal injury at the hip. After receiving bad treatment from indifferent hospitals, he had eventually been brought to the humane Rehab with severe bedsores on his bottom. The poor man had to lie on his stomach for months, as the sores took their time to heal. Actually, with the exception of Mahema, all the patients were afflicted with bedsores, to the extent that the mild stench of decayed flesh had become a prevailing presence in the Rehab.

Lalchand owned a small sweet shop where he sat for too long. He liked the wares in his shop so much so that he simply gobbled up huge amounts, dripping with ghee. He kept putting on so much weight that he found it difficult to get up. A day came when he was unable to get up at all. His weight had pressed the spinal cord at the lower level so much that it became starved of nutrients, notwithstanding all that he ate. He was brought to the Rehab. When I first saw him, Lalchand was not obese at all and had in fact become thinner than me. He was able to walk with the support of his wife on one side and a walking stick on the other.

Each person had a story to tell.

But what struck me was this: while the wives of the male patients stood by their husbands, the husbands of most of the women patients had abandoned their wives. Often egged on by their kith and kin, these men simply remarried.... And there were enough parents around, willing to give their daughters in matrimony to such wife-deserters.

The enlightened doctors of Christian Medical College (CMC Hospital, for short) had found a niche for Dr Mary Verghese, when she had become a paraplegic herself after a road accident. It was thought that she would understand and be sympathetic to the plight of her patients on one hand and be a shining example to her wards on the other. So, the hospital administration had sent her on a special training programme to an institute in the US founded by Dr Howard Rusk, the father of physical medicine and rehabilitation. The CMC Hospital management built the rehabilitation centre at Bagayam and the wheelchair friendly house right next door, specially for Dr Mary Verghese. But, she chose to stay in the main hospital in Vellore and visited Bagayam merely twice a week. Those who ran the Rehab—the administrator, the therapists, the orthotic gadget designers, the nurses, the gardeners, the helpers—were all extremely dedicated people, who were especially kind and considerate to Mahema, the only quadriplegic there then. A strong sense of Christian charity prevailed.

It was during the first week of Mahema's stay at Bagayam that the truth of her situation hit her with full force. When I went to Bagayam from Madras, the following weekend, she requested me to wheel her away from the others to the mango grove and cried her heart out to me.

'Oh, Mano,' she whispered, 'Dr Makhani told me that I would walk, but everyone here seems to know that I won't.'

'I did warn you at JIPMER to be prepared for such an eventuality, didn't I?'

'Yes, you did, and I was partly prepared. But Mano, I secretly nurtured a hope. Now, I have an overwhelming sense of finality.... This is it.... I am now surrounded by disabled persons like me.... And yet, I don't at all feel that I belong here.' She began to sob again.

My heart ached to see her cry. I held her limp hand in mine and said, 'Actually, Mahe, you're the only quadriplegic in this place now and as such, physically, you are far worse off than the others. But, you have one advantage which the others lack.'

'What's that advantage, Mano?'

'You alone have ME as the spouse. None of the others here have this advantage, do they?'

'You are a conceited chap, aren't you?' she said laughing and crying at the same time. After a pause she added, 'Come to think of it, you are absolutely right.' She laughed and cried even more.

Fortunately, time did not hang heavily on Mahema's hands. During the day, she was fully occupied with the therapy and rehabilitation related activities. An extremely handsome medical student named Mahendran—who had heard about Mahema through his cousin in Madras—visited her one evening. The following evening he introduced a whole group of his classmates, both men and women, to her. One of them, Renu, brought some ice for Mahema one morning. That evening, she brought her classmates, named Johnnie, Liz, Deepa, and Arvind. The students began coming in droves. They invariably parked Mahema in her wheelchair near the small lily pond—the pride of the Rehab—and sat around her. They entertained her by teasing each other and narrating college anecdotes. One of the students, named

Pattu, played the guitar and the students sang for Mahe.

I told her, 'At JIPMER, it was the young doctors and here it's the students. I can see that while I'm away in Madras, there's no dearth of entertainment for you.' I was pleased to see her surrounded by young people.

It was now five months after the accident and at long last our car was repaired to my satisfaction. So, I drove to Bagayam from Madras in our car, taking our daughter with me. It was Suja's birthday. When we reached the Rehab, I saw Mahema at the mango grove with a big group of medical students. She had organized a surprise birthday party for Suja with the help of the medicos.

'You're wearing a sari,' I shouted out with joy. She wore the cream-coloured sari with cream embroidery work that I had gifted her for Christmas.

'Liz and Deepa tied the sari for me, by rolling me in the bed like a rolling pin,' said Mahema, beaming. She also wore a bronze chain that an American friend, Peg, had gifted her. Her hair had grown enough to make her look as if she had a short bob. Someone had dabbed lipstick on her lips.

I told her, 'You know, you look thoroughly contemporary now and not like Goddess Parvathi.'

Mahema was radiant with joy, when she saw how delighted her daughter was with the surprise party. Later, when she was alone with me, Mahe observed, 'I am determined to provide as natural and happy a home as possible for Suja…. Please help me, Mano….' She looked up and said, 'Please help me, God.'

Before the advent of television in India, those with severe mobility constraints depended wholly upon visitors for entertainment. Many patients in the Rehab at that time had virtually no visitors. These patients sat silently and stared vacantly at nothing in particular. They just sat all alone, with boredom writ on their blank faces. I could now understand why they all rushed out to see Mahema when she arrived at the Rehab. Mahema had provided a welcome break from their monotony. It occurred to me that I could make slide presentations to these patients, as I had done at JIPMER. The environment here was far more suitable for such shows. Surprisingly—perhaps not surprisingly—Dr Mary Verghese was unenthusiastic about my idea.

'Most patients do not understand English and many don't know Tamil,' she told me.

'But Doctor,' I replied, 'these slides would give them visual pleasure.'

'They face serious problems—physical, emotional, and financial. Pretty pictures will hardly give them any pleasure. Thanks for your thought, but I'm afraid that a slide show, especially on America, is unnecessary.'

9

When Mahe was in JIPMER, I used to go to the secluded cashew grove to spend time alone with myself. Now in Bagayam, I went to the mango grove, early in the mornings, climbed and sat on a branch of one of the mango trees to reflect—and think about the past, present, and future. I especially enjoyed thinking about the wonderful Oberlin years, which I wish to recapture now, in a coherent way. I went to the US in July 1969—twelve years after I had completed my bachelor's degree in Madurai in 1957—to work on my master's degree in chemistry at Oberlin College. Mahema and Sujatha were to join me a year later—after Mahe completed her master's degree in English literature in Madras.

We spent the final night before my departure from Madras in a small bedroom with a mat on the floor and two pillows....nothing else. Predictably it was a wild night. So Mahema kept repeating 'primitive man...primitive man...primitive man'. This energized me further and made me wilder.

The Reserve Bank of India in those days allowed only a pittance as currency exchange to students for transit expenses. Despite this limitation, with the help of a dynamic travel agent, I managed to travel by seven different airlines, seven different types of aircrafts with five stopovers, thrice at the airlines' expense, and with nine touchdowns.

Mahe wore one of my favourite saris—a white cotton one with delicate white designs printed all over—to see me off at the airport. We had some private time together before other dear ones came to the airport to bid me goodbye. With tears rolling down her cheeks, she gave me a small packet. Earlier on, she had noted my itinerary, and the packet had a set of her letters to me, to be read at my stopovers—in Athens, Copenhagen, Manchester, and other places. This thoughtful gift made parting a little less difficult. I felt happy that Mahe and I excelled in the art of giving each other valuable gifts, which were not expensive.

This is a page from one of her letters.

To be read at Athens.

How quickly you have flown away from me! At Athens, you'll be in the midst of classic beauty ..... architecture which could so aptly be called, as Hopkins did 'frozen music'. As you walk amongst the ruins. I want you to think of how Suja, you and I will share this lovely experience two years from now. You must not feel sad ....

I looked back into a diary I was keeping during our courtship. It was most interesting ..... On the 27th of July 1963 ... you visited me for the first time on the Thunderbird... You pretended not to have written a letter, and then suddenly gave me a lovely, pat one! You wanted me to read it before you, so that you could watch my reactions - then

My brother Divakar and his fiancée, Mary, received me at the Chicago airport. Later in his apartment, Divakar handed me an aerogramme from Mahe that awaited my arrival, which she had mailed the day after my departure from Madras. In this letter she accused me of having been primitive during the night before my departure. Her whole body ached, but her heart ached far more for the primitive man. My response was a series of cartoons on the primitive man and his mate in my letters that followed. In my favourite one, I loosely adopted Bernini's famous statue of Pluto and Persephone, for the cartoon. While Persephone has a painful face, the primitive man's mate has a dream-like expression, not unlike Mahe's at the wedding dinner.

At Oberlin College, I shared a neat little apartment with an Indian graduate student in the dormitory, Asia House. Asia House was a co-educational dormitory where men and women students stayed in two wings of the same building. It was an active, lively place. With its mosaic of tiled roofs, brick and ivy walls, pillared canopies, a little chapel with stained-glass windows, a quadrangular lawn and crab apple trees, Asia House was a lovely place.

The academic pressure was gruelling, especially during the first semester, when I had to make a quantum jump academically, to reach the higher level of chemistry in the college. Besides there were varied excellent programmes, exhibitions, plays, concerts, slide shows and more, all free. There were weekend travelling opportunities and many dinner invitations. Despite all these, I found the time to write elaborate, colourful letters, full of illustrations, to Mahe. How did I manage all these? Firstly, I was highly motivated. Secondly, all systems worked with super efficiency and there was no wastage of time. Thirdly, the way chemistry was taught fascinated me and in a way, the academic pressure was also a stimulant. Above all, I honed my time management skills further. I slept less and I left the chemistry department building, 'Kettering', only around three in the night, to go back to Asia House. During the brief walk I used to go through in my mind what I had studied. My breakfast was invariably a bar of chocolate that I ate while walking briskly to the 8 a.m. class.

When I studied organic chemistry, I read out aloud the portion from the textbook and recorded what I read into a tape recorder. Later, while working on detailed illustrations for my letters to Mahe I would simultaneously listen to what I had recorded on a tape. So I spent the time on the illustrations free while I 'studied' chemistry. I used to 'speak' what I was going to write to Mahe in my letters while shaving or taking a shower, a rehearsal of what I was going to write to Mahe, so to speak. These are only some examples of my time management.

Then summer gave way to fall. I was so moved by the autumnal beauty. I included many pictures of autumn in my letters to Mahe. I went to the Niagara Falls and Rochester with a fellow graduate student, Margie, in her car. I sent a detailed letter of these visits to Mahe. For the salutation page, I used a set of real autumn maple leaves and addressed Mahe as 'My Beloved Autumn Maple'. While I was working on the salutation page, Marty Ackermann, a professor, walked into my little laboratory, had one look at the sheet of paper and said, 'Yes, maples are beloved aren't they?' This was 1969.

I was equally enthused by the beauty of winter snow, which gave me the opportunity to send more pictures and descriptive letters to Mahe.

The students, especially the women students, were very friendly with me. So I did not feel lonely. Nevertheless, I missed Mahema greatly. From the distance, I grew even more fond of her. This fondness prompted me to send a card for our sixth wedding anniversary with a beautiful picture of Mahe in profile and a circular stained-glass window all aglow, with the caption, 'You are like a stained-glass window of a chapel'.

Then spring made her brief, sparkling visit to Oberlin, bringing with her abundant sunshine, balmy weather, and flowers galore. Following the spring, Suja and Mahe came, but unlike spring, they came to stay at Oberlin. I received them with great joy. On the day of their arrival, I was delighted to listen to Suja, just four then, describing with great enthusiasm in Tamil, her experiences in the flight, what she saw from the plane windows, and their visit to Malcolm MacDonald's stately estate, Raspit Hill.

On the day of their arrival, I awaited the night with great anticipation. That night I played softly a record of classical guitar music and approached Mahe in bed. I thought that after a long journey, with jet lag, she would be tired. So I was very gentle with her. Later, as she clung to me she observed, 'So, you have become a gentleman now, have you? I thoroughly enjoyed the gentlemanly way.' Soon, she added, 'But Mano, I must also tell you that I like the primitive man a wee bit more.'

Saying this, she filled the room with her tinkling laughter. I told her that the classical guitar music she heard would be the beginning of our unions after our reunion. So each night from now on, when we went to bed together, we would be hearing the classical guitar songs.

She smiled and answered, 'Yes, I know. After a few years, when we hear the songs, nostalgic memories of this period would flood our minds.'

She was tired after all. With her head resting on my arm, with her bare body close to mine, she slipped into a deep slumber before even slipping into her nightie.

I began thinking about the past few months. In February 1970, I learnt that the positions of the programme director and the house director, held by a husband and wife team at Asia House, would fall vacant from the following academic year. I was delighted, as I was sure that with my strong support, Mahe would manage both jobs splendidly. I applied for the jobs on behalf of Mahema. But the college was hesitant. How would a South Indian woman, with a very South Indian upbringing, manage to handle the job in a permissive, co-educational dormitory? So I worked very hard to convince all concerned that the job held by my wife would be as much a boon for the college as it would be for us. Poor Mahe had to send me a stream of documents and other material, even while she studied and wrote her final MA examinations. I made an artistic, convincing portfolio as the application, with many strong recommendations, including a brilliant one by the venerable Malcolm MacDonald.

The selection committee was very impressed with Mahe's overall credentials and the manner in which I presented the application. The job was offered with a personal touch. Therefore, Mahema was now with me at Asia House.

With Mahe's head still resting on my arm, I began thinking about the immediate future. We would soon be going on a tour of New England and the New York State in the two-year-old car that I had bought just three weeks before the arrival of my daughter and wife. During the trip, we would stay with many families of Oberlin friends. We would prepare South Indian dinners for them. I was glad again because the chemistry professors liked me and approved a special summer research scholarship. A nice part of Oberlin's most beautiful edifice would be our home. We would be amidst a group of bright students of ethnic diversity. Mahe's job would offer both of us unlimited scope for creativity in different areas. We would invite a host of guests to Oberlin, Asian scholars, musicians, dancers, artists, and others with whom we would....

Mahe interrupted my thoughts by stirring in bed. With her head still resting on my arm, she moved closer towards me and put her arm around my shoulder. Her eyes remained closed.

I asked her gently, 'Mahe, have you woken up?' Without answering me in words, she nodded her head affirmatively. I felt her head shake in my arm. Perhaps she had been awake for some time.

Then I asked her, 'Mahe, would you like me to take you again?' Now her affirmative nods were more vigorous. 'She liked the primitive man a wee bit more than the gentleman, did she?' I thought. So let her have the primitive man now. 'Ah, but then,' I thought, 'it would be inappropriate for a primitive man to use a soft comfortable mattress for action.' So, I got out of the bed, lifted her from the cot and placed her—not too gently—on the carpeted floor, without a pillow.

Moments earlier, I was thinking about our near plans for the near future. Now that she had opened up the path for me to give and to get from her intense pleasure, I suspended my thoughts about the future and plunged into the present.

~

We swiftly moved into the director's 'double apartment'. Here two dissimilar, first floor, frontage apartments had been attached together. So the double apartment had a private corridor, two drawing rooms, two bedrooms, two kitchenettes, and two bathrooms. This was just as well. This gave us the opportunity to refurbish one drawing room in Western style and the other in Indian style. We decorated the Indian room with two beautiful South Indian brass lampshades, and an open bookshelf with a strong Indian imprint that I designed. An oil painting by Mahe or me, on a South Indian theme, adorned the wall above the bookshelf, with a 10-inch Thanjavur bronze statue of Parvathi on the shelf.

I was bubbling with ideas for Asia House. Mahe had her own innovative plans too. Happily we were able to implement much of our creative thoughts for the programmes. One of our favourite projects was this: Thrice a month or so, we invited a group of men and women students, along with a faculty member or a dean, with his or her spouse or family, for an elaborate Indian dinner. For the meal, we first arranged a temporary low table with four wooden planks just 6 inches above the carpeted floor and covered the planks with an exquisite South Indian handloom tablecloth. At the centre of this table, Mahe placed a carved Indian vase with flowers in it. We placed folded finely woven mats along three sides of the table.

After socializing with our guests, in the Western drawing room, either Mahe or I would go into the 'new' Indian dining hall with a student, heat the food, and arrange the dishes on the low table, switch the record player in the adjacent room, open the door, and request the guests to have dinner with us.

The rich aroma of Indian food, the pleasing sight of the differently arranged table, the soft sound of veena or sitar music, would evoke a very positive response from our guests. Why every now and then, some students would run to their rooms to bring their cameras to photograph the arrangement and to be photographed with the guests at the 'table'. The drawing room was not large and we had furnished it sparsely, but tastefully. The items of decoration were not too expensive. And yet our guests loved the ambience.

One evening, we invited the college president and his wife along with a group of Asia Housers for dinner. During the course of the dinner, the president observed that those students who got invited by us were really the lucky ones. One girl laughingly told him, 'Mahema and Mano invite, in rotation, all seventy-five students of Asia House—many of us more than once. They also invite small groups of two or three for informal South Indian breakfast at their kitchen table.'

Three days later, Mahe received a copy of a letter written by the college president to the finance department. In this letter, he observed that he was extremely happy that as the programme director, Mahema has been inviting all the students of Asia House to delicious Indian dinners in her apartment. The students also got the opportunity to interact with professors, deans, and their spouses in a congenial environment. But he was surprised to find out that the Devadoss couple were doing this at their own expense, which was far beyond the call of duty. So, he advised the finance department to reimburse the expenses incurred by us on this project.

We were deeply touched. Mahe told me that sensitive thoughtful acts like that of the president and ever so many others here, were among the reasons that made Oberlin an outstanding college. Mahe thanked the president, but informed him that this project was from our heart, an expression of our love for the college and the students of Asia House. So we did not want reimbursements. Mahe and I believed in giving what little we could, where we thought we should.

Now that Mahe was with me, I did not have to write long, illustrated letters to her. Instead, I made beautiful posters and A4-size flyers for Asia House programmes. Creating these in different styles gave me a lot of pleasure. My posters became collectors' items.

With Mahe's leadership, Asia House throbbed with activities. In a college where excellence was taken for granted, a student of Asia House, Tom Hamburger wrote, 'Dear Mahema, How do you do it all? How do you do it all so well? Tom.'

Mahe said that she did it all so well because of the unflinching imaginative support I gave her! Yes, I gave her all the support I could to make her programmes more colourful. As an example, let me briefly describe just one programme, which became close to our hearts.

Mahema made her own presentations too. Among these, her multifaceted programme, 'The Unique Drape of the Sari' was the most outstanding. Earlier on, through an elaborate arrangement, she managed to procure fifteen gorgeous Kanjeevaram handloom silk saris, with rich borders, all from Madras, especially for the programme. She bought for herself one of these, a very elegant but a bit less gorgeous sari, to suit her personality and keep the cost low. She kept this a total secret from me so that she could surprise me by presenting herself in it on my very special day—the day I would receive my master's degree.

Before the programme, we printed a hundred copies of an exclusive brochure on saris. Her texts ranged from lyrical to practical, backed by many drawings by me. For instance, I did eight drawings in a single sheet, pictorially showing, step by step, how a sari was worn. Another had two diagrams for Mahema's texts, describing how the tight blouse and the petticoat were to be stitched. I presented just one sheet with two drawings of mine. I drew two sari clad women, one with excessive traditional modesty and the other with voluptuous hip-hugging modernity.

This presentation by Mahe gave me ample opportunities to make attractive posters and a nice flyer.

On the evening of the programme, Mahema left hundred copies of the brochure on the table in Shipherd Lounge at Asia House. The lounge was filled swiftly and the giveaway brochures were all taken. So, we had to print more copies later. Let me give just some salient aspects of the programme.

Before Mahema began her presentation, we played a record of nadhaswaram music to give an Indian flavour and set a festive mood. After Mahema's brief speech, she draped a sari, explaining the steps, on a statuesque girl who presented herself in a blouse and a petticoat. Some Asia Housers came as models, wearing Mahema's saris in different styles, as worn by traditional women in different regions in India, such as Coorg, Maharashtra, Gujarat, and Tamil Nadu. Among them were white Americans, an African–American, a Chinese and a Japanese girl. One Asia Houser observed that the girls had been transformed into colourful butterflies. Then the fourteen saris were displayed for sale at cost. The saris were snapped up and the people lingered on, enjoying the South Indian snacks that I had prepared.

This programme elicited such a keen interest that Mahema had to make repeat compressed presentations at different venues. A colourful newspaper article made its appearance.

A week or so later, two Asia Housers, a girl and a boy, came to our apartment. The girl was in one of the saris of the programme. She said her boyfriend, who stood beaming, gifted her with the sari and proposed to her and she accepted both. Later, happily, at least three of the Asia Housers received their degrees clad in saris.

Mahe received accolades aplenty. For instance, the director of East Asian Studies, Professor Dale Johnson, wrote a two-page note on Mahema. I remember a line from this: 'She organized intellectually stimulating, aesthetically satisfying and culturally enriching programmes.' The associate dean of students, Rose Montag, wrote, among other things, that Mahe was a beautiful sort of magical presence. Invitees to Asia House later invariably wrote heartwarming letters. One visitor wrote, 'I cannot tell you how much my visit to Oberlin College and Asia House means to me. It was a pilgrimage of fellowship which will shine in my life.'

The informal, 10.30 p.m. 'study break', often with snacks, that Mahe instituted, became very popular with the students, as they deserved and needed a break in studies. Often professors, deans, and their spouses too joined. In the little town of Oberlin, no house was more than ten minutes drive to Asia House. For one such programme, Mahe asked the students to come in Asian costumes, if possible. For this light-hearted study break, Mahe wore a madisar sari. Normal saris are six yards long, while madisar saris have a length of nine yards. In those days, all South Indian Brahmin women and none others—wore madisars. But by the 1960s, only some older Brahmin women clung to the custom and no young woman wore madisars, excepting as a bride, because tradition demanded that a Brahmin bride at the ceremony should wear red madisar. People began calling any old woman wearing madisar as madisar maami. Rightly or wrongly people—even many Brahmins too—began thinking of madisar maamis as parochial, old fashioned, and even narrow minded.

Mahe came out of our bedroom as a madisar maami. In order to match her attire, I decided to present myself as an ammaanji. An ammaanji is a marriageable male cousin of a woman. But in time, this term came to be associated with a dim-witted, unattractive male. So, I wore a pair of ear studs and a large red pottu (dot) on my forehead, and made a middle parting in my hair. These aspects were looked down upon as archaic and utterly unsophisticated. I thinned my huge moustache to an insignificant level. I wore a dhoti and covered my bare upper torso with an angavasthram (body cloth). When I presented myself to Mahe, she had a hearty laugh.

We walked together down the corridor, she as an old-fashioned, narrow-minded madisar maami and I as a lacklustre, unattractive ammaanji, to Shipherd Lounge. When we entered the lounge, the students had one look at us and screamed with glee, 'Oh, Mahema, Oh, Mano, you both look sexy!'

After talking about what we wore, Bob Reed, a student at Asia House, asked me, 'All the men and women students in the dormitory keep kissing away, here, there, everywhere. How come we never see you both kissing each other?' Elise Porter, a woman student observed, 'If you kiss each other on the lips, in this sexy outfit, you'll look threefold sexier.'

I told the students, 'Well, Mahema is intellectually emancipated, but she has had a very South Indian upbringing. She will certainly feel very shy, if I tried to kiss her on her lips, in public.'

After a pause, I added, 'Come to think of it, I've never seen a sari-clad, Indian woman being kissed on the lips—not even in photographs or in movies, let alone in real life.'

All this was way back in 1971. Bob held my camera in his hand and said, 'Oh, come on, Mano, kiss her. I'll take a shot. Then you can have a record of what is normally not seen.'

I tried to kiss Mahema on her lips. But she resisted me, blushing and turning her face away from me, while holding me at bay with her forearm.

I turned, looked at Bob and said, 'See what I mean?' At that moment he clicked the camera.

Later, I replicated the photo in a colour drawing, for our eighth wedding anniversary.

This drawing became one among Mahema's and my favourites....

~

A year after Mahema and Sujatha joined me at Oberlin, we went on a twenty-three-day, 7,000-mile, summer camping tour in our Plymouth Fury car. Hari and Gayathri, a newly married, Tamil Brahmin couple, went with us....

During this tour, we were moved by the majesty of the Grand Canyon, the breathtaking beauty of the Grand Tetons, the calm tranquillity of the Great Sand Dunes, the dignity of the Rocky Mountains with the snow-capped peaks and pine tree slopes, the bounty of nature's extraordinary footprints that are millions of years old, especially so at the Petrified Forest, the Painted Desert, and the Badlands, the sheer power of the mighty Yellowstone River, and more. We enjoyed the human imprint too—the abandoned cliff-dwellings at Mesa Verde and the huge stone faces of four US presidents, blasted out of Mount Rushmore—an unprecedented landmark that epitomized the then American penchant for grandiose ideas. We were thrilled to see elks, bison, moose, and other wildlife grazing or roaming freely and fearlessly, as though they were the lords of the magnificent landscapes that they surveyed....

All the five of us—Mahe, Suja, Hari, Gai, and I—spent a good deal of daytime within the confines of the car and most of the nights within the confines of a nine-by-nine foot tent. Amazingly, we managed not to get on each other's nerves. We hired a romantic little, one-room log cabin at the North Rim of the Grand Canyon.

The campsites were invariably laid in beautiful locations—in wooded regions. One could simply pitch a tent in an empty slot in a campsite at any national or state park or forest, for up to three days, all free. Some very small campsites were primitive, while some large ones offered facilities—free modern water closets, coin operated showers, clothes washing machines and the like. A coin-operated shower gave Mahe and me the opportunity to take a shower together, more importantly it presented us with the desired complete privacy that we eagerly sought, for you know what. Some campsites offered free educational talks or slide shows of high quality by the rangers.

Fortunately for us, the petroleum companies were then engaged in a price war, so petrol was cheap, especially in the western states, selling at 29 cents per US gallon. My Plymouth Fury was a large, dependable workhorse of a car, with no fancy features. So it gave good mileage. Hari, at that time, was in the gap between completing his masters' degree and getting a job. So Mahema and I took care of the cost of petrol and shared the other expenses with them.

We cooked our own, simple yet tasty, nutritious vegetarian food and for dessert we ate fruits. Occasionally, we stayed with friends, which was a welcome break, when we could do some of the things we could not at the campsites. For our onward journey, our hosts gave us packets of sandwiches and cakes. So, our food expenses too were low. At the end of the tour, we realized with relish that the 7,000-mile, twenty-three-day tour had cost for all five of us a mere 220 dollars, which included the photographic expenses.

The tour was one among the most memorable, moving, exciting, educative, joyful events in our lives....And oh, I had the good fortune of being able to take many stunning photographs. Along the way, Mahe had picked up informative booklets and pamphlets about the places of our visit. We gained all these at such a low cost. Why, Hari laughingly said that had he and Gai stayed in their apartment instead of joining us on the tour, it might well have cost him a bit more. Talk about value for money. This is one of the enlightened aspects of the American system.

I had one disappointment with the camping trip though. The campsites were invariably in beautiful surroundings, which evoked a strong sense of romance. I would have loved to spend a night, one whole night, all alone with Mahe in the tent, which was like a cozy little cave in a forest. But this was not to be.

As soon as we came back to Oberlin, we returned all the sleeping bags, the Petromax lamp, the sleek little cooking stove and utensils to the Schoonmakers who had loaned these. We kept the tent and the night lamp in the boot of the car, as the Renfrows from whom we had borrowed these were out of town. This was vacation time. But soon, I began going to the chemistry department to work on the summer scholarship project.

A professor, whose daughter was Suja's kindergarten classmate, was going on a three-day boat trip with his family, and wanted Suja to go along with them. Suja jumped with joy. So did Mahe and I. We jumped with joy because while Suja was away, we decided to spend one night in the tent in a state park not too far away from Oberlin. The flooring of the tent was of three layers. The bottom layer was of a tough waterproof material, the top layer of heavy-duty canvas with a thin rubber foam in between. So, I decided that we did not need a mattress. The flooring, in fact, would be a bit more appropriate for me as the caveman with his mate in the cave like tent.

So, apart from the tent and the night lamp, we took with us only two pillows, a towel, some sandwiches, a large can of water, a small jar of cider, paper plates, cups, napkins, and a trash bag. Excepting the mangalyam, Mahe wore no jewellery. We did not even take a watch or the camera.

On a Thursday evening, we drove to the park. The sky remained bright late in the evening on this summer day. We were happy that ours was the only tent in the park. Mahe and I took long walks in the gently winding path, surrounded by large trees. For our first wedding anniversary, I had drawn a picture, surprisingly, of a similar path, surrounded by tall trees, with tiny figures of Mahe and me in it, with the caption, 'Life with you is like walking through the woods.' Now at the state park, I felt happy that we were doing what I drew years earlier.

The light began to fade. We had our supper outside the tent. By then it had become dark. We washed and wiped ourselves, went into the 'cave', barefoot, lit the night lamp, and zipped the doorway shut, but leaving the windows open. The weather was such that, without clothes all through the night, we neither felt warm nor cold.

And what a terrific night it had been.

~

Now sitting on the mango tree behind the rehabilitation centre at Bagayam in July 1973, I thought with great relish about the details of our night in the state park in July 1971. I felt that this night, in a way, further strengthened our marital bonds. I began thinking about the physical relationship between a husband and wife. A chauvinistic male, might subconsciously think of his wife's body merely as a source for his gratification, on account of which she too would derive some pleasure. The physiological reality is that the wife can receive far, far greater pleasure than her husband would get in bed. There are two reasons for this. Firstly, a woman's body is endowed with more erogenous zones than a man's. Secondly, after seven years of married life, if the husband gets three peaks in one night—as in the night of the tent—one could think of it as some sort of achievement. But the wife can get many crescendos in one night and this, night after night, if the husband was imaginative.

Very early in our married life, I decided to approach my wife in bed with the intention of giving her great enjoyment. Her response was very positive and so proactive that I ended up getting far greater pleasure. Thus I felt that this is yet another case where, in 'giving' more, one gets more.

While I was engaged in such happy thoughts, I heard a voice calling out 'Misthar They-vathos!' I was asked to go to Mahe's room for breakfast. I jumped down from the mango tree and walked back to have my breakfast.

10

Mahema stayed at the Rehab for six months. This was a period of learning, not only for her, but also for me and others in the family, to cope with the new way of life after her return home. It was also a period for equipping Mahema with specially designed gadgets—the tools of trade for a quadriplegic, so to speak—some of which were essential and others, desirable.

During her stay there, I learnt to change the indwelling catheter hygienically. As the catheter drained urine continuously, collection receptacles were always needed. An ordinary football rubber bladder, suitably altered and tied to the knee while she sat on the wheelchair, became an unobtrusive, inexpensive, well-concealed urine collector, which did not hinder mobility. She acquired many such devices. She was like a pitiable bride collecting her woeful trousseau for her new life.

But of all the items collected, Mahema found the hand splint most dear to her. It was a gawky-looking piece of aluminium-and-leather, which could be fixed to her right forearm, extending from the palm to the elbow. Mahema learnt to write with a pen attached to the splint, using her shoulder muscles. After weeks of struggle, with sweat pouring down her face, all that she could show on paper were a few wobbly alphabets—each several inches tall.

But would she ever be able to fine tune her writing so that she could correspond with her friends scattered all over the world, write verses and articles when the spirit moved her? She could write checklists on her memory pad, she thought. Why, she could even write her own cheques and not depend always upon me to dole out the money she wanted.

She could not make any finger movement, but was determined to relearn handwriting by disciplining the gross shoulder muscles to get the precision and sensitivity of the finger muscles.

Mahema practised so diligently that a stage came, when the size of the alphabets was as small as—well, nearly so—it had been before the accident. Earlier Mahema had had a convent educated girl's handwriting—very legible, neat, and predictable. But now her handwriting had a certain free spirit of its own.... Her new handwriting had a pluck, a certain panache that the earlier disciplined one had not possessed.

The part-time psychotherapist of the Rehab once asked Mahema's parents, 'Your daughter has no siblings and you two are quite old. Do you harbour secret fears that after your time, your son-in-law might simply abandon your daughter, or make her life miserable?'

Mahema's father replied: 'We harbour no such fears. Indeed we are sure that he'll take care of her, as he would a princess. God will always guide him, even if Manohar fails to recognize that it is God who guides him.'

Meanwhile, the mini-palace on Palace Road had to be readied to receive its princess. At that time, Mahema's parents were finding it increasingly difficult to maintain their large house. Before Mahema came back home, they moved to a smaller portion of the large bungalow and my family moved downstairs to occupy the main portion of the house. Mahema's father rented out the apartment upstairs to the family of a captain of a ship. His wife was so afraid that a thief might climb into the terrace using the sturdy stalk of the mullai creeper that, without telling us, she arranged to get the creeper chopped off. This was a sharp hurting reminder of the irrevocability of Mahema's and my changed situation.

But then, life must go on.... I built ramps near the front and rear steps. I reoriented some of the doors and removed all the thresholds for the free movements of the wheelchair. As a surprise homecoming gift for Mahema, I prepared a small wall specially for projecting my colour slides.

When Mahema had left her house with her family the day after Satya's wedding, the plan had been that she, Suja, and I would return home from Madurai on the fifth day. But really, Mahema's return home was a long time coming.

Now after ten months, I drove her in the same car in which we left, back to her cozy nest. That late October evening, the sky was overcast heavily with monsoon clouds and the air was refreshingly cool. It was seven in the evening when I honked at the gate, heralding the arrival of the princess. Mahema's parents rushed out and swung the gates open outwards like outstretched, open arms. My mother had drawn a beautiful kolam near the front steps with the words: 'Welcome Home'. From then on, in the years to come, a kolam with a brief caption became a family tradition for any special event in our household.

The trained helper and I removed the folded wheelchair from the boot of the car, unfolded it, and deftly transferred Mahema from the car to the wheelchair. At once Sujatha came running, sat on Mahema's lap, without disturbing the rubber bladder tied right below Mahema's knee, and giggled when the wheelchair was rolled up the ramp to the veranda. As Mahema was at the front door, I played Handel's exuberant and triumphant 'Hallelujah Chorus' on my powerful stereo system. There was a profusion of arum lilies, asters, and tuberoses in the drawing room, their gentle perfume filling the air. Mahema sat at the entrance of the house with her daughter on her lap, silently absorbing the fragrance, the sights, the sounds, and the love. When the brief musical piece ended, I switched off the record player. She did not utter a word. My mother, who characteristically stayed in the background and who was normally not demonstrative, nevertheless came forward, gave Mahema a kiss on her cheek and said, 'I am glad that you are back home, my beloved daughter.'

It was then that Mahema broke down and cried. She cried and cried.

Actually, the readjustment since her return home was hard on Mahema. After all, she was born in this house, had grown up there, and gone to the church as a bride from the same house. She had come to this very abode—packed with countless happy memories now, to lead a vastly different kind of life. Before she returned home, she had the support of an efficient, service-minded hospital administration, to meet the day-to-day problems that pounced on her from all sides. Now, her family had to fend for itself. She was aware that her condition made life difficult for everybody.

Acquaintances who had not taken the trouble to visit her at Pondicherry or Vellore, now came in droves, many looking at her as an object of curiosity. One day, I took Mahe, my mother, and Sujatha to a flower show at a horticultural society. Many visitors stared so hard at Mahema that Sujatha became very upset and began crying. All in all, it was not a pleasant outing. After this experience, Mahe was reluctant to go out. She became quiet, less communicative, and tended to withdraw into a shell.

It was around this time that K. V. Mohan came into our lives. He made an unannounced visit to our home.

'Hi, I'm Mohan,' he said exuberantly, 'I heard you were involved in a road accident and you can't walk anymore. Well, I was involved in a road accident too and virtually escaped from the clutches of Yama Dharmaraja himself.'

Mahe knew his talented sisters as they were old Santhomites. She had heard of Mohan and occasionally seen him tearing down Santhome High Road on his powerful Red Indian motorcycle, but had not met him before.

'I knew you,' Mohan told Mahema. 'From the time you were a Stella girl and I was at Bede's School then. All the Santhome boys

knew of you then as the pretty maiden of Palace Road,' he laughed
boisterously.

At the time Mohan walked into our house, Mahe and I were
listening to a sitar record by Debu Chaudhuri. Mohan talked
superlatively about the album and the stereo system. Superlatives came
easily to Mohan. He asked Mahema, 'Do you like Ravi Shankar's
sitar playing?'

'Yes, very much.'

'A week from today, Ravi Shankar is giving a recital at the
university auditorium. Why don't we all go?'

Mahema was reluctant. I pointed out to Mohan that the hall
had a big flight of steps and we would need four pairs of hands to
carry the wheelchair with Mahema in it. Mahema would need a
seat along the aisle. Mohan replied nonchalantly, 'Don't worry about
anything, Mano. I'll make pukka arrangements.'

But, he did not make any arrangements at all.

As soon as he and I transferred Mahema from the car to the
wheelchair in front of the auditorium, Mohan simply disappeared.
Only then did he buy the tickets, which were allotted in the middle
of a row.

I asked him: 'What about the two extra pairs of hands?'

Mohan replied, 'It's all arranged.'

Then he looked around, spotted an acquaintance and shouted.
'Hey, Ashok, come here, boss. Long time, no see.'

He told Ashok expansively, 'Ashok, meet my great pal Manohar
and his charming wife, Mahema. Boss, I need your help to take the
lady up the steps. So please stand by.'

He looked around again and shouted, 'Dai Seenu, come, come,
da. I want my friends to meet you.'

He introduced Seenu to us as a fantastic veena player. He told
me, 'So, here are the extra pairs of hands.'

The four of us carried Mahema in her wheelchair up the imposing
flight of steps. Once inside the auditorium, Mohan rearranged the
seats of some other acquaintance so that we could get a wheelchair-

friendly location to sit together.

At the dinner table that night, Mahema laughed heartily as she narrated Mohan's antics to my mother and his peculiar brand of pukka arrangements, all the dots and dashes falling perfectly in position. Mohan began visiting our house, off and on. He often brought his pals. One evening he brought a talented guitarist, Visu, who filled our house with vibrant flamenco music. Visu, in turn, brought his wife, Chitra, a well-known Bharatanatyam dancer. Then one day, Mohan brought with him a young woman doctor, who, he later told me, was the daughter of the man who had later married Han Suyin, the author of *A Many-Splendoured Thing*. I thought that Mohan's claim was far-fetched, but it turned out to be true.

Mohan took Mahema and me to restaurants, musical recitals, and movies, always making pukka arrangements in his own fashion. He was a gifted mimic and made Mahema laugh. I had feared that after her long stay in hospitals, Mahema had tended to go into a shell when she came back home. I had not been sure how to lead her out of the shell. Mohan had barged in and unknowingly tore apart the cocoon that Mahema had begun weaving around herself.

Happily, members of our church youth group, both young women and men, began visiting our house regularly. Soon, ours became an 'open house' for them. They immensely enjoyed my new recipes. Many of them were gifted singers and guitarists. So, our house often reverberated with music. They took us to the church and out to movies, restaurants, and music recitals. Three young men, Floyd, Jerry, and Shekar were so especially supportive of Mahema that she called them her 'Three Musketeers'. Samuel Selvakumar was one among the youth group members who visited us regularly. He moved to Bangalore. Later in life, professionally, he was phenomenally successful and became an imaginative, generous philanthropist. Earlier, when he was a married young man with a five-year-old child, he warmly invited us to be his guest at Bangalore. Indeed, he persuaded hesistant Mahema to take the trip. So, in 1991, I took Mahema on her first train journey after the accident with two helpers to Bangalore, and we enjoyed the very warm hospitality of the Selvakumars, met many dear ones, saw many places, and returned to Madras with joy.

Mahema began going out regularly with me. But wherever we went, particularly to places with flights of steps, we always had to look for obliging strangers to help carry Mahema in her wheelchair up or down the steps. Many strangers willingly came forward to help, but often neither had good coordination nor did they listen properly to my instructions. Mahema frequently ended up having rather jerky rides up or down the steps.

I thought of a way of taking Mahema on her wheelchair up or down flights of steps with the help of one extra person instead of three. I welded carefully designed iron clips to a pair of iron pipes. After hooking the pipes to the wheelchair frame, it was possible for two persons to lift the wheelchair like a 'stretcher-chair' or a palanquin. I, of course, would take the load-bearing rear position. This worked reasonably well. I teased her saying that the wheelchair was the palanquin of the Princess of Palace Road, and I a mere rear-bearer of the palanquin.

One afternoon, Sujatha's school took the children to a show in Museum Theatre. Mahema and I went to Museum Theatre at dusk to pick up our daughter after the show. But the performance had not ended. The premises had a deserted appearance outside but inside, the children were squealing with glee.

'Instead of waiting in the car, why don't we go up and see what's going on from the corridor?' I asked. I caught hold of a man who agreed to help me take the 'palanquin' up the fourteen steps. However, halfway through, the man declared that he was not able to hold the front any longer, lowered the iron pipes awkwardly in the front to rest them on a step and slunk away, promising to fetch someone else. But neither he nor anybody else turned up. I could do nothing except wait like a rear-guard with aching arms till a nun came out, saw the strange scene, and hurriedly brought someone else to relieve me. From then on I decided not to seek help from strangers to take the wheelchair up the steps in the 'palanquin' mode.

A typical wheelchair has two large wheels, one each under the armrests and two very small fully-swivelling wheels in front, on either side of the footrest. Two handles are provided on top at the rear, on either side of the backrest, to enable a person to roll the wheelchair by pushing it from behind. One day, it suddenly occurred to me that by holding the wheelchair firmly from behind and tilting it through thirty to forty degrees, such that the two large wheels were firmly rooted on the ground and the two small, front swivelling wheels dangle freely, it would be possible for me to take the wheelchair up or down flights of steps—gently raising or lowering it, one step at a time, without help from anybody else. In other words, I would be able to raise or lower Mahema up or down flights of steps, all by myself. I tried this on the front steps of our house with the empty wheelchair, while Mahema was in bed. It worked. I then tried lowering and raising the wheelchair with my daughter sitting in it. To my delight, I was able to achieve this task without any problem. Sujatha thought that this was fun and wanted me to take her up and down the steps, again and again, which I did obligingly, as it gave me the necessary practice.

Mahema was very reluctant to go down the steps. She looked at me with pleading eyes. Her eyes almost said to me that she did not want to go through another crash. By then, my mother had come to the front veranda.

She asked me anxiously, 'I hope, Manohar, that you aren't doing something rash.'

Mahema's parents came out.

'Really, Manohar,' my mother-in-law admonished me, 'how can you roll the wheelchair down the steps, for heaven's sake? Be reasonable.'

My father-in-law was sterner. 'I'll hold you personally responsible if a mishap occurs,' he warned me.

But Sujatha told her mother, 'Amma, you'll like it, let Appa do it.'

Standing behind the wheelchair, with Mahema sitting in it, I gave the wheelchair, the backward tilt and brought it to the steps so that the two large wheels stood at the brink and the two small wheels hung in the air, far above the steps. Mahema was quite nervous but she implicitly trusted my judgement and did not scream or create a scene. I gently lowered the wheelchair to the first step down. The wheels hugged the vertical portion of the step till they touched the flat portion of the step, rolled over the flat portion to the brink of the first step and began the descent to the second step. This process was repeated till the wheelchair was on the ground. Continuing to hold the wheelchair tilted backward and not pausing at all, I began the ascent one step at a time till it was on the veranda floor. I moved the wheelchair sufficiently back and brought it to the horizontal position. I locked the wheelchair, came in front of it, looked at Mahema triumphantly with arms akimbo and asked her, 'And what do you have to say now?'

Mahema replied, 'Not bad, not bad at all.'

After a pause she added, 'As a matter of fact, Mano, this was the smoothest ride I've had up and down a flight of steps,'

Beaming, Suja asked her mother, 'Didn't I tell you that you'd like it?'

I knew that if ever I slipped or even took a single wrong step during this manoeuvre, it could mean a calamity for Mahema. Therefore, from that day onwards, I stopped using leather-soled shoes or slippers and began to use only footwear with rubber soles, which had a better grip.

This simple discovery that I could take the wheelchair up and down steps by myself gave Mahema a certain freedom of movement. I could transfer her now without the help of others, into the front seat of the car, fold and load the wheelchair into the boot of the car. My Herald car had a floor-shift and an individual passenger front seat. I tied a belt that went around Mahema's waist together with the backrest of the seat so that if I jammed the brakes, she would not be thrown forward.

I took her up and down flights of steps in her wheelchair countless number of times, including aircraft steps, sometimes to the third floor of a building. Why, many years later (on 20 October 2001) when I was sixty-five, I even took her up and down on an escalator. This was in a new departmental store in which at the time, the escalator was the only means for Mahe to go up to the first floor.

One winter evening, I took Mahema to the Pavilion restaurant in the newly opened Taj Coromandel Hotel. A helpful waiter removed a chair from the table for four and I positioned Mahema's wheelchair in that slot. I sat on the adjacent side of the table so that I could feed her easily.

I told her casually, 'Incidentally, Mahe, today is the second anniversary....'

'Yes,' she replied. 'I even said a prayer in the morning.'

It was two years earlier on this day that we had been involved in the car accident. The waiter at this new hotel was an enthusiastic, young management trainee. On hearing the talk about an anniversary, he quietly moved away and soon reappeared beaming with a big vase of fresh flowers, set it on the table with a flourish and said, 'Many happy returns of the joyful day.'

Mahema smiled sweetly and said, 'Thank you.'

She then requested him to bring a couple of candlesticks. 'My husband can't see properly in dimly lit rooms,' she explained to him.

The man moved away to bring the candles. As we waited for the candles, Mahema told me, 'I'm cold.'

'Don't worry,' I replied. 'The candles and a bowl of hot soup will no doubt warm you up. Once the restaurant gets filled, you may even feel warm, what with all the sizzling steaks whizzing past, this way and that.'

'But Mano, if you don't do something now, my teeth may begin to chatter.'

It was winter, and the brand-new air conditioners worked efficiently—perhaps too efficiently for Mahe.

I chuckled and said, 'Relax, I've come prepared.' I pulled out the heavy silk shawl I had gifted her three days earlier, on our wedding anniversary, and covered her shoulders with it.

Seated at right angles to Mahema, I watched her profile. Her hair had regrown fully but was less profuse now. She had gained some weight. In the mild glow of the candle light, her serene yet radiant face looked attractive. I had always liked Mahema's gently pouting lips and remembered that two years earlier, a couple of hours before the accident, this was more or less the way she had looked—then, in the yellow morning sunlight and now in the yellow candle light.

I alternately fed Mahema and ate myself. To simplify the process, I used the same cutlery and plate for both.

A lady, who seemed very sure of herself, entered the restaurant and stopped to look around for somebody. In the process, she spotted Mahema, and made a beeline towards the table. As the lady came close, Mahema said to me, 'Here comes Mrs Leela Xavier.'

The lady took the vacant seat opposite Mahema. 'Hello, Mrs Xavier,' said Mahema.

The lady said smilingly, 'Don't worry, I won't play a gooseberry. I'll leave you to your own devices in a minute. I'm dining here with my sister-in-law. Actually, she's supposed to host the dinner, but hasn't turned up yet.... Well, she's not known for her punctuality.'

'How are you and how's Mr Xavier?' asked Mahema.

'We're fine,' she replied.

'After Nigeria, we moved to Venezuela. My husband seems to have become the favourite of the petroleum guys. I've come to India on a long visit now, leaving my poor husband all alone in Venezuela. I arrived in Madras only a couple of days ago.... I heard that you were in the States. Somebody had told me that you were in Opal Inn College. Is there really a college with a silly name like Opal....'

'It's not Opal Inn. It's Oberlin College.' I said interrupting her.

'But we have returned to India for good,' added Mahema.

'I can see that you've returned with your raging romance perfectly intact,' she said teasingly.

'Well, I continue to like Mahema, I suppose,' I replied.

'Merely like her!' she exclaimed with great amusement. 'Talk about understatement! You don't know how very, very romantic you both look…a gorgeous shawl for the lady, a big vase of flowers on the table…candlelight for the occasion…my, my…one feeding the other…eating from the same plate…you know it's almost mushy.'

'Well, in the first place I had to drape the shawl to keep her warm. You see, Mahema's spinal injury….' I began.

'Injury?' asked Mrs Xavier, her expression of mirth suddenly changing into one of sobriety. She looked at Mahema carefully, then turned to me and said, 'She doesn't look like an injured person. Oh come on, you're just pulling my leg, aren't you?'

I realized that as she had been away in Venezuela, she had not heard about the accident. The wheelchair was completely concealed from her view by the table. Its arms and rear handles were fully covered by the shawl.

'As a matter of fact,' I told the lady, to dispel any doubts she had about the accident, 'Mahema is sitting in a wheelchair right now.'

'A wheelchair?' asked the lady in astonishment. She peeped sideways and below and saw the black tyres and the shiny chrome of Mahema's wheelchair. Mrs Xavier's expression became grim.

'You see,' I continued, 'the air conditioner may be refreshingly cool for you and me. Mahema, however, feels cold because after the accident, her internal thermostat doesn't work well. So, I was obliged to cover her with the heavy shawl.'

The lady was too taken aback to ask how, when, where, or why the accident had happened. 'As for the flowers,' said Mahema smiling, 'the kind-hearted waiter brought the vase erroneously thinking that we were celebrating the anniversary of some happy event.'

The lady's jaw kept dropping and she did not utter a word. 'I have to feed Mahema because she can't eat by herself,' I said.

Mahema added, 'I'm paralysed below my shoulders, you see.'

'If I don't have the additional illumination from the candles, I might end up feeding Mahema nasally,' I joked.

'Yes, Mrs Xavier, my husband's retinal degeneration has been relentless. He's slowly going blind,' said Mahema.

'We are very sorry to disillusion you, Mrs Xavier,' I said, 'but the truth of the matter is that it's not so much romance, but rather the sheer necessity of our situation....'

Mrs Xavier could take it no longer. She got up even before I could complete the sentence and dashed out of the restaurant, never to return for the dinner appointment with her unpunctual sister-in-law, whoever she was.

'Well,' I said, 'she said that she wouldn't play gooseberry and promised to leave us to our own devices, and that's precisely what she has done!' Mahema giggled.

Had she visited Mahema five months later, Leela Xavier would have found Mahema in a far worse state. And that was how Osman Ali Khan—an enthusiast of my art work—found her, when he visited our house in mid-May, during the height of summer.

'Why is she breathing so hard? Why is she finding it so difficult to speak?' he asked me when we were alone.

'Her body temperature goes up in the hot season because, after the accident she stopped sweating below her shoulder level. So, the cooling mechanism of her body has been thrown out of gear. If the ambient temperature goes above 105°F, she develops symptoms of high fever.'

'But you told me sometime ago that she does not have touch perception. Does this mean she has heat perception, if she finds heat unbearable?'

'Oh, that's the irony. If a red-hot metal were to come in contact with her body, she would not scream because she just wouldn't suffer any pain. This really happened, you know. Once, her bare foot rested directly on the hot exhaust pipe of a friend's old car, because there was a hole in the floor board. By the time she could smell the burning flesh, the sole of her foot looked like an overripe tomato.'

Osman Ali Khan flinched, but I continued, 'It is precisely because the subcutaneous nerve ends cannot pass on messages of heat perception to the brain that the sweat glands in turn do not get orders from the brain and start producing sweat. Consequently, she doesn't sweat and so she becomes hot.'

'Why is she suffering from a cold and cough, now, in the heat?' asked Osman.

I replied, 'Well, the other day, when the mercury touched 110°F, my mother telephoned me at the office to say that Mahema's body was literally burning and that she had become delirious. As an emergency measure, I advised my mother to rub Mahema's body immediately with ice cubes and then wipe her with a towel dipped in ice-cold water. By the time I reached home, she had cooled off reasonably but had picked up this severe cold and cough. As the chest muscles too are paralysed in most quadriplegics, they cannot bring out the phlegm easily and they take a long time to get rid of a cough.'

'Is there no solution for this problem?'

'Unlike most other problems she faces, there is a solution for this one. If she stayed in an air-conditioned room, she'll not suffer.'

'Then why the hell didn't you buy a damn air conditioner?' burst out Ali Khan. He was normally soft-spoken, but he used strong words now because he was angry with me.

I laughed. 'It's like Marie Antoinette saying, "Why don't they eat cake?" The accident has wiped out our savings. An air conditioner is beyond my means. Besides Mahema tells me that she would rather go through this summer ordeal than see me get into a debt trap.'

'You rascal,' scolded Osman, not without affection, 'why didn't you tell me all this earlier? If the solution is as simple as an air conditioner, an air conditioner she shall have. Tomorrow, she'll receive my gift of a brand-new air conditioner. Will you take care of the 7/20 wiring and the service contract?'

The following Sunday, Osman Ali Khan visited Mahema. She was seated blissfully in the air-conditioned room and welcomed Osman chirpily.

'I hope to see you exactly the way you are now, Mahema— cheerful and cool,' observed Osman.

11

Many friends from Oberlin College visited our home after Mahema returned home. Soon after the Chinese thaw towards the US, China-born professors at Oberlin like Paul Arnold and his wife Sally and China-scholars like Professor Johnson came on a pilgrimage to India. On their way back home, most of them made a detour to Madras to meet Mahe and me. A long line of Oberlin students too kept visiting us. We in turn received the visitors with great pleasure.

Larry Shinn kept the promise he had made when Mahema was at JIPMER and returned to India. He used our house as his headquarters and commuted to Pondicherry and other places, to collect material for his research paper on Auroville. While he stayed with us, Larry helped me and Mahe in many ways. It was around this time that I began to find it increasingly difficult—especially after dark—to drive my car, on account of my declining vision. Larry offered to drive me and Mahe wherever we wished to go. He was so tall that it was a perennial surprise to me that this American could get into the driver's seat of my little Herald car. However, Larry not only managed this feat, he learnt how to deftly transfer Mahema from the wheelchair to the car, and also take the wheelchair up and down staircases.

Mahema and I received an invitation from Mr and Mrs Christadoss for a dinner party preceded by cocktails.

Mr Julius Christadoss was a rich, hospitable, large-hearted man, who had a penchant for ostentation. His daughter's wedding was to be solemnized in July at St George's Cathedral, followed by a reception at Abottsbury. He invited a small group of about 200 select guests to an extravagant cocktail party followed by dinner, on the sprawling lawn of his bungalow. Actually 'lawn' is a euphemism. In the water-starved summer heat, there was only dry earth and no grass. Pansy, his wife was very fond of Mahema. She telephoned Mahema to say, 'If you wish, you and Manohar can skip the reception, which is for everybody, but do come for the dinner.'

'Pansy akka, our American friend whom you met at Nalli Silk….'

'That tall, handsome fellow?'

'Yes, yes. Professor Shinn is staying with us now. May we…?'

Before Mahema could complete the sentence, Pansy said, 'Of course, do bring him along for the dinner. He'd enjoy the cocktails in dry Madras, I'm sure.'

When she said 'dry Madras', she meant it metaphorically because prohibition was in force then. But Madras was dry in a literal sense too. As the monsoon had failed the previous year, there was acute water shortage. However, the city, which is normally parched in July, occasionally received sharp showers—the spillover of the Southwest monsoon. It so happened that, just two days before the wedding, the Madras sky became very cloudy and as the wedding day approached, the clouds became ominously darker. The weather forecast was that heavy rains were highly likely in the evening and fishermen were warned not to venture into the sea. Mr Christadoss was very upset to think that the rain might ruin the grand dinner party he had planned meticulously. As a precautionary measure, he hurriedly booked the ball room in Hotel Connemara as an alternate venue. The guests were suitably informed that the party would be held either on the lawn of his bungalow or the ballroom of the Connemara, depending upon the weather.

Larry Shinn, Mahema and I arrived at the bungalow, on time—
by eight in the evening. Mr Christadoss received his guests warmly.
'Dr Shinn, I presume,' he said. 'My wife talked about you. We
are honoured to have you here.'

Larry answered, 'Sir, the pleasure is entirely mine.'

A battery of photographers flashed away. Mahema smiled broadly
and said to Mr Christadoss, 'So, the weather has become very
cooperative after all.'

Mr Christadoss took her hand in his. 'It's also a question of
faith,' he declared proudly. 'See, Mahema, Periyakutty's prayers are so
powerful. I knew that only she could restore good weather through
her prayers. So, I earnestly requested her to pray and she did ever
so fervently. Now you can see the result for yourself. Isn't there a
lesson for you here, Mahema?'

He went on, not waiting for Mahema's answer, 'The lesson is
that faith can work miracles as it has now. Here's Periyakutty with
her extraordinary power of prayer. She can make you walk if only....'

'But Mr Christadoss, I had a spinal injury. Medical science as
it stands....'

'I'm disappointed in you, Mahema. If Periyakutty's prayers can
stop the rains, they can also make you walk.'

He then turned to Larry, 'I believe you are also an ordained priest,
Reverend Shinn. Perhaps, you should guide Mahema spiritually and
show her the true path.'

I thought to myself, 'If he has so much trust in Periyakutty's
prayers, then why did he arrange an alternate venue for the party?'

But I, of course, kept this thought to myself.

Cars began to roll in. A large lady got down from a large car
and said, 'Oh, Julius dear, I'm so very, very delighted that the sky
cleared specially for the party.'

Mr Christadoss's attention shifted to the new arrivals and he
moved away to greet them and possibly to spread the word about
Periyakutty's special prowess in praying.

There were drinks aplenty, though prohibition was in force. A posse of policemen was on hand to ensure security and to regulate the traffic. Just as in many other places, drinking went on merrily, right under the nose of the constabulary. But then, the law enforcers had been assured of their share of alcohol, after the guests had had theirs.

Soon the food began to arrive. There were richly garnished crisp chicken kebabs on silver trays, steaming mutton biryani on huge porcelain platters, dressed salad in wooden bowls, unshelled giant prawns cooked in wine and arranged on clear Corningware, whole baked fish in Petri dishes, and much more. I was getting ready to plunge into the food and so was Larry. Suddenly, a large drop of water hit my forehead with force, another my face and yet another, my head. Within seconds, the sky opened up and there was a downpour of unbelievable intensity. Women dripping with jewels moments were now dripping with water too, their make-up running down their noses. There was utter confusion. The guests and waiters dashed pell-mell for cover. The bungalow soon became packed with people, and the drawing room carpet was caked with mud.

Larry, Mahema, and I remained where we were. Wheelchairs turn obstinately sluggish in slushy soil. Mr Christadoss's sister, Dora Kurian, brought an umbrella and held it over Mahema's head—certainly an act of kindness, but really an exercise in futility. In the meanwhile, the kebabs became wet and limp, the biryani soggy and cold. The schools of fish swimming in the shallow pools of the Petri dishes and the giant prawns inside the Corningware, which now overflowed with water, stared unblinkingly at the wheelchair and the group of four.

I told Dora, 'I think it's time we went home. We shouldn't linger here, Mrs Kurian, till the roads get flooded. Then, if the car stalls, we'll have a bit of a problem on our hands.' I said this smilingly, looking pointedly at Mahema. Larry brought the car close to Mahema. He then lifted her quickly from the wheelchair and gently placed her in the front seat of the car. I folded the wheelchair, loaded it into the boot, and jumped into the rear seat. We took off, after hurriedly thanking the elderly lady. As Larry backed the car, we saw bright sparks—like mini-lightning flashes—at some distance, coming from the temporary electric wiring of the searchlights that were trained on the lawn and the bungalow. Immediately, the electric supply failed, plunging the whole place into darkness.

I was surprised to find the roads already flooded. There was no let up of the rain which continued to come down in torrents. 'At least the well won't go dry now and the water level in the reservoirs will go up,' I said.

But Mahema was not thinking about the water situation of the city. 'All that lovely, lovely food,' she said yearningly, her mouth watering and her teeth chattering, 'entirely wasted and I didn't have even a morsel.'

I teased her, 'Don't worry, Mahe, we'll have a grand treat of dried up bread at home.'

Although she was shivering with cold, Mahema guided Larry vigilantly and pointed out the right roads to him. Hunched up over the wheel and without uttering a word, Larry navigated the car cautiously through shin-deep water. The drone of the engine in the third gear sounded like that of a slow motor launch, the movement of the windscreen wipers like drums beating a rhythm, Mahema's chattering teeth like fast telegraphy and the splattering of rain on the roof of the car like a relentless spray of arrows hitting a warrior's shield.

'You're very quiet, Larry,' I observed, but the professor held his peace.

'Please do share your profound thoughts with us, Reverend Lawrence Shinn,' demanded Mahema.

'The lady, Periyakutty, whoever she is, said her powerful prayer to stop the rain, didn't she?' asked Reverend Shinn, rhetorically. Shaking his head disapprovingly, he added, 'SOME prayer, that.'

The closed confines of the car resounded with uproarious laughter, which drowned even the droning, the drumming, the chattering and spattering sounds in the car. After we reached home, my mother hurriedly made some uppuma for the three of us—humble fare that was a far cry from what we had missed at the wedding reception. But then, uppuma had never tasted better. When I narrated the events of the evening to Sujatha and my mother, there were gales of merry laughter all over again.

'Perhaps,' I said, 'God in heaven is laughing too.'

When I retired to the bedroom, Mahema, Larry, and Suja continued to sit around the dining table, chatting and laughing. I felt happy that during the thirty months after the accident, Mahema had not merely survived but had in fact flourished. In Bagayam, two years earlier, Mahema had vowed that—with my support and the grace of God—she would provide as natural and happy a home as possible to Sujatha. Now, I was gratified that she had, in her own quiet way, really done it. I lay in bed and began composing the next stanza for the verse on Mahema. Within two weeks I completed the stanza:

Friends, relatives and doctors rallied around her
Touched, encouraged and thankful we were
Their support and fellowship helped us unfold
A new way of life o'er the ruins of old.
Our house now echoed with tinkling laugher,
A happy home renewed for our darling daughter.

In 1975, Geoff D'Graff came three weeks after Larry left. Geoff had been an Asia Houser during Mahema's tenure at Oberlin College. Once, when we were at Oberlin, he had asked me, 'You know, Mano, many, many of us are in love with Mahema...doesn't that bother you?'

I had replied nonchalantly, 'It doesn't bother me one bit...that is, as long as Mahe doesn't reciprocate the love.'

Now, Geoff, who was on his way back to the US from Chiang Mai University in Thailand, had decided to spend a couple of weeks at our house.

It was during Geoff's stay with us that I had a sudden setback in my right eye. I found this out by chance, while using my right eye to look at a millimetre graph sheet through a hand-held lens. I noticed that very close to the point I was looking at, the green checked lines of the graph seemed to have two smudges, and that these pale green smudges moved with my right eye to whichever part of the graph I looked at. The smudges had specific shapes. Looking at a dot without moving my eye or head, I could draw on the graph sheet the precise amoeba-like shapes of the two smudges. However, I could not see the smudges when I looked at a blank white sheet or a plain brown packing paper. I realized that my retina did not 'read' the visual messages in the region of the smudges and the brain perceived this region as the average of the surrounding region. This was why I could not see the smudges when I looked at a monotonal flat surface. I realized that if I closed my left eye, I could hardly read normal printed matter, as the dead parts of the retina in my right eye were in the macular region, very close to the centre.

I explained all this and more to Geoff. I had heard about 'sympathetic ophthalmia', a condition in which whatever happens to one eye is often repeated in the other. I told Geoff about my apprehension that if my left eye became similarly afflicted, the consequences could be dire.

During the weeks after Geoff's departure, I kept checking and redrawing the smudges in my retina. I noticed with trepidation that the smudges were slowly spreading and obscuring the vision in my right eye a little more. Fortunately my left retina did not have blind regions near the macula.

A letter arrived from Geoff. He had checked on my retinal problem with a knowledgeable ophthalmologist in Washington DC, who had told Geoff that one of India's foremost retinal experts was probably one Dr S. S. Badrinath, who fortunately lived in Madras, and that I should consult him at once.

In the years to come, I was to see Dr Badrinath grow in stature and inspire the admiration of both the weak and the powerful. Mahema and I were to include him and his wife Dr Vasanthi among our most beloved friends. Sankara Nethralaya, the brainchild of the Badrinaths, grew into a fine, world-renowned eye institute. But at the time when I developed those infamous smudges in the retina of my right eye, I did not know of Dr Badrinath at all. It was ironic, I thought, that

I heard of the great doctor through an Oberlin friend all the way from Washington DC. And this happened well before the advent of the internet and other magical tools of information technology.

When Mahema contacted him, Dr Badrinath was working at a small clinic with two assistant doctors, at Vijaya Hospital. He was obviously quite well known even then. Mahema had great difficulty in trying to fix an appointment with the doctor, as his calendar was full for the next three months. However, Mahema's persuasive powers won, and he reluctantly agreed to see me a couple of days later. The doctor was rather taken aback to see his new patient's wife in a wheelchair. Mahema had talked with great concern over the phone only about my sight and not a word about her own plight.

After my eyes had been dilated, Dr Badrinath peered into my right eye and carefully drew on a pad, a picture of the affected area in the macula of my retina. The smudges that I had drawn earlier were almost identical to the ones drawn by Badrinath. The doctor studied my graph sheet with interest. I explained to the doctor how I had managed the drawing and the doctor looked at me with renewed interest.

When Badrinath completed his thorough examination, I requested the doctor to give me an honest assessment.

'Use your eyes as much as you can,' answered the doctor. 'However, you must avoid very harsh light and ultraviolet rays. Normally, degeneration of the retina is gradual, but the rate of degeneration varies from patient to patient and again from time to time for the same person. Unfortunately, retinitis pigmentosa has its own secret agenda and there is no way of knowing its timetable. So there is an element of uncertainty. However, what is certain is that retinitis pigmentosa is relentless and there is no known cure for this syndrome. Let us hope that in your case the decline is very gradual.'

I laughed and asked, 'Can I then assume that I may well die before I become totally blind?'

Laughing in his own characteristic way—something I would have many occasions to hear—the doctor said, 'Yes, that could well happen, especially as none of us knows when our own end will come. Let's hope that you will live long enough to take care of your wife and that you will not become totally blind either.'

We received the doctor's frank opinion, completely devoid of sugar-coating, with composure. As we were about to leave, the doctor told Mahema, 'Because of your very special situation, I will make you a promise: If ever your husband faces an emergency, you may come to me without prior appointment. I'll somehow find the time to see him.'

And over the years, Dr Badrinath kept his promise.

On our way home from the doctor's clinic in the afternoon, I felt that Badrinath's kindness was, in a sense, the doctor's response to Mahema's situation and an expression of the admiration for the concern with which she dealt with my problem, while keeping her own in the background. There was something about her personality that made many doctors spontaneously lavish kindness on her—even if they could not always offer her satisfactory medical solutions. Dr Rajan brought his assistants as well as complicated dental equipment to our house, just to spare her the trouble of going to his clinic. Dr Mohandas was a pillar of support. Dr Abraham, Dr Subramaniam, Dr Ajith, Dr Mariappan, Dr Guna, Dr Tommy, and many others became close family friends.

Of course, not all doctors were uniformly considerate. Some used comforting words, but would not budge an inch when it came to collecting their fees. One or two were impersonal and business-like.

And, one—just one doctor—was exceedingly unkind to Mahema.

As quadriplegics have no control over bowel movements, an upset stomach is a bane and can turn into a source of utter social embarrassment. Quadriplegics are natural candidates for chronic gastrointestinal problems, including amoebic dysentery, as they depend upon others to feed them. They can never be too sure that the fingers of those who feed them are always clean.

Occasionally, Mahema did suffer from an upset stomach. Dr

Raghu Bhushanam, a well-known gastroenterologist, was one of the doctors who was unfailingly kind to Mahema. He gave her special attention whenever she consulted him. About four years after the accident, Mahema once suffered from a severe gastrointestinal disorder, which did not respond even to strong medication. Dr Bhushanam told her that he would examine her more thoroughly as an outpatient at one of the government general hospitals where he worked, using their newly acquired endoscope.

The following morning, I drove Mahema to the particular government hospital, took her up the huge flight of steps to the first floor—all by myself—and waited with her in a small room assigned for endoscopic examination. It was here that she received a volley of insults from a doctor who was a total stranger....

The wait was long and Mahema felt bored as she sat passively, while I stood silently behind her. Suddenly there was a flurry and a retinue of doctors, two male nurses and two orderlies swiftly filled the room.

'Dr Raghu Bhushanam?' I asked trying to locate him.

'The chief is held up in the ward. He'll presently join us here,' replied a junior doctor, helpfully.

A doctor in his early forties took the lone chair at a small table. Apparently, he was the second in command.

He asked Mahema matter of factly, 'Name?'

'She replied, 'Mrs Mahem, Devadoss.'

'Age?'

'Thirty-six.'

He scribbled something on a chit pad.

'And what's your exact problem?' he asked.

'My stomach has been upset for about three weeks, doctor. I've been eating bland food, but with no improvement. Medicines haven't helped either.'

He turned to look at the others who stood around and said with a smirk, 'She doesn't look as if she's on a diet, does she?'

I did not like his comment but kept quiet.

The doctor asked a few perfunctory questions which she answered.

He then said, 'Okay, lie down on this examination table.'

'Doctor, I can't get on the table by myself and....'

'Oh, yes, you jolly well can.'

'No, doctor, I can't even get out of the wheelchair....'

He looked at her sullenly and said, 'Don't fuss, I say. Get moving.'

I was becoming angrier by the second.

Tears welled up in Mahema's eyes. 'I'm sorry, doctor. My husband and one of the orderlies can transfer me into....'

'Oh my God,' he said interrupting her yet again. 'Our orderlies are here not to pamper every hypochondriac who lands up here at the GH.'

Looking at the tears that began rolling down her cheeks, he preached. 'And don't wallow in self-pity. If you refuse to get out of the wheelchair, you'll end up staying there forever.'

The bitter irony of what he said seemed to slap my face.

Even as she wept, Mahema replied, 'I don't want to be pampered, doctor. I need help only because I'm a quadriplegic.'

At long last, I thought the fact that Mahema could not get out of the wheelchair would penetrate the thick skull of the man. But the physician's reply shocked me.

'Now,' said the doctor derisively, 'she is trying to impress us with medical terms.'

'DOCTOR,' I intervened loudly so that everyone's attention shifted to me, unambiguously. Now lowering my voice to the normal level, I said, 'Kindly listen to what I have to say and don't interrupt me. My wife had a spinal injury between C4 and C5. Since then she has been paralysed below her neck. Only God Almighty can make her get out of the wheelchair on her own now. And you insist that she must. I may pardon you for your ignorance, but your insolence, I will not tolerate.'

'Measure your words, mister.'

'You ought to have measured yours in the first place,' I shot back. 'Did you measure your words when you cheekily said that my wife doesn't look as if she is on a diet? In the first place, she did not say she was on a "diet". Perhaps you are not aware of the fact that, for complex reasons, quadriplegics tend to put on weight, even if they do not eat much. An unsettled stomach makes the life of a quadriplegic even more difficult. Do you have the licence to ridicule her merely because she isn't thin like a stick?'

Now the plump doctor sat silently stabbing at the chit pad with his ballpoint pen. I continued. 'You have made sweeping pronouncements about my wife, but what do you know about the dignity with which she bore the pain, or the grace with which she faced the trauma? How dare you accuse her of wallowing in self-pity?'

There was pin-drop silence except for the sound of the pen making smudgy indentations on the chit pad.

'I know that some of you doctors think that medical jargon is the private turf of physicians on which lay persons shall not tread. If you think that quadriplegia is one such hallowed term, you are wrong yet again. The word finds a place even in concise dictionaries, used by ordinary mortals like my wife. Besides, she used the forbidden word only after you obstinately insisted that she get up by herself to lie down on the table. How else can a person in her position explain her plight to a pompous ignoramus?'

The light-skinned doctor became quite red. From where I stood, the man's bald head seemed like a tomato to me. Suddenly the doctor stood up, threw the pen on the table and declared, 'I'm leaving.'

I blocked the doorway and said, 'One last thing, doctor. I had to bring my wife in her wheelchair up the steep flight of steps, all by myself, without help from any of your corrupt orderlies. Now, I have a request: instead of displaying your smartness by putting down hapless patients, why don't you channelize it into arranging for the installation of a lift?'

The man pushed me aside and rushed out without replying.

The group—without the chief and bereft now of the second in command—stood around listlessly.

'We are leaving this place because the behaviour of that doctor is unacceptable. But before we do, I would like to know his name with initials and his designation. I'd also like to have the names of one or two of you as witnesses. I wish to take up this matter to the higher authorities. If no justice is done, I'll go straight to N. Ram of *The Hindu* to expose the unkind attitude of a government doctor towards a suffering patient.' I said.

No one responded for a while. Then one young doctor said, 'Sir, I request you to drop the matter. After all, you have punished him enough already.'

I thought to myself, 'Yes, the physician was obnoxious but he has been sufficiently humbled in the presence of the very "subordinates" he had tried to impress.'

I slowly grinned and replied. 'I agree, doctor, I believe you are right. I'll drop the matter.'

The tension broke and everyone relaxed. One of the doctors picked up a swab of sterile cotton wool and gently wiped away Mahema's tears. I was touched.

'Do you want the chief to examine her?' a doctor asked.

'Yes,' I replied. 'Actually, it was Dr Bhushanam who suggested that I bring Mahema to the general hospital, so that he can examine her here.'

'Then why don't you wait a little longer? The chief will be here anytime now.'

Even as the young doctor said this, Dr Raghu Bhushanam breezed in.

'I'm so sorry, Mahema, I was held up,' he said and turned to his retinue. 'Gentlemen, you've already met the lady. She has traumatic quadriplegia. The serenity with which she has accepted her personal misfortune is an inspiration to all who know her.' Then he said a little impatiently, 'But why haven't you prepared her for the check-up as yet? Surely, you didn't expect her to get out of the wheelchair by herself, did you? Come, come, move her onto the table.'

The doctor switched on the endoscopy machine. Two young

doctors lifted her onto the examination table which was at a high
level. I heaved the middle part of her body.
    'If I don't do this, her big bottom will stay behind!' I told them.
    'Shut up, Mano,' said Mahema laughing.
    The group laughed too, full of goodwill.

12

While I was in the US, I received a formal letter from a large, Bombay-based company, The Standard Batteries. The letter informed me that this company had taken over the smaller, Madras-based British company, Oldham, at which I was still an employee, but on lien. The Madras unit had now become a division of the Bombay company. The letter informed me that my terms of employment would in no way be adversely affected.

The chairman of the Bombay company, L. D. Char, knew and liked me. As a chief guest of a seminar and a symposium where I had presented scientific and technical papers, he told me at a party later, that he had an open offer for a job for me in his firm. In other words, he was keen that I should become his employee. I was amused that I had stumbled into becoming his employee, while I was in the US, enjoying the summer vacation in a college. I was happy too, because the chairman of the Bombay company could see my potential, which would make my job even more interesting. This letter came two or three weeks after Mahe's and my rapturous night in the tent at the park, not far from Oberlin. Around the time the letter came from Bombay, the Renfrows had returned to Oberlin. When Mahe and I drove to their residence to return the tent and the night lamp, Mahema cried. I could perfectly understand why. The tent meant so much to both of us.

Soon the college reopened. By then I had completed all my course requirements, which meant no more examinations. The chemistry department offered me the position of a Laboratory Instructor for the academic year 1971–72. My income doubled. In appreciation of Mahema's excellence in work, she received a raise in her salary. I was free to sit in any class as and when I wished. This was the strength and beauty of the American educational system.

As a Laboratory Instructor, I made many simple, innovative, artistically creative contributions to the chemistry department. Let me give just one example....

The chemistry department had acquired a state-of-the-art ultraviolet spectrographic machine. It had a roll of graph sheet, which came out like a long tongue with a delicately inscribed spectrogram. While all the ultraviolet spectrums were measured in metric system, I was surprised to find that the graph sheet was in an inch scale instead of a millimetre one. I was appalled that the least count of the scale was one-third of an inch—an awkward gross length of about 8.47mm between two parallel lines.

While I was in eighth standard at school, I had learnt in the geometry class how to divide any straight line into any number of equal divisions, ingeniously without even using any measurements. It became a useful tool for my artistic work. Now, using this method, coupled with my artistic abilities, I subdivided a line with a length of one-third of an inch into ten equal parts between two parallel guide lines. I did this on a small snippet of a tracing paper, stuck it to a thin, stiff, transparent tiny plastic piece and hung it on to the UV machine with a twine. The user of the machine could align this piece to the graph and read the spectrographic peak more accurately between the lines, so to speak.

This academic year was even more enjoyable and enriching. The students, the faculty, and the deans who knew us, loved us more. My research work and my thesis were satisfactory to my research guide.

The college was very keen that we should stay on, but we were determined to return to India. We wished to serve our nation in whatever little way we could. The provost of the college, Ells Carlson, wrote, 'Mr and Mrs Devadoss were loved and admired by the whole community. Oberlin would have been very fortunate if Mr and Mrs Devadoss had been willing to stay on. They decided however to return to their home in India.'

The final months of the academic year became extraordinarily precious ones for us. The months were studded with jewel-like incidents. I defended my thesis. As I waited in my room, Professor Renfrow took me to the mini-conference room, all wreathed in smiles. The chairman, Professor Schoonmaker said, 'You've done it, Mano.'

That evening Mahe had organized a programme on the Philippines, with a Filipina schoolgirl who stayed with an American family in a nearby town. At the beginning of the programme Mahe gave the happy news about me, to an enthusiastic response. The girl served tasty Filipino snacks that she had prepared in our kitchenette. She talked humorously about the Philippines, sang, and performed a complex dance to recorded music from her country. The girl was very eager to spend the night with us. Mahema telephoned and obtained the permission from her 'American mother'. The girl went to sleep in our bedroom with Suja and Mahe. I lay down on a grass mat in the 'Indian room', and began reading George Orwell's *Animal Farm*. About an hour or so later, Mahe slipped into the Indian room, removed her dressing gown and stood in her night slip. She said that Suja and the girl were sound asleep. She let her negligee slip down on to the floor, came and laid herself down next to me and said. 'I want us to celebrate your triumph now. After the celebration, I'll put on my clothes and quietly go back to the bedroom.'

Before her 'American mother' came the following morning to take the girl away, she hugged Mahe and cried. She then turned to me, gave a quick hug and said, 'I am glad I gave my performance on your day of victory, so you will always remember me.'

Like many, many other invitees to Asia House who made their

mark, I knew I would always remember this girl. But I am writing about her as she gave a beautiful finishing touch to my 'day of victory', as she put it.

Later, one evening, the chemistry faculty had a formal dinner, where I was awarded membership in the Sigma Xi Society for excellence in my research work. Professor Bill Renfrow told me that he would be sending a very brief paper, based on my research, in both our names to the prestigious *Journal of Organic Chemistry*. He hoped the journal would publish it (the journal did).

As part of my research requirement, I made a slide presentation, based on my thesis in the chemistry department. Many Asia Housers attended. So the auditorium was full. After completing the scientific presentation, I made a brief artistic one, with appropriate slides. I thanked the chemistry department, the college, and the country for giving us the opportunity to gain such a wide spectrum of knowledge and experience. I then showed some of my best slides, taken at the college and during our travels. I also showed some slides of the four seasons. I ended my talk presenting ten close-up portraits of leaves–from summer to autumn.

I started with a slide of emerald green leaves, then yellowish-green ones, greenish-yellow and yellow leaves, followed by orangish-yellow, yellowish-orange and orange-coloured leaves, followed by reddish-orange, orangish-red and finally ruby-red leaves. Instead of verbally stating the colours, as a chemistry man, for each picture, I stated the predominant wavelength of the colour. Of the visible spectrum VIBGYOR, my slides covered GYOR.

Not surprisingly, the audience liked the brief artistic part of my presentation more than the earlier scientific one. I thought to myself, 'Certainly, "Gas Phase Thermolysis of Sulphonyl Azides" would not excite many Asia Housers.'

Professor Bromond, an excellent, sensitive photographer himself, declared my slides were stunning. The chairman, Professor Schoonmaker said that he was glad that I was taking with me those spectacular slides of America to share with our dear ones in India.

That night, Mahe stayed in the beautiful sari that she had worn for my presentation. I knew that she wanted to give me the pleasure of untying it before taking her to bed. But before I undressed her, she gave me an intense kiss and said, 'Mano, I'm very proud of you.'

She made me happy.

The following morning, Mahe told me, 'Yesterday's event, Mano, was also your informal goodbye to the chemistry department. Shouldn't we have an informal goodbye event in Asia House?'

I agreed. So, I developed a drawing of an open, exquisite Indian bullock cart, a man driving the cart with his wife and little daughter in it. Mahe wrote a beautiful text. We had been regularly printing our pamphlets, brochures, invitations, greeting cards, and the like in the college printing press. The man in charge would study the matter, ask pertinent questions, and do a satisfactory job well on time. But he did not indulge in friendly chats. Now, he looked at the drawing, studied the text, raised his head and asked, 'Are you leaving Oberlin?'

I said, 'Yes.'

He was quiet for a brief moment and then said, 'Oh, that's a pity. I so enjoyed printing your work. I even came to know a bit more about Asia through your work.'

I was touched.

Our goodbye programme was a slide show, 'Asia House Through the Seasons', with my slides and Mahe's running commentary. First I showed a set of slides that had captured the edifice from various angles in different moods. Then we showed a set of slides of various programmes and activities of the dormitory. I interspersed these with pictures of the stained-glass window all aglow, the beautiful tiled roof with the tiles in harmonious hues and the sun dappled ivy. The seasons were represented by the crab apple tree as seen from our bedroom window. The first slide showed thick foliage covering the branches in summer. The autumnal picture showed no leaves but with little red berries aplenty. In the winter picture, the snow-laden tree appeared darker by contrast, standing on a carpet of snow. The picture looked more like a monotone brown ink drawing on a white sheet of paper than a photograph. The early spring slide showed tiny green spots all over the branches. The next picture showed green buds. These were sepals of the flowers. The next one showed white buds all over them...the tree was full of white blossoms hiding the branches.

A week or two before the students would begin to scatter far and wide around the globe, Mahe and I decided to have a picnic lunch in the courtyard of Asia House to enjoy the sunshine, the balmy weather, the view of the crab apple trees in full blossom and the pleasing, buzzing sounds of thousands of honeybees that thronged the trees fully covered with flowers.

Many students took the time to sit and chat with us, as they came and went on their own businesses during this time of academic pressure. Many pulled out their cameras, clicking away. Cathy Shaffer, an Asia Houser, later sent a photograph with a handwritten note. In the photograph she named the nine students who happened to sit with the two of us at the time she took the shot. In her note she wrote:

> One of my treasured memories is this day when I walked into the courtyard and found you both sitting in the sun. When you said you came to listen to the bees, I suddenly found the air filled with the low hum from the blossoms in the trees. As we sat there, a group of friends collected to talk and to enjoy the sweet harmony of the day that we found you so much a part of.

> With love
> Cathy Shaffer

Many other students too expressed similar sentiments.

The final programme was a study break at 10 p.m.. This was not on any Asian theme. Instead it was an informal Western music fest where, among others, a talented pianist and a gifted flute player of the dormitory gave a recital. As this was examination time, we expected only a moderate gathering. But Shipherd Lounge at Asia House was packed with people. Along with the students, there were faculty members, deans, administrators, and some of their spouses. The lounge was full, because the students had planned a beautiful surprise for Mahe, Suja, and me. After the flute and piano recital, Scott Wilk sat at the piano and to our utter surprise he began singing. He sang as he played the piano; lyrics that he had especially composed for Mahe, Suja, and me.

Goodbye lovely lady
Goodbye smiling man
Goodbye little girl, pigtail and all.
Goodbye friends
Goodbye loving patience,
Goodbye guiding light
And crayon girl home from nursery school.

Now the time is almost ended
And though I wish it were not so
Now the time is almost ended
India calls you and you must go
So be well, dwell in happiness, harmony and peace
Be of good health, of good spirits
In your works find your release, your release.
Goodbye friends,
Goodbye lovely lady, goodbye smiling man
Goodbye little girl, pigtails and all.

We received many gifts from Asia Housers. Ray Siefer made a brief wonderful presentation, during which he handed over a generous gift on behalf of the college community. Ray concluded his presentation saying, 'But let's go back to the beginning because that's where it all started and really that's how it should end. All of us love you, Mahema.'

There was a hushed silence in the lounge. Then someone began clapping and others joined. Soon the entire gathering rose and gave her a prolonged standing ovation. I too stood up and applauded enthusiastically. The image of Mahe sitting there with her stretched arms resting on the table, with her head laid on her arm, as she wept quietly, has been permanently engraved in my heart. It was a bitter sweet event for those in Shipherd Lounge, a poignant moment of mingled sorrow and joy, a time for much tears and laughter.

Late that night I did my last poster, three symbolic figures, representing Mahe, Suja, and me, with the caption 'You Touched Us beyond Words'. The students loved it.

A month or so later, I composed a stanza on Mahe at Oberlin for my ongoing verse, which I present below:

When she worked at Oberlin College
(That treasure-trove of wisdom and knowledge),
With her beauty, excellence, and a sense of duty,
She endeared herself to the college community,
Her Oberlin years she savoured with relish
And returned to Madras with memories to cherish.

The senior students stayed at Oberlin to receive their degrees, while the others left in droves after their examinations. Soon, families of graduating students began arriving. The morning of the commencement day dawned bright and clear. The sky was pure blue, the grass was very green, the weather was gentle and the air was fragrant. Oberlin had done away with capes and caps. I wore a tie for the first and only time in the US—my favourite, raw silk, Italian tie. Mahema dressed up and came out of the bedroom. When I looked at her, I was amazed. There she stood, clad in a new tasteful Kanjeevaram silk sari—one I had not seen before. However, I could guess that she had reserved for herself one of the saris she had procured from Madras to wear on this day. But what took my breath away was that she also wore a profusion of fresh jasmine blossoms in her hair.

'Oh, Mahe, you are wearing jasmine,' I yelled.

On seeing my utter astonishment and on hearing my enthusiastic response, her face took on a glow of joy. I gave her a hug, the jasmine buds touching my forehead. But how did she ever manage to get an abundance of such fresh jasmine at little Oberlin? Verna Kanu, an Asia Houser from Hawaii was graduating, and Mahe had persuaded her parents to bring from Hawaii a small basket of freshly plucked jasmine buds. They had flown into Cleveland the previous evening and gifted the basket to Mahe who, after I slept, strung them together, keeping the flowers in the 'other' refrigerator, to give me this wonderful surprise.

I had to leave early to take my assigned place, while Mahe had her fellowship with families of Asia Housers.

Pete Seeger, the chief guest, was an intellectually inclined folk singer. His ballads—often incisive, sometimes witty—were on sociological subjects such as upliftment of the downtrodden, equal rights for Afro–Americans, responsibilities of the rich and the mighty, pollution control, and the like. Some songs were his own, while others were by like-minded people.

The commencement presentation began. Introducing the chief guests, the young president of the college, Bob Fuller, said, 'There was a time, in the early McCarthy fifties, when Pete Seeger was not welcome at many colleges in the United States. But in those days he was welcome here.' He then said that while Fuller himself was a student at Oberlin, he recalled listening with fascination to verse after verse sung wonderfully by Seeger.

Seeger began his presentation first by strumming his banjo. He said, I quote, 'I won't forget that seventeen, eighteen, or nineteen years ago, some of you weren't born and others were students. We had some good music in an old church. I remember being told that the steeple of the church had never been put on because in 1860 it was voted to take the money saved for the steeple and give it to help the fight against slavery'.

A little later he said that Oberlin had a proud part in the 'Underground Railroad'—a euphemism for helping the Blacks from the south to escape slavery to the north. Aptly, his first song was about the 'Underground Railroad'.

After a couple of meaningful songs interspersed with his relevant observations, Seeger spoke about José Martí, the Cuban exile, and played Martí's poem 'Guantanamera' and began singing the song— one of Mahe's and my favourite haunting melodies. He taught the gathering to sing the refrain, 'Guantanamera, guajira Guantanamera'. He said repeating the line twice would cover nearly half of the song. When the entire congregation sang in unison, Tappan Square reverberated with 2,000 or more voices. It was stirring. Some students had tears.

I thought it was a moving culmination for our wonderful time at Oberlin. One among the most precious days in my life. A precious 'day'. I did not know at that time that the afternoon would not be all that precious.

~

Soon the ceremony of awarding the degrees began. The students stood in an orderly line and, as their names were announced one after another, they received their degrees on the podium from Seeger. Their friends applauded and sometimes cried out 'voooo'. When my turn came, I was taken aback to hear a group of students yelling out loud and clear, 'Jai Tamil Nadu'. I knew at once it was Mahe's handiwork. This was followed by a very long applause accompanied by enthusiastic hooting. I was touched and a bit embarrassed. Perhaps the students thought that, if Mahe deserved a standing ovation, I should at least get a long applause. Human nature is such that, if there was vigorous clapping by some, then others would join too. So the smooth flow was briefly disturbed.

We knew that after the ceremony, the new degree holders and their families would leave Oberlin seemingly in a hurry. Soon Asia House would be forlorn. Mahe had wanted to have a 'home celebration' with a special South Indian lunch. By chance, three days earlier, a distant cousin who lived in the nearby town of Akron telephoned me. So, I promptly invited him and his wife for lunch on the commencement day. He said that his wife's friend and her husband were with them. So I requested him to bring them along.

After the commencement function and friendly chats with some dear ones, we returned to our apartment in the now empty Asia House. Soon, we heard a knock at our door. I thought our guests had arrived a bit early. That was not so. A man whom we did not know was there. He said that Pete Seeger was having a lunch with a small group and he cordially invited us to join the group. We would, of course, have loved to. But we were soon expecting our own guests. Mahe asked me, 'Can we not ask your cousin to come for dinner instead of lunch?'

I told her, 'That wouldn't be proper. Besides, my cousin told me that they were going out somewhere this morning and would drive here directly from there. So, there is no way we could contact him.'

Later we learnt that Seeger wanted to know why I was given such a tumultuous applause when I received my degree. Apparently people talked about Mahema and me in glowing terms. They had also told him that we were determined to return to our motherland even though the college was keen that we should continue. Seeger liked meeting people from different cultures, from different countries, so he wanted us, 'the ideal couple' to join him at lunch. But sadly, that was not to be.

We had invited our cousins to come at 1 p.m., with the hope that they would arrive by 1.30 p.m. Time kept ticking. While the group had lunch with Seeger, we waited. Not to waste time, Mahe began writing to our parents about the commencement and I began writing about the 'jasmine surprise'. At 2.10 p.m., Mahe said, 'Oh Mano, we could easily have had a fellowship with Seeger and our friends, and come back on time to receive our guests.'

I told her, 'What to do? If only the students were at Asia House, we could have requested a student or two to stay in the apartment to receive our guests. Then we could have rushed back as soon as our guests arrived.'

Our guests finally arrived at 2.35 p.m. As soon as they came, two of our friends from some other dormitory came to say a quick goodbye to us. When they left, my cousin's wife's friend's husband—

let me call him Mr P—asked me, 'From where did you get hold of these hippies?'

I asked, 'Hippies?'

And then with a suggestion of sarcasm I said, 'Well, one hippie is going to Johns Hopkins to study medicine and the other hippie to Stanford to do her PhD.'

His response was, 'Tall claims.'

After reheating the food and after resetting the dishes on our usual 'floor table' we took our guests into the Indian room. My cousin said, 'I'm hungry and the aroma is so appetizing.'

Mr P said, 'Couldn't the college have provided you a dining table?'

I said, 'The dining table at the kitchenette can seat only four,' and with sarcasm again, I added, 'unfortunately there are six of us. So, we are forced to sit on the floor to eat our lunch.'

I could see that sarcasm was wasted upon him.

Our guests enjoyed the special lunch. My cousin asked Mahema later, whether the large building just on the opposite side of the road, was a church.

Mahe replied, 'Yes, "First Church" is its name.'

My cousin said, 'It seems to have something like a pedestal for a steeple. But there's no steeple.'

I told him that in 1860, the Oberlin community opted to give away the money intended for the steeple to help the fight against slavery.

Mr P said, 'That was a hundred years ago. Could not the silly Oberlin people have built a steeple any time during the course of a century?'

I could have told him about the historic significance and the symbolic relevance of not installing the steeple. But I did not want to waste my words. So, I only said, 'They could have but they didn't.'

Later still, reacting to an ordinary happening, Mr P, in a convoluted manner—and not subtly—implied that he was a peacock and that I a turkey and laughed at his own joke. Actually it was his laughter that sounded like the 'gobble gobble' of a turkey. I saw Mahema's face becoming red with anger. She excused herself and went into the bedroom. After some time, I followed her. When she saw me, tears welled up in her eyes. But her words were eloquent. 'I am unable to bear the thought that on this golden day, we had to give up the fellowship with Seeger and friends, only because we had to extend our hospitality to a nasty stranger. The fellowship could even have paved the way for a long-term friendship with Seeger.' Long-term friendship was not far-fetched. There have been numerous instances in our lives when such friendships had blossomed with mutual enrichment.

I told Mahe, 'You are not easily provoked. But I saw that you became very angry.'

She said, 'I became angry because he insulted you.'

I answered her, 'But Mahe, he didn't diminish me by his unkind words. Instead, he only diminished himself. Actually he began diminishing himself when he made his pronouncements about "the hippies", the dining table, and the steeple.'

She was thoughtful for a moment. She smiled and said, 'During the course of the past months, God had gifted us with many gem like events. Today, He has withheld just one gem, replacing it with a rotten egg. Instead of complaining about the rotten egg, we should rejoice that we have received many gems.'

I admired the quality of her thought.

We rejoined the group in a better frame of mind. During our brief absence, something must have transpired between the four of them. From then on, till they departed, Mr Peacock was overly civil and courteous.

That evening, Mahema and I decided not to brood over the disquieting events of the afternoon and not to talk about it in the future as such talks would serve no useful purpose. Indeed, I buried the bad memories with the knowledge that I could retrieve them if the need arose. Now after four decades, I decided to exhume the substance to write about the incidents—in this book—altering some inconsequential details to camouflage the identity of the people concerned, while keeping the content unaltered.

Mahe, as I guessed, did not change into a simpler sari or her nightdress, to give me the pleasure of untying the beautiful commencement sari. She had kept nearly half of the strung jasmine in the refrigerator. Late in the evening, she discarded the flowers in her hair, which had begun to wilt, and wore the fresh-looking blossoms from the refrigerator.

When I saw the fresh jasmine in her hair, I told her, 'Tonight I'd undress you so completely. Excepting the jasmine you'd wear nothing else—not even a chain, a bangle, or ear studs. So, I'd take to bed my Mahe and her jasmine, with exclusion of all else.'

I noticed just a tinge of red on her face. I said, 'You're blushing, Mahe, and this after eight years of married life!'

Mahe smiled shyly and said, 'You know Mano, throughout our stay in the US, tonight is the only time I give myself to you with jasmine in my hair. That would be a fitting finale for the commencement celebration of my beloved husband.'

13

Among all the helpers that we employed to take care of Mahema, old Radha was perhaps the most extraordinary. She was efficient, punctual, and, above all, very regular. Though she often gave the impression of being a cold, detached person, I discovered that a certain brand of humour lurked within the seemingly hard exterior.

One evening, she telephoned me to say, 'Aiyya, I won't be coming to work for a few nights. My husband is dead.'

I had known that her husband, a wastrel, had been ailing for some time.

'I'm sorry, Radhamma. When did he die?'

Radha replied calmly, 'About five minutes ago.'

'What?' I cried in astonishment. 'He died just five minutes ago and yet you are out talking to me from a telephone booth?'

'Well, nobody knows yet that he's dead, you see. I locked the front door of my hut and came out to tell you. If I asked someone else to inform you, then our slum prudes would have decried me for thinking about my employer while my husband lay dead. So, I have to do this a bit secretively.'

'It's really good of you to inform me. What will you do now?'

She replied matter of factly, 'I'll go back to my hut, beat my chest, and scream loudly. My neighbours will rush in to find out what happened. And, of course, they'll come to know that my husband has just died.'

I could not help but laugh.

A few years later, Radha did not turn up for work one night, nor did she send word, which was rather uncharacteristic of her. The next morning however, she visited our house to personally assure us that she would report to work that evening. She had a bandage with bloodstains around her head. She looked as if she had been plucked out of an old Tamil movie. I guessed that the head injury symbolized the reason for her absence the previous night. She explained that a man in her slum had hit her with an iron rod.

'What? An iron rod?'

'Yes, aiyya, that was exactly what he did.'

'How horrible. He must really be a mean, cowardly, disgusting fellow to hit an old woman like....'

She interrupted me. 'No, aiyya, he had a fully justifiable reason to hit me. I hit him first with a broomstick, right in front of his cronies, you see.'

Mahema and I burst out laughing. Radha seemed very pleased with herself. 'Like you, the police, and later the doctors laughed heartily too,' she said with satisfaction.

This was Radha at her best.

Usually, Mahema was transferred from the bed to the wheelchair by two women, one holding her body and the other her legs. Over the years, Radha began to find transferring Mahema from the bed to the wheelchair, with another helper, more and more difficult. Alas, a day came when she was no longer able to do this task. I helped her to get a lighter job in a clinic. She had come to work in our house when Sujatha was a child of seven and left when our daughter was a married woman of twenty-four. During the course of her seventeen-year employment, Mahema's father, mother, and also my mother had passed away.

Soon after Radha's departure, the young girl who worked as a live-in, also had to leave, as her family had arranged her marriage, in her village. Mahe and I found to our surprise that the stability that had existed in the realm of helpers was abruptly upset with the departure of the old woman and the young girl. A parade of women of all shapes and sizes came and went.

A woman who walked with an elephant-like gait, though she was rather thin, assumed that her swollen leg would be well hidden by her sari. But her peers found out while she slept soundly, that she had elephantiasis. When I suggested that she be treated for her condition, she retorted that her leg was not swollen and swung out in a huff, with her elephantine gait.

Immediately after her came a woman whose legs were not swollen but who shivered in the evenings like her predecessor and had high fever. She claimed that she shivered because the water in our house did not agree with her and went back to her mosquito-ridden hut to enhance the malarial parasite count in her blood. The next woman had an ugly gait. The day helper, Josephine, confronted the newcomer who sobbingly confessed that she was infected but placed the blame squarely upon her husband. Josephine was unimpressed and sent her away without even consulting her employers. I promptly forgot the real names of the three women, who had come and gone in rapid succession, but only remembered them through the years as Filarianne, Malarianne, and Gonorrheanne.

Then came a slightly plump, young woman who was spritely and for a change, positively helpful. She voluntarily took on additional jobs like darning, ironing, and the like. Mahe and I became fond of her. However, the way she dressed and walked provoked the other helpers to call her 'Jil-jil Rani' (loosely, Tinsel Queen). Every now and then, she would receive an evening phone call. She would at once declare that her uncle had been admitted in a hospital, change into a gaudy sari, put on cheap make-up and chew betel-leaf to make her lips red.

Soon, a man would arrive in an autorickshaw and take her away, purportedly to the hospital. She would return only the following morning. I realized that all that a call girl needed was a decent shelter, a cover-up occupation, and ready access to a phone, all of which we unwittingly provided to Jil-jil Rani. When I warned her that I might have to monitor the calls that she received, she readily agreed. However, that very evening she went away to see yet another uncle in yet another hospital, never to return.

But, among all the stay-in helpers who did not stay for long it was Mottachi who left an indelible mark on our household. The nun who sent her had told Mahema that the helper she was sending was a shy, gentle, and kind-hearted person. I soon found out that the newcomer was anything but shy, gentle, and kind-hearted. As soon as she arrived, Mottachi began pontificating on the various deficiencies of the other helpers. She obviously chose not to endear herself to her peers, who derisively began calling her 'Mottachi', as she had a shaven head. The new woman did not sit with the other helpers to eat. Instead, she sat on a low stool, held a wide-mouthed aluminium pot between her knees and ate directly from the pot.

One evening, Mahema and I had a group of friends for dinner. It was a lively evening with much laughter and merry-making. The last guest left around midnight. Mahema and I went to bed an hour later. We had hardly slept for an hour, when we were woken up from deep slumber by a gurgling sound. We saw Mottachi standing before us, shivering with fear and blabbering something totally unintelligible.

'What is it?' asked Mahema with alarm.

Mottachi's reply was pure gibberish.

I told the woman comfortingly, 'Don't be afraid. Tell us. What is the problem?'

From her incoherent babble, we finally gathered that there was a ghost moving about the drawing room. She claimed that the spirit had summoned her. She was terrified.

Gaja, the night-helper known as the Giantess, had by then heard the commotion and had come into the bedroom to find out what was going on. I got out of the bed to go to the drawing room to investigate.

Mahema said, 'No, no, Mano, I won't let you go. Maybe a burglar is there.'

I calmed her down. 'If there's a burglar already in the house, I am as unsafe in the bedroom as I would be in the drawing room.' I requested Gaja to accompany me because of my vision problem. The Giantess went along very reluctantly.

As we approached the drawing room, we heard a faint, quivering, whistle, whereupon the Giantess promptly abandoned me and ran back to the safety of the bedroom. I switched on all the eleven lights in the drawing room but could discern neither a spirit nor a human being nor an animal of any sort, not even a mouse. Thereafter, Mottachi and the Giantess refused to leave the bedroom, and curled up on the floor to sleep, drawing their courage from one who could not move and another who could not see!

The following morning, the day helper, Josephine, came in and observed, 'Amma, Mottachi is squatting on the kitchen floor with her head between her knees. The women in our slum who indulge in a night binge of country liquor often sit the same way with a hangover in the morning. I hope that Mottachi didn't stealthily drink something last night, after your party.'

Just then, Gaja came running up with an empty rum bottle.

'Amma, amma,' she said, 'Aiyya had left an unopened bottle of rum on the table. I found the same bottle lying empty, hidden under the fridge.'

'Jesus,' said Josephine, 'the stupid woman has drunk the whole bottle of rum. No wonder she's having a miserable hangover.' Fortunately, it was only a half-bottle.

'Oh, that's why she had hallucinations in the night,' said Gaja with delight.

'Aha,' I said, 'the havoc was wrought last night by a spirit, after all.' Everybody laughed.

'She couldn't keep her spirits bottled up for long, I suppose,' said Mahema, her expression serious, but her eyes twinkling.

All of us laughed uproariously, as poor Mottachi sat with her head between her knees, suffering silently.

Through the following days, the other helpers teased Mottachi mercilessly. For instance, Josephine would say, before she went home, 'Amma, lock up the cupboards or else the spirits will escape.' All these taunts from the other helpers were like water on a duck's back.

But what about the quivering whistle that Gaja and I heard on the night of the ghost? It turned out that the whistler had been none other than the new night watchman. Whistling was his way of announcing that he was indeed on his street patrol.

One evening, Mahema and I had been warmly invited to the wedding of the daughter of our dear friend, S. Muthiah. Our good friend, Rochelle, had also invited us for a dinner party later that evening. We had decided to attend the wedding reception and then go on to Rochelle's house. Our driver Rajan was unwell and on leave. Mahema's helpful friend, Gita Ram, offered the services of her chauffeur for the evening. Mahema's night helper, Gaja, was also on leave that night but had promised to report to work the following morning.

Mottachi felt uneasy and nervous about staying all alone after dusk in the big, old house when we were away. I told her that she had no reason to be afraid as long as she kept away from spirits.

That evening, Mahema wore her gorgeous Kancheevaram sari, deep olive green, shot with blue—the one she had worn at Satya's wedding, the night before our car accident. As this was a traditional, grand wedding, Mahema had her necklace and other gold ornaments taken out from the almirah and wore them. She looked rather nice.

After two enjoyable social engagements, we returned home at midnight. Gita's chauffeur was on pins, since he had to catch the last commuter train to get home. He helped me transfer Mahema from the car into the wheelchair and left in a hurry. I rang the doorbell repeatedly but had no response from Mottachi. I opened the door with the spare key that Mahema had in her bag and discovered that Mottachi had left the house bag and baggage, leaving the rear door wide open. I cursed her, bolted the rear door, and wheeled Mahema into the bedroom.

So there was no Josephine, no Rajan, no Gaja, no Mottachi, nobody. Even the Mathews, our tenants, were not in town.

We were all alone. Mahe was wearing her jewels and was clad in a beautiful sari. I was fifty then. I lifted her from the wheelchair all by myself, carried and gently laid her on the bed. Before removing her jewels and undressing her, a happy thought flashed across my mind. I remembered a similar incident that happened twenty-three years earlier. Like now at that time we were all alone. Then too she was wearing her jewels and was clad in a beautiful sari. I had lifted her, carried and laid her gently on a bed and later had proceeded to remove her jewels and undress her. This was on the night of our wedding day and Mahe was my bride. Now, I smile and reminded her about the long-ago 'event'. She too smiled. I removed Mahe's ornaments and placed them on a low stool nearby. Just as I began rolling her in bed to untie her sari, the electric supply went off, plunging the whole house into darkness and silencing the air conditioner and the fan. I opened all the bedroom windows and the door. Fortunately, it was not a hot or muggy night and there were not too many mosquitoes. I went back and resumed the process of undressing Mahe. The heavy silk sari slipped down and fell on the floor. I removed all her undergarments. I detached the rubber bladder from her knee, connected her catheter to the urine bottle, and propped up her pillows. I could not find the key to the shelf to get her nightgown. So I covered her with a bedsheet and told her, 'This will do for now.'

Just then, the talking clock said in a nasal, eerie tone, 'It's 1 a.m.'

I asked Mahe, 'Where's the alarm clock? Where's the torchlight? I want to set the alarm at 4.30 to turn you in bed.'

She replied, 'Don't bother with the alarm clock. You can turn me as soon as you wake up in the morning. Now, go to sleep.'

I cast off my silk dhoti, jubba, and underwear, had a shower, put on a lungi and came out of the bathroom. By then, Mahema was fast asleep. I tiptoed to my bed in the darkness, but inadvertently stumbled over the low stool and knocked down Mahe's precious ornaments. I did not even try to retrieve them from the floor for fear of trampling on them.

'I'll attend to all this in the morning when there is light,' I told myself wearily. I lay down on my bed and slept within minutes.

I woke up with a start, hearing Gaja exclaim in alarm, 'What happened, what happened?'

The morning sunlight was streaming down through the eastern windows and all the eight tube lights in the bedroom were now blazing, hurting my eyes.

'How...how...however did you get into the house?' I asked the woman.

'Why, the kitchen door was wide open and that's how I came in,' she replied.

'Oh, no,' groaned Mahema, 'Mottachi has left the rear door as well as the kitchen door wide open.'

'But where's Mottachi?' asked Gaja.

'Obviously she's no longer in our employment as of last night,' I enlightened the Giantess.

Gaja surveyed the room in utter amazement. Everything Mahema and I had worn the previous evening—that included Mahe's jewels—lay scattered all over the floor. The windows were wide open and yet the air conditioner was on. The ceiling fan which now revolved at full speed had shifted the bedsheet covering Mahe, to reveal that she was not wearing a thing. Gaja's expression of concern swiftly changed into one of great amusement.

'Aha,' she said, with a chuckle, 'I see that you two had a wild night. We can't trust and leave you both all alone in the house, can we?' she said, her eyes dancing with mirth.

Now it was Mahe's turn to survey the floorscape. 'The way our things are lying all over the floor reminds me of the rollicking night before the day of the accident,' she told me and giggled. This was the closest to her earlier silver bell laughter that I heard after the accident.

'What a rare coincidence,' I observed, 'this was the very sari I had untied that night, fourteen years ago.'

Mahema was silent. I turned to look at her. I saw a teardrop at the corner of her eye.

14

During our courtship in 1963, Mahe and I used to talk a good deal about the art and architectural treasures of Europe. So in a letter I did an ink drawing of a few of those treasures floating in the air with the tiny figures of Mahe and me at the bottom right edge, looking at the treasures with the caption: 'If dreams came true dear'. In the early 1960s, there were formidable constraints in India for tourism abroad. So, our dreams were unrealistic but we dreamt anyway.

Now, in 1972, on the way back from the US, our dreams of a European tour came to fruition. We travelled extensively around Europe for forty-five days. Our real experiences of 1972 exceeded our far-fetched dreams of 1963.

We visited so many art galleries and museums that each morning, six-year-old Suja would ask us which gallery and museum we were visiting that day. Our European experience of course extended far beyond art, artefacts, and architecture. We immensely enjoyed such varied natural beauty, theatre, concerts, a wide range of cuisine, and even a bit of shopping. Above all, every now and then, we stayed with dear friends, which added a new dimension to our enjoyment, and enabled us to reduce our expenses.

There were a few moments of anxiety in Europe—something we never experienced during our extensive travels in the US. We hired a Volkswagen Beetle from Hertz at Geneva and extensively drove around country roads in Switzerland. One late evening, as we drove back through narrow mountain roads to our friend's home, where we stayed, it was beginning to get dark and cold. For miles on end we did not see a single house or a vehicle. I told Mahe that if the car broke down, we would be in real trouble. Our friends were relieved when we reached home, well after dark.

The following morning, we left for Zurich, again avoiding the Autobahn and enjoying the scenic beauty. Around ten in the morning, I noticed on an incline upwards that the clutch began to slip. So, I drove to the nearby town. The slip became so bad I had difficulty taking the car on a formidable steep road. However, I just managed to coax the car to a petrol bunk in the town. Within twenty minutes, we were on our way in a bigger car, a Vauxhall. We were amazed by the super efficiency of the Swiss–American combine.

A few days later, when we surrendered the car at Zurich, the lady at the counter said that the rate for the bigger car was higher. I was ready to argue. But she raised her hand to stop me. She said that because of the 'inconvenience and anxiety' that was caused by the car that broke down, the company would charge only the rate for the smaller car. Further, she said we would get a 15 per cent discount. Because of the exchange of cars, we saved some money in petrol too. Later, when we drove around in hired cars in England, I hoped that these cars too would cause 'inconveniences'. But I had no such luck. The cars did not give any trouble in relatively flat England.

One night in Paris, we were in a small underground metro station, which appeared deserted. A hefty middle-aged man in an overall walked straight towards Mahema unsteadily. I looked around and could find no one on the platform. I became a bit nervous. But to my surprise, the man knelt down in front of Mahe and began saying something vigorously, but with a slur, in French. Every now and then he removed his cap, swung it, at the same time bowing low and beginning his recital again. I asked Mahema not to move. Suja, who was standing with me, looked at him with curiosity. A refined looking man entered the platform. He had one look at the scene and came to me and asked softly in perfect English, 'Shall I call the police?' I did not want the police but requested him to stay with us till we boarded the train. The man smiled and said that the drunk thought that the lady was a Hindu Goddess. I told him that, when I met her first, I had thought so too. He laughed. We saw a train approaching. Mahe who sat there unperturbed, stood up and flashed a smile at her admirer. So the man bowed deeper in acknowledgement. She walked around him and thanked the other man for his moral support. Earlier, when the hefty man walked directly towards Mahe, I had a sense of anxiety. But it turned out to be one of amusement. The two men—the one who knelt and the one who waited with us—actually endeared themselves to us, each in his way.

There were a few unpleasant instances during our European tour which did not have such happy endings. However, excepting for some loss of money, material and time, we came out of them unscathed. The rest of the time was sheer joy.

We ended our European tour with our stay for a week at Raspit Hall, Malcolm MacDonald's stately estate. It was for us a great finale. Malcolm was a gracious host, who showered us with his affectionate hospitality. After spending a few days at Oldham in Denton and a few days at the Standard Batteries in Bombay, I returned to work at the Madras factory during the third week of August in 1972. At that time, there was acute electric power shortage in Madras. At once, I took up a project of saving power. The company's main product was miners' cap-lamp batteries—which, unlike most others—were fully charged in the factory itself. I felt that a power consuming process, namely 'formation', could be completely eliminated, if suitable changes were incorporated in the preceding and following processes. I made meticulous experiments with satisfactory results. Indeed, I was able to eliminate the formation process altogether. There was also a reduction in labour, process time, and material consumption. I made a lucid, long internal report, which was sent to Bombay and Denton. The American Consulate General at Madras invited me to have a photographic exhibition of scenic America, which received an excellent response. Soon, the Photographic Society of Madras invited me to make a slide presentation of our life in the US. There were more invitations, in all of which Mahema fully participated. These gave us plenty of joy.

I had been to Kodaikanal for the first time ever in May 1964 with Mahe, five months after our wedding. I was simply enthralled. The Appasamy cottage commanded a magnificent view. Later Satya's father, Shanth Appasamy, told me that he had never seen more beautiful pictures of Kodai than the photographs that I had taken—not that there were many pictures of Kodai floating around, then. After two more visits to Kodai in the 1960s, Mahe and I had considered the idea of a book on Kodaikanal with my colour, black and white photographs, oils, watercolours and ink drawings, and Mahema's text. A couple of months before leaving Oberlin, we had talked with the provost of the college about financial support for our Kodai project. He had laughingly said that, if we presented an application as artistically and as forcefully as I had earlier for Mahe's Asia House job, then the college would have difficulty rejecting the grant.

After settling down in Madras in 1972, we sent an application to Oberlin for financial support for the Kodai book project. This grant would enhance the probability of getting the book published. Just then, word reached us that the board of trustees of American School in Kodai, which had become the International School, was very keen that Mahe and I should join the school as English and Science teachers respectively. The school management, under the leadership of Professor Riez of American College in Madurai and Professor Jaswant of the Indian Institute of Management (IIM), Ahmedabad, felt that our credentials were impeccable. In our case, the school had to provide just one living quarters for two teachers! On our part we were delighted...even thrilled. Teaching is relatively a nobler profession. We loved teaching and immensely enjoyed the company of young people. Above all, we would live in beautiful Kodai, which would be a great boon for the book project. So we eagerly looked forward to meeting Professor Riez in Madurai, soon after Satya's wedding.

Vidyodaya Girls High School in Madras was founded by Mahe's grand-aunt Swarnam Appasamy (in whose house garden my marriage with Mahe had been agreed upon in 1963). Her daughter Vimala, a pragmatic idealist who virtually dedicated her life to the school, was particular that Mahe should join the school and at an appropriate time, take over the leadership. So a position was open for Mahe at Madras, whenever she was ready. As for me, I had many options in Madras and would choose a service-oriented job, while keeping my creative candles all aglow. So we had the luxury of returning to Madras from Kodai whenever we chose to.

Earlier on, we had had many dreams and all those came true, surpassing our fond expectations. Now we began nurturing many brave new dreams. Among these, we dreamed of pursuing earnestly the art of giving that was close to Mahe's heart. We believed that our new dreams too would come true.... And why not? Dreams coming true was something we grew quite accustomed to.

I told Mahe on our ninth wedding anniversary, in December 1972, 'Verily, verily my cup runneth over.' Three days later, the accident happened. It seemed to me that the cup which was overflowing had suddenly crashed down and had broken into shards. I had felt shattered.

Yes, that road accident that had been unfair, caused by a thoughtless lorry driver who simply had not cared, had consigned my beloved wife to a life in a wheelchair. Had her tragedy been limited merely to a life in a wheelchair, then I would not have found it so hard to bear. But oh, the curse that had mercilessly fallen upon her was far, far worse.

I have already written about the trials and tribulations of quadriplegics. In India—why even in affluent countries—quadriplegics did not live for long. I was determined to stretch Mahe's life as far as possible. Now, Mahema was being loaded with powerful drugs and I feared that this might dull her sharp mind. She would be dependent all her life, needing twenty-four-hour attention. Her medical expenses would spiral. From then on I felt it would be harder for her to give than to receive.

One of the relatively minor sad outcomes of the accident was that we did not get to meet Professor Reiz in Madurai and had to forget about the Kodaikanal project. It was again, a bit of a sad day, when I wrote to Oberlin College, withdrawing our application for a grant for our Kodai project. But I saw one positive outcome. The bond of affection between Mahe and me—which was very strong before the accident—became stronger than ever before.

After the accident, my job at Oldham became crucial. My colleagues and the personnel in the technical department were highly supportive, although one or two in positions of power did take advantage of my vulnerability. While paying attention to Mahe's condition, I also had to ensure my job security. So even while Mahe was in Bagayam, I spent my spare time there to prepare insightful internal papers. Later I presented them in well-designed folders.

A seventeen-page paper that I prepared while in Bagayam entitled 'Orientation of Perforations in Pg Tubes' created a bit of a stir. The paper was sent to Schönberg, in Sweden, the inventor of Pg tubes, who, I was told, observed that I was an asset to the company. So, the small-time manipulators could not suppress me. I was amused to hear that one or two of the blue-eyed boys of the boss in Bombay were not jumping with joy about me, the new intruder.

By early 1975, many months before I met Dr Badrinath for the first time, I had noticed that I could not see properly with my right eye. Soon, I had realized that the macula (centre) of the retina of my right eye had degenerated. There was a justifiable anxiety that a similar situation could arise in my left eye too. What should I do at such an eventuality? Mahe observed that since the accident, I had not gone on a holiday anywhere at all. I needed a change. She suggested that I should either go to Meghalaya, where my dear cousin Prema's family lived, or to Nepal, where our Oberlin friend Al Dieffenbach lived. Now, by early 1975, we had evolved a system to care for Mahe. So, after a meeting with officials of the coal sector in Calcutta, I took ten days leave and went to Meghalaya.

It seemed to me that, wherever I turned, there was a worthy place to make an on the spot sketch. I 'saw', sketched, and photographed far more than I thought I would. I also had some out of the ordinary, interesting experiences, but that is another story.

By the mid-1970s, German Rotring engineering pens were easily available in Madras. I designed a compact leather case to hold a set of those pens and a bottle of Rotring indelible black ink. I designed a pad using a thick, strong hylam sheet base and a cover made of waterproof, tough transformer lamination paper and kept in it cut pieces of British Scholar art paper. I also designed a shoulder bag to hold the pad and the pens.

I went to Nepal too on a two-week holiday, after a meeting with a couple of officials at the Research Designs & Standards Organisation (RDSO) at Lucknow. The grand beauty of Nepal was stunning. There was so much to 'see', sketch, and photograph.

~

When I first met Dr Badrinath in late 1975, he observed that while I had only a rather narrow cone of vision in my left eye, fortunately the central region of the retina had been unaffected. So he said I could use the central vision to read and draw as much as I could, as long as I used comfortable levels of illumination. We decided that I should spend much of my spare time working on ink line drawings, which were easy on my eye. My style of ink drawings was time consuming, which in turn would affect my reading. Mahe immediately offered to rearrange her schedules so that she could spend a great deal of her time reading to me while I drew. Reading for hours on end would strain her voice, so I made her sit very close to me so that she could read softly in her mellifluous voice. That worked out wonderfully. I felt closer to her. She read book after book. We discussed the salient points as we went along and laughed together at the humorous passages. I could draw non-stop for long stretches because, listening to what was read softened the tedium. She kept track of the material I needed while I drew, and watched the progress of the artwork with enthusiasm.

My friends Renu and Roy and their two children often went from Madras to Kerala in their car. They warmly invited me to go along with them. They stopped the car and waited whenever I wanted to work on in situ drawings.

Roy used to tease me by telling Mahe, 'Your husband claims to have vision problems. But he spots any shapely woman in a mundu on the road well before I can.'

Mahe would laugh, saying, 'Don't I know? He has selective vision.'

The director of Max Mueller Bhavan invited me to present a multimedia art exhibition on Kerala. Mahema was totally involved in the project. The exhibition, held in early 1978, was a sensation in a gentle way. Fine articles appeared in the press about the exhibition and about us. *Kumudam*, the very popular Tamil magazine, featured a cover story on us with overwhelming response. I felt perhaps this was a new beginning.

In December, 1972, I had told Mahe that we had made a new beginning and that the future held many promises. But then the accident happened. Within a few years after the accident, I had lost useful vision in my right eye and became a one-eyed Jack, so to speak. And yet in early 1978, I felt that the future held promises, though the promises would coexist with uncertainties. We were able to give our daughter Suja a near-normal home environment. Life was becoming so enjoyable that I had to often remind myself that Mahe and I were severely challenged.

Then, Mahema's father was bedridden at ninety. Supported by my mother, Mahe's mother looked after him with devotion. Mahema spent quality time with him and read the Bible for him. He passed away in late 1981. This was hard on Mahema but, characteristically, she recovered soon.

Within five years after Mahema's return home from the hospital, many good things happened in our lives. Mahe took up teaching

spoken English on a one-to-one basis. Among her students were
the then Japanese Consul General's wife, two school-going sons of a
German professor at the Indian Institute of Technology (IIT), a couple
of Yugoslavians, Indian housewives, and Indian male professionals.
Mahe enjoyed the company of her students as much as they enjoyed
hers. Some had hilarious stories to narrate to her in broken English,
which she corrected, while others shared their tales of woe with her.
So, she also had to embark on counselling.

Our greeting cards had become collectors' items. From 1974
to 1975, to everyone's delight, the director of Oldham Division at
Madras wished to use our cards for the company. Our director wrote
appreciative letters to me for the artwork and Mahe for the text.
Through word of mouth, people started visiting our house to buy
cards. Mahe began giving away the profits from our cards.

I gifted all my on the spot sketches to Mahe. These were snapped
up by her students and visitors. The money she earned from all the
above was not all that much, but it did take care of a good deal of
her medical expenses. The money also gave her the ability to help
the needy.

By mid-1975, I had lost all useful sight in my right eye, and had
a relatively narrow cone of vision in my left eye, which was slowly
becoming narrower. And yet it was after mid-1975 that my artistic
productivity touched new heights. Moreover, the quantum of reading
of books, by Mahema and me (together), had been very high too. It
was a happy irony that the possible threat of an early loss of eyesight
had spurred me to move into a higher gear of artistic creativity. In
the bargain, I also joyfully ended up reading more books than I
would have under normal circumstances.

Alas, in 1981, it was confirmed that I was just beginning to
develop a cataract in my 'seeing' (left) eye. It was very small like a
pinpoint then, but it would grow. In January 1982, Mahe told me
one day, 'You and Suja need a break. You have plenty of earned leave
to your credit. I would like you both to go to the US on a long
tour, before your cataract worsens.'

I replied with a tinge of sarcasm. 'It is a noble thought no doubt,' and asked, 'Pray, who is going to finance the luxury tour?'

Mahe replied, 'Well Mano, we have relatives and friends all over the US who would only be too happy to have you both as their guests. As for the plane ticket, I can raise the money by selling a few of my gold ornaments. I am anxious that you should see new places and socialize while you still have some vision. It would also do a lot of good for Suja.'

I was deeply touched.

Yes, at that time the support system for Mahe was good. It would be nice if Suja and I could go to the US. But I was reluctant to allow her to sell her jewellery

Mahe arranged the plane tickets through friends at Oberlin. Suja and I travelled extensively through the US and a part of Canada for two months. Our stay at Oberlin was a true homecoming. My art exhibition and Suja's Bharatanatyam recital, held in Asia House, brought much joy all around.

Just three months after our return to Madras, Mahe's mother who was in her early eighties, had a bad fall and died within a week.

Most patients with retinitis pigmentosa developed cataract early. The cataract began to develop in my eye when I was only forty-five. Medical literature warned that many retinitis pigmentosa patients go into depression after the cataract surgery because often the retina would have degenerated at an accelerated pace. The cataract in my eye was slowly growing. After a stage, I became blind for many months. What with a cataract in one eye and extensive retinal degeneration in the other, my art came to a grinding halt. But I took extraordinary trouble—with the dedicated support of the technical department staff—to make sure that my 'temporary blindness' did not affect my performance in my workplace.

If my vision did not improve after the cataract surgery, as the technical literature warned—what should I do? If that was to be the case, I could write a book and learn Carnatic music.

Mahe said, 'But Mano, why should you wait till after the cataract operation? You could start writing the book now.'

I accepted her suggestion. Based on my boyhood, I planned a book on growing up in the historic temple town of Madurai. The book would include the escapades and preoccupations of a set of schoolboys, of which I was a very active member. Over the years Mahe had listened to my boyhood stories with great interest. She kept reminding me about writing the book, but I kept postponing ir for various reasons. Then one day Mahe made me sit next to her and began reading what she had written in order to give me a push start. She began to read: 'It was called the Green Well. It still is. Such an appropriate name, for greenness was its very essence....' Then she had gone on to describe the rural irrigation well and the pranks of a set of schoolboys there. I was moved. So I began writing about the well in detail and about the activities of my school friends and me in the well.

What I began eventually became the seventh chapter in the book that was published fourteen years later in 1997.

My newly appointed secretary, Malini, at Oldham Madras, was willing and eager to type the text. I informed the company that Malini would be helping in my book project and added that if the book got published, it would bring a bit of credit to the company too. I began dictating from late March 1983.

It was my intention to weave into the book the heritage, the festivals, social changes, the music, the scenic beauty of the surrounding countryside of Madurai and much more, to make it into a wholesome colourful fabric. Mahe began reading to me books and articles on Madurai, particularly the doctoral thesis 'Madurai' by late Devakunjari.

Soon I was ready for the surgery. Intraocular lenses were to become common in Madras only two years after I had my surgery in August 1983. Dr Badrinath performed the cataract surgery. When he was about to begin the surgery, the pace of my heart beat remained the same. He observed that, for most people, the heart would begin to beat faster. I said, 'When you perform the surgery, why would the heart beat faster?' He smiled and with that happy note the surgery began.

Three weeks later, Badri patiently tested my eyes to prescribe glasses. Finally, the doctor handed me the reading card to check my near vision with a +15 glass. After reading the smallest type on the card, I requested him to give me one with a type still smaller. Laughing in his characteristic way, he said, 'Sorry Mano, this is the smallest type we have.' As the biological lens inside the eye had been replaced by an external glass lens, the images that fell on my retina were a little bigger than before. So, I could read fine print with less difficulty now. The retina had not degenerated at an accelerated pace. I rejoiced that in my protracted losing war against retinitis pigmentosa, I now had won a victory in one battle. I stood up and gave Badri a hug.

On the way back home, I told my monster, retinitis pigmentosa, 'You have not triumphed over me. Actually, your earlier threat that you might rob my eyesight only motivated me to become an author. Now I am an author–illustrator of my book. Ha!'

15

When I was temporarily blind, my original thought was that I should begin writing a book 'only' after the cataract surgery and again 'only' if the retinal degeneration was such that I would be unable to pursue artwork. On the other hand, if the retinal degeneration was not significant, then I would resume art and drop the book. In other words, it was a question of either drawing or writing, but not both.

Fortunately, because of Mahe's imaginative initiative, I began working on the manuscript well before the surgery. Fortunately again, I could resume artwork after the operation. So, instead of either this or that, it came to pass that I could do both.

I often thought Madurai and its surrounding countryside would lend themselves splendidly for ink drawings. I could put my heart into the artwork that would go to illustrate *Green Well Years*. So the book would have both pen portraits as well as pen-and-ink portraits of my dear Madurai. I began visiting Madurai frequently, and roamed there like a vagabond on sketching expeditions. Unfortunately, after the cataract surgery, I was not able to draw on the spot as satisfactorily as I did before. I now had to use a graph sheet and make pencil sketches and not ink ones. Later, I began carrying a pair of binoculars to see the details and sketch these on a separate graph sheet. I took photographs too.

After returning to Madras, I typically completed the artwork thus: after poring over all the material I brought from Madurai on a single topic, I prepared an accurate outline drawing with a 4B pencil on an A4 paper.

Fortunately in the early 1980s, Xerox machines had come into India. Oldham acquired one. I made an enlargement of my line drawing on a larger A3 transparency, stuck it at the back of a British Scholar drawing paper, illuminated the pair from behind on the easel (that I had designed) with a glass base and completed the drawing in intricate detail with Rotring ink pens.

Every time I made changes and corrections in the manuscript, poor Malini had to retype the text again and again in the manual typewriter, which was time consuming and tedious. Conveniently, electronic typewriters became freely available in India. The technical department acquired a high-speed electronic typewriter with floppy disc and hence had unlimited memory. Now Malini could breeze through all the changes and corrections. The dark, crisp prints were easy on my eyes.

The very first ink drawing I made especially for the book was of Spencer's at Madurai. It illustrates an amusing incident involving four middle-school boys on the pavement, with Spencer's forming a larger backdrop.

Correspondingly, the text also had a larger sociological narrative relevant to the time. Mahe observed, 'This does not look like a mere story illustration. This is an intricately done, exquisite piece of artwork.'

I happily told her, 'This is how all the illustrations in the book are going to be, for each and every story illustration there would be a larger background, both pictorial and sociological.'

While I was in high school, one late winter afternoon, two school friends and I walked upstream along the Vaigai riverbed far from the madding crowd of Madurai. That evening we bathed in the colourful glorious sunset, the silvery river water turning into gold.

The very next artwork I took up was to present this scene in the book. It was an interesting challenge to capture this glorious moment, vibrant with colours, all in black ink. I presented the view as seen from a higher plane, with the three of us appearing like insignificant specks, standing in the water. Here too the text would cover some larger historical and sociological backdrops.

While Mahema was in Bagayam, where many disabled persons stayed under one roof, I was able to observe the widely differing levels of compassion that different disabled persons evoked in the minds of others. I have already written about it. Now, Mahema and I were totally in the mainstream of society, despite our respective disadvantages. Over the years, I had many opportunities to keenly observe the differing reactions of different persons towards a given physically handicapped person. I realized that from the perspective of a disabled person, there were, by and large, six major kinds of people.

The ideal ones, among the six types, were, of course, those who had both the ability and the willingness to extend sustained help to the disabled. My list of people who constantly went out of the way to help Mahema and me was, fortunately, very long indeed.

A majority of people, however, belonged to the second category. These persons were overly eager to help a disabled person, usually in a tentative and ad hoc manner. Their eagerness however was short-lived. They were often not sufficiently equipped or motivated to sustain the help that they came to offer. A good example of this type was the man at the Museum Theatre, who had readily come forward to help me carry Mahema's wheelchair up the steps like a palanquin, only to suddenly leave me in the lurch, without completing the task.

I thought of the third category of people as those who exploited the very vulnerability of the disabled. An autorickshaw driver who exhorted a higher fare from a man in crutches belonged to this group.

But I did not feel bitter when I encountered this type. They were, after all, openly or subtly, knowingly or unknowingly, obeying the Darwinian Law of the Jungle. I also thought that many of the exploiters of the less fortunate had perhaps themselves been victims of exploitation, especially during their formative years.

The small section that made up the fourth group generally avoided a disabled person as they were either too busy or too embarrassed or plainly afraid that they might say or do the wrong thing.

The fifth category of people was so totally self-absorbed and so completely wrapped up in their own little problems—often brought upon themselves by their own actions—that they totally failed to see or care about the misfortunes of the disabled.

The sixth category of persons was the worst. They were callous, insensitive, and derived some sort of perverse pleasure in making a disabled person feel very small.

An usher in a musical hall was a typical example of this kind. Mahema and I enjoyed attending some of the fine Carnatic music recitals that took place during the music festival held at Madras in December–January, for which the city had grown famous. One evening, as I was engaged in the somewhat awkward process of transferring Mahema from the wheelchair to an aisle seat, with the help of a rasika in the Music Academy, a hired usher said to Mahema, 'Why do you ever come to places like this, when you can't even walk? Instead of making yourself a nuisance, you ought to stay at home and watch TV.'

I told the man, 'I suggest that you mind your business of ushering and keep your views to yourself.'

However, the rasika who helped me went straight to T. T. Vasu and complained about the usher's uncalled for rudeness. The then president of the academy gave the hired usher such a drubbing that the man cowered like a mouse before Vasu. Later, whenever T. T. Vasu saw Mahema in the academy—where he seemed to live during the music season—he always made kind enquiries to her, which the ushers did not fail to note, and they behaved accordingly.

I was angry with the usher. But then, he was only a temporary hand, whose limited abilities did not allow him to go far beyond ushering. To him a wheelchair must have seemed an incongruity, an alien object in a music hall. So, his unkind words perhaps stemmed partly from ignorance and partly from arrogance.

But what I found most difficult to condone was the insults that the doctor at a government hospital had hurled at Mahema, a patient in a wheelchair and in a hospital, of all places. Fortunately for Mahema, Dr Raghu Bhushanam had soon taken command and after the endoscopy, had assured her that she had nothing whatsoever to worry about. Mahema had returned home that afternoon in a happy frame of mind.

That night when we went to bed, Mahema told me, 'There I was, tied down, unable to move, a damsel in distress, while the nasty dragon breathed fire. I could only cry, but the dragon had no pity. Suddenly you stepped in like a knight in armour, drew your sword and in a duel of words tore the menacing dragon to pieces.'

After hearing what Mahema had to say, I smiled. I was glad that the doctor at the hospital had been nasty to her. For it had been this doctor, after all, who had inspired Mahema to call me her knight in armour for the first time ever.

As my vision declined, I first avoided driving my car in crowded roads at night time. A few months later, I stopped driving after dusk. Later still, I stopped driving on crowded roads even in the daytime. Then a day came, when I announced to Mahema: 'I feel nervous when I drive now. I think I should stop driving altogether, before I hit somebody.'

She agreed. 'The traffic is so chaotic in Madras that even those with normal vision would feel insecure driving on our roads,' she said.

I engaged a few full-time drivers, all of whom had to be sent away, sooner or later for one reason or another. Then a boy named Rajan arrived. Rajan had very limited driving experience, but I liked his positive outlook and helpful disposition.

Mahema always sat in the front seat of the car and not in the back seat with me. It was easier to transfer her from the wheelchair to the front seat. Besides, as she was mostly homebound, she would have the opportunity of seeing more from the front seat of the car, whenever she went out. Unlike the Herald car which I had owned earlier, the Ambassador did not have a separate passenger seat in the front and I could not tie Mahema down to the seat now. Instead, I would lean forward from the rear seat and hold her shoulders so that she would not be thrown to the front, if the driver jammed the brakes. Late one afternoon, we went out in our car, with Rajan at the wheel and I holding Mahema's shoulder as usual. The car drove over a rough patch causing Mahema to suffer pain in her neck at the region of her spinal injury. At the next traffic light, I gently massaged her neck to give her relief. Just then an autorickshaw stopped alongside our car. A passenger in the autorickshaw with a boom-boom voice whispered to his co-passenger, which I could hear, 'Look at the lecherous fellow in the back seat of the car. He is leaning forward and fondling the woman in the front seat. All this in broad daylight on a public road.'

Just then the traffic lights changed and the autorickshaw puttered away, ahead of the car. I laughed. Mahema asked, 'What's so funny?' I replied, 'I'll tell you later.'

Years later, as a middle-aged man, I bought a new air-conditioned NE 118 car, which came with bucket seats and shoulder safety belts. The safety belt completely eliminated the need for me to lean forward to hold Mahema's shoulders. Now I could sit back and relax. But I would quip, 'Alas, Mahema, from now on, the road-users shan't be seeing me "fondle" you. So, we'll be denying them the satisfaction of decrying the erosion of moral standards in Madras!' But I was wrong....

When Mahema went out for long stretches of time, the rubber bladder tied on to the knee would bloat up with urine which had to be emptied as early as practicable. For this reason, we carried a plastic bottle in the car. If we returned home late after a dinner party and if the rubber bladder became too full, Rajan would stop the car in a lonely, dark place and move away discreetly. I would get down from the car, open the front door, bend down and position the disposable plastic bottle at the outlet of the rubber bladder under Mahema's sari and empty the urine into it. I would then adjust her sari, dispose of the bottle, wash my hands, and call Rajan back. This was done with privacy as the open door blocked the view from the front and I myself standing outside and leaning inwards, blocked the view from the rear. This operation was warranted only occasionally. But, every time I had to do this, Mahema would feel very sorry for me.

One day, as I emptied the urine, 'Poor, poor man,' she whispered into my right ear which was close to her face, 'you have to not only wage battles like a knight on my behalf, but also empty my urine like a menial on public roads. What can I give you in return? Come, I'll give you a kiss.' Saying this, she leaned forward and planted a kiss on my face. Just then, a midnight scooter suddenly emerged from a lane and turned into the road. As it turned, its headlight momentarily caught Mahema kissing me—like a flash-lit snapshot through the large windscreen of the car. The scooterist swung the vehicle to make a U-turn and trained its headlight on the car, where I stood. The pillion rider jumped out and came very near me to find out what the devil was going on.

And, what did he see?

He saw that a middle-aged man in a folded silk dhoti, who stood bending down outside the car, had inserted both his hands under the sari and between the legs of the middle-aged woman in a grand sari, who sat in the car, who had been kissing him moments earlier.

That was exactly what he saw!

'Madras has become really decadent,' he decreed loudly and walked back to the scooter in utter disgust. Mahema and I laughed all the way home.

But this incident of 'decadent Madras' occurred many years later.

Going back to about four months after Rajan became our driver, Mahema, Suja and I went in our Ambassador car on a picnic, one late afternoon to St Thomas Mount. When we reached the foot of this hillock, Rajan—and not the car—stalled. 'I have never driven a car before on a hill road, saar, and I am quite nervous about doing so now, especially with Amma inside.'

I exchanged seats with Rajan and began driving up the hill with ease. I assured Mahe that I was far less unsure of driving on hill roads than on flat city roads. 'This might sound incongruous,' I added, 'but it's absolutely true.'

At that time, I had acute tunnel vision and night blindness in one eye and virtually no useful vision in the other. The hill road was narrow and did not demand a wide angular vision. With an upward slope on one side and a downward slope on the other, it was highly improbable that anyone would dash into the path of the car from the side—as they sometimes did on flat roads. Besides, there were hardly any pedestrians or bicyclists on a hill road and above all no cycle-rickshaws at all. When I began driving the car—now after a gap of nine months—my spirit soared.

As soon as the car reached the top, Suja got out and jumped around like a pogo stick. Mahema enjoyed looking at the city of Madras spread out down below, and the airport runways to the south, where airliners took off and landed as noisy as thunder and yet, as smooth as silk.

Mahe was in an upbeat mood. She also enjoyed my chicken sandwiches and my fresh homemade tomato juice with ten other ingredients that included a dash of gin. Most of all, she enjoyed the glorious winter sunset from the higher vantage point.

But unfortunately, we could not linger on the top of the hill. No sooner did the sun descend behind distant trees, we had to go down the hill before darkness would spread her mantle upon the scene. I drove to the foot of the hill and handed over the wheel to the driver.

This was the last time that I ever drove a car. A few years earlier, I had allowed Mahe's driving licence to lapse. Now, the time had come to allow my licence to lapse too.

During the 1980s, in general, Mahe did not suffer much. The systems were all in place. I was invited by two powerful art promoters to contribute my ink drawings (along with artworks of many famous artists) to a roving art exhibition, *Kala Yatra* by Sara Abraham and an annual art show *Ah, Madras* in The Gallery by Sharan Apparao, which received excellent reviews. For *Ah, Madras,* reviewers used phrases like 'the inimitable style of Manohar Devadoss'.

Our twin disabilities disallowed many simple activities and some of the basic pleasures of life that others take for granted. With time, the disallowances were only to pile up against us. In spite of this, we tried to lead as happy a life as practicable, for as long as possible.

The varied sources of happiness were like big and small gift-wrapped packages, stacked in a large cupboard. It was true that Mahema and I did not have access to most of these packages of joy. But then, it was also true that there were some that remained within our reach, if we took the trouble.... Music, for instance. We enjoyed many genres of music. Fortunately, we had ample opportunities of listening to live performances as well as recorded music.

Good books were another source of happiness. Mahema read a lot to me and we discussed the book as we went along.

Our disabilities could not stop us from enjoying good food. I liked inventing new recipes and at least a dozen persons suggested that I should write a cookbook.

And what about humour? I believed that a physically disabled person with a keen sense of humour was a more complete human being than a humourless person who had no physical handicap. Ironically, the very physical disability could in itself be a perennial source of humour.

The fellowship of friends and relatives could be an abiding source of happiness.

What about creativity? I had ample opportunities to be creative in my workplace and at home. Mahe and I ensured that our creative candles were aglow, overcoming the many constraints imposed upon us by our two monsters. Above all, we were able to pursue the art of giving to the extent we could, which was a source of great joy.

16

The wheels of Mahema's chair turned on.

Now Suja was a young lady pursuing her master's degree. She had done well academically. She was also a lively conversationalist and a fine photographer. Though she enjoyed intellectual freedom, she had grown up with certain social restraints. Our cousin Mithran, who had been fond of Suja from her childhood, asked her to a dinner party to which he had also invited many talented young people.

'We shouldn't overprotect our daughter, we must allow her to go out on her own, meet other young people, and be exposed to a party environment. After all, Mithran is one of our well-wishers,' Mahema told me.

I agreed.

Thus Suja attended her first party alone, as a young adult. The following morning, Suja confided to Mahema that at the gathering, she had ended up spending much of her time conversing with just one person, a young American who worked at the US Consulate. She had met him twice earlier when she had attended programmes on American literature at the then USIS.

Later, Suja and the young American, Michael, began exchanging telephone calls and their favourite books. Suja did not hide from

Mahe the keen interest that Michael was beginning to show in her.

On Suja's birthday, a huge bouquet of roses arrived from Michael. A few days later, Matthew, one of our friends and a respected Indian official of the USIS, visited our house at a time when I happened to be out of town. After talking with Mahema about the good old days, he said, 'You know, Mahema, I have worked in the consulate for many decades with many Americans. Michael Pelletier is among the finest.'

Mahema replied, 'Yes, we hear that he has many Indian friends.'

Mathew replied, 'He also approves of many Indian customs.... at least the traditions as followed by cultured Indians....their family ties, their food, their music.... He does approve of the Indian way of arranged marriages and that is why I invited myself to your house today.'

Mahe said, 'I don't understand what you mean.'

Mathew drew a deep breath and went on, 'Michael likes, for instance, the Indian way of a family member—usually an uncle or an aunt—asking a girl's parents for the marriage of their daughter to his or her nephew.... Well, Michael's uncles and aunts are far away. So, I have the honour of playing the role of his Indian uncle to request you properly for Suja's hand for Michael.'

Mahema was completely taken aback. She could only say, 'Well... well, well. It's an extraordinary situation, isn't it? What can I say? Mano is in Delhi now. I have to talk with him and Suja, before I can give you even a hint, either way.'

Later that evening, Mahema told Suja about Mathew's visit and the proposal he brought on behalf of Michael. Mahema could not fathom her daughter's expression. It seemed a mixture of thoughtfulness tinged with joy, anxiety, and amusement.

Suja told her mother, 'Please talk with Appa and let me know what your views are. Remember, Michael's job will take him to far away countries and if I marry him, I won't be able to live with you or be near you.'

Mahema and I thought deeply about the proposal. We did some

soul-searching. Finally one day, at three in the morning, I told Mahema after turning her in bed, 'We have always promised ourselves that we will never let our daughter become our prop, our security blanket. It is now time to let Suja fly free and not keep her in our little cage.'

Mahema replied, 'I agree with you, Mano. But let us first have an open, frank talk with Michael before we take the final decision.'

Mahe telephoned Michael the following morning to say that she and I would like to meet him and talk things over. He promptly invited Mahema, Suja, and me for dinner to the consulate bungalow. He told Mahe that his cook excelled in preparation of Western dishes and wondered whether she had any preferences. Mahe gave him a detailed list of American specialties that I liked and another list of what she liked.

Michael was taken aback, but soon recovered enough to reply, 'I will serve exactly what you would like to have, Mrs Devadoss.'

Later, I would tease Mahe saying, 'I'm sure Michael must have had second thoughts about marrying our daughter when he found out that you could be so demanding even before you became a full-fledged mother-in-law!'

His eyes twinkling, Michael would observe, 'On the contrary, Appa, when she ordered such a detailed menu, I became quite sure that she had already made up her mind about the marriage alliance!'

But all this teasing came later. Mahe, Suja, and I went to Michael's house for the special dinner. After the dinner, I requested Suja to relax in the garden. Mahema began talking about Michael's wish to marry her daughter.

'In your society, you have ample opportunity to get to know the girl and her parents before marriage. How did you decide that our daughter is for you without getting to know her or us, all that well?'

'You will be surprised to hear how much I know about you and your daughter…about your Oberlin years, the photography exhibition that you had at the US Consulate….Your car accident, and so much more. Mathew, Mithran, Sister Sheila, and so many others who have known Suja from her childhood have talked about her to me. Really, you are no strangers to me.'

'Well, we are pleased,' I said, 'you must also have heard that I have a problem with my eyes. Suja does not have retinitis pigmentosa but she may carry the recessive gene.'

'Well, your cousins have told me that not a single person, other than you in your family, for generations, has had your vision problem, so it must be a freak occurrence. Besides, I count on the good genes you two have passed on to your daughter, especially, Mrs Devadoss.'

'But, I have to tell you,' I said, 'that notwithstanding the genes, temperamentally, Suja is very different from Mahema.'

Michael said with a smile, 'What you mean is that Suja is no dollop of ice cream.'

I laughed. So, Michael even knew that Suja and I called Mahe 'Ice Cream', after an article in *Kumudam*.

Michael talked to us about his family with affection. They were French Canadians who had emigrated to Maine in the US. They were a close-knit family and his grandmother had always lived with them and never in an old people's home. Michael assured me that his parents knew about Suja and approved of her.

Mahema's countenance was wreathed in smiles. With her limited hand movement, she pressed my arm gently with hers, to express her approval. I too liked the young man. I said to Michael, 'Once we talk to your parents and hear their acceptance, we'll be very happy to give our consent.'

Michael looked at his watch: 'My parents would have woken up about two hours ago. We can call them now, before they leave for work. Would you like to talk with them?'

He dialled his parents in Maine and after an animated conversation with them in French, he held the phone to Mahema's ear.

When the little family of three returned home, instead of beaming and smiling, Suja began weeping. 'I don't want to abandon you both,' she said, crying uncontrollably.

Mahema too started crying. I did not know what to do or say. Eventually, I managed to pacify my daughter and convince her that she should not feel any remorse. I added that if ever anyone made her feel guilty that she was deserting her parents—all she had to do was to tell that person sweetly, to talk to me and not her.

For a wedding in India, it is usual for the bride's parents, their siblings as well as the bride's siblings to rally round and help with the preparations in every way. Neither Suja nor Mahema had siblings and my two brothers were far away in the US coping with their own problems. Fortunately for the family, the absence of siblings was more than compensated for by innumerable close friends and some relatives. The outpouring of support made the period between the formal engagement and the wedding a magical one for Mahema.

Michael's parents, siblings, and grandmother flew to Madras to attend the wedding, as did many Oberlin friends with their families. I was overjoyed that it was yet another Oberlinian, David Gallup, who solemnized the wedding. Suja was a beautiful bride. As the bridal car glided to a stop near the noble columns of St George's Cathedral, Reverend Gallup came up smiling to receive the bride. During the bridal march, the bride's hand gently rested on my arm, and the bridesmaid, Tess, walked two steps behind Suja. Because my vision was impaired, it was not I who led the bride, but rather it was the bride who led me. I held my head high and walked with dignity, although I was quite nervous lest I inadvertently step on Suja's sari and make her trip and fall.

David Gallup's reading of I Corinthians, Chapter 13 was impeccable. When he ended the reading with the words, 'And now abideth faith, hope, love, these three: but the greatest of these is love.' Mahema's eyes filled with tears of joy.

It had been decided earlier that during the recessional, after the wedding ceremony, Michael's father, Moe, would wheel down Mahema right behind the bride and the groom and that his mother, Pat, wearing a sari for the first time in her life, would walk with me and guide me, immediately behind Moe. I was very pleased with this arrangement, which seemed symbolic of the union of two families rather than merely of two individuals. The pipe organ came alive, filling the cathedral with the powerful and triumphant notes of Mendelssohn's 'Wedding March' and the congregation stood up. As we walked down the nave, repeatedly bowing to the congregation, I told Pat, 'You know, Pat, during the bridal march, I was quite nervous that I might step on Suja's sari and make her trip and fall.'

Pat replied, 'You didn't, and actually managed very well.'

I quipped, 'Ah, but then, I might step on your sari now.'

Pat came her reply: 'The marriage ceremony is over and it really wouldn't matter even if you stepped on my sari now and made me fall!'

I relished the Pelletier brand of humour. I reckoned that it was rather unusual for a conversation like the one Pat and I were having, to take place during the recessional march of a wedding ceremony.

Later that evening, at the dinner party, Suja's friend, Priya, held my hand and said, 'Oh, uncle, this was the very first Christian church wedding service that I've attended. The ceremony was so wonderful I think it's worth falling in love with a Christian boy just to get married in church!' Her friends agreed enthusiastically.

I had set aside some money for my daughter's wedding and planned to draw the extra amount I would surely need from my provident fund. But, I had actually spent only a portion of the money that I had kept in reserve. So, it had not been an expensive wedding and yet many described it as 'classy' and even 'grand'. I realized that a tastefully organized wedding need not necessarily be an expensive one. Fortunately, I did not have to spend any money on seer varisai as the American mappillai came with a house equipped to the hilt. But above all, their friends had extended their support and service as their wedding gifts—limousine-service, flowers, music, et al.

During the following months, Mahema and I came to love our son-in-law. Mahema said that she now felt that she had a son. I heard in her words, an echo of my mother's when she said she had gained a daughter in Mahema.

Mahema and I often visited Michael and Suja in their elegant house. Sometimes, Mahema would spend the day with Suja, taking a helper with her. She would sit in the bedroom, taking in the beauty of the serene lawn and the greenery of the trim garden. Mother and daughter would share precious moments of togetherness, which brought Mahema deep satisfaction. Months sped peacefully. Mahema and I experienced the joy of having settled our daughter happily and comfortably. My heart was full of gratitude.

One day I told Mahema, 'Mahe, I really wish to return all the kindness we've received over the years, in some concrete way. I've been thinking it over. Perhaps I can have a one-man art show and present the sale proceeds to Sankara Nethralaya. What do you think?'

Mahema sat silently in deep thought with an expression bordering on concern. I wondered whether she was going to tell me that we should keep the sale proceeds for ourselves for our own future security. But when she spoke, I realized that her only concern was for me.

'Mano,' she said, 'your vision is not what it was even a year ago. Your style of detailed pen-and-ink drawings will take so much time to do. You have to do your work on your drawings for the book too, which cannot be sold. How can you ever expect to finish the twenty-five to thirty drawings you'd need for a one-man show with your demanding, full-time factory work?'

I replied, 'Well, for one thing, I can stay up every night until two in the morning. You can read to me for longer stretches.'

Mahema's eyes brightened with a new idea. About two years earlier, Suja had encouraged Mahema to make light-hearted drawings using her splint. Now Mahema said, 'Mano, can I join you in your endeavour? I would like to contribute eight to ten water colours to the exhibition.'

I was thrilled. It would be as challenging for Mahema to work on ten water colours with her quadriplegia as it would be for me to complete thirty meticulously executed pen-and-ink drawings, with my retinitis pigmentosa. We shared our thoughts with Michael and Suja that evening.

Michael said, 'Amma, maybe, it should be a family affair. Suja can surely contribute her artistic photographs to the exhibition.'

Badri and Vasanthimma of Sankara Nethralaya welcomed the idea with great enthusiasm. Klaus Schindler of Max Mueller Bhavan readily agreed to sponsor the art show. Chitra Chockalingam of Heritage, told me that she would be honoured to have the exhibition in her gallery, which was just next door to Max Mueller Bhavan. And, M. S. Subbulakshmi Amma, the nightingale of South Indian classical music, graciously agreed to inaugurate the exhibition by singing one of my favourite 'Meera Bhajans'. All this happened as quickly and easily as a breeze blowing.

Now, much labour lay ahead. Mahema read to me until midnight, but I continued to work for another two hours. If I became very sleepy in the wee hours, I took a quick, cold shower to get rid of my drowsiness temporarily, so that I could work a little longer before going to bed. Mahema did her paintings, ably helped by her secretary, Graceamma, who changed the brushes and colours as Mahema wanted. Suja woke up early in the mornings and wandered through Madras to create special artistic photographs for the exhibition.

Time marched on, and the day of the exhibition dawned—crisp, refreshingly cool and with a cloudless, clear, blue sky. But the political firmament was heavily overcast. With the rising sun, came the news that the ruling party of Tamil Nadu had been sacked by the Centre, late on the previous night. Many people involved in the organization of the exhibition thought that the art show would have to be called off. However, despite the palpable tension in the state, the programme was not cancelled. And almost all the invitees attended the beautiful function on the lawn of the Max Mueller Bhavan, which was peacefully tucked away from the rude din of the arterial roads. In the soft evening light, when M. S. Subbulakshmi sang 'Mere tho Giridhara Gopala', I thought, 'I never, ever dreamt that a day would come when this saintly singer would sing a song of my choice, honouring my family and me.' It was a very moving experience. Then, to my delight, she spontaneously sang a second song, 'Naagendra Haaraaya'.

After she sat down, Desikan, who compered the function, said with a voice trembling with emotion, 'Time stood still when she

sang.' Later she lit the lamp which we had brassed after it had broken
on our ninth wedding anniversary.

Well before the exhibition closed on the fourth day, all of my
pen-and-ink drawings, Mahema's paintings and Suja's photographs had
been sold. There was excellent press coverage. I liked all the articles
on the exhibition and in particular, Geeta Doctor's, that appeared
in the *Indian Express*:

> Rarely does the inauguration of an event such as an art
> exhibition move an audience to a state of high emotional
> experience. This happened when M. S. Subbulakshmi sang
> at an outdoor ceremony.... Filled with a radiant grace, the
> living legend of Madras appeared to salute the spirit of the
> two older artists, as she wove her garland of song....

In the same article, she wrote about Mahema thus:

> ...Mahema Devadoss is a poem to courage. With rare
> detachment and dignity, she spoke of what it means to
> be a person paralysed from neck down, a condition that
> she has had to endure for the last eighteen years due to
> a car accident. The exhibition was their way of thanking,
> she explained, the doctors and the people who had helped
> them on their journey, which continued to be rich and
> rewarding....

Many years earlier, just after the accident had taken place, I had
expressed my hope to Professor Larry Shinn that in spite of the
consequences of the devastating car accident, Mahema and I would
be able to conduct our affairs in such a way that we would continue
to put together a portfolio of happy events, the memories of which
will remain rich and glowing. I was now sure that this exhibition
would be one among the many jewels in this portfolio.

Two months after the exhibition, a sweet old Christian lady held
Mahema's and my hands and said, 'God will reward you both richly
when you go to Heaven.'

I replied with a wink, 'On the contrary, Aunty, God has warned us not to expect any rewards in Heaven since we have already reaped more than our fair share of earthly rewards in terms of goodwill, affection, and even prestige.'

Dr Badrinath arranged a luncheon meeting for a small group at the Madras Club in April, to formally accept the cheque from me and to receive a donation on the same day from another well-wisher of Sankara Nethralaya, who had come from Bombay. At the meeting, Badri gave an impromptu speech about Mahema and me for a full four minutes and told the gathering that the collection from the exhibition exceeded my take-home salary for a whole year at that time. The group applauded most enthusiastically. He then, turned to the other well-wisher and said, 'Mr Burgawa, we thank you for reposing your trust in us. We accept with humility your most generous gift.' I found out that the amount that the philanthropist gave was about 115 times more than what Mahema, Sujatha, and I, by our joint effort had raised.

Later, I told Mahema laughingly, 'Badri talked more about us and our paltry donation than about Burgawa and his huge contribution.'

Mahema replied, 'Perhaps Badri thought, ours is like a widow's mite, that Christ talked about in one of his parables.'

Badri had organized the luncheon in a non-air conditioned lounge of the club because of certain dress restrictions that the club observed. With its high ceiling, huge bay windows and shady trees, the Madras Club was a relatively cool place even in the height of summer. Mahema, therefore had assured Badri that in early April, she would be quite alright in the non-air conditioned lounge of the club, even at midnoon. But it was an unusually hot day and towards the end of the meeting, she began to feel hot. After lunch, we dropped Suja and Michael in their house and proceeded to ours. But halfway towards our house, the car had a puncture. A long nail had pierced a tyre. Rajan stopped the car under the partial shade of a tree and swiftly changed the wheel, with my help. A parked car was like an oven and by the time Rajan restarted the car, Mahema had become very hot and was finding it hard to breathe.

The stretch before the Foreshore Estate stank more than usual that afternoon. Mahema warned me in a feeble voice that she might throw up at any time. Rajan and I raised the glasses in an effort to keep out the stench. But this made the car even hotter inside. By the time we reached the Foreshore Estate, Mahema became mildly delirious, burning with high temperature. I asked Rajan to stop at Hotel Romus and dashed into the non-vegetarian eatery. A boy there was going about filling glasses with water from a large stainless steel jug. I grabbed the jug from the startled boy, went to the car and poured the water all over Mahema. I returned the empty jug to the boy along with a five-rupee note, all of which surprised the adolescent even more. I told Rajan, matter of factly, 'Thank Heavens, the jug was full of cool water and not iced water. Had I poured iced water on her, she would surely have caught a terrible cold.'

Mahema soon felt less hot and told me, 'Thanks, Mano, for the bath, though you've ruined my freshly laundered and pressed silk sari.'

I countered, 'And what about the new upholstery in my car?'

As mentioned earlier, I had spent only a portion of the money I had kept in reserve for my daughter's wedding, which was safely in the bank now. During the sixteen months after my daughter's wedding, I had saved some more. As a hedge against inflation, I had earlier decided to buy a small housing plot. Now, I had second thoughts. Instead of buying a piece of land for the distant future, I could instead sell the Ambassador car, pool my resources and buy a brand-new air-conditioned car to take care of Mahema's immediate needs. A few years earlier, only imported cars had good air conditioning. But now, reliable Indian-made air-conditioned cars were easily available. Michael and Suja too approved of the idea.

Two weeks after the luncheon meeting at the Madras Club, it was time for Michael and Suja to leave for Nigeria, where Michael had been posted.

About three weeks after Michael and Suja departed for Nigeria, I bought a new air-conditioned car. As soon as I reached home in the new car, I went straight up to Mahema and delivered a brief speech, 'If the philanthropist, Burgawa, had chosen to come to Madras before April or if Badri had arranged the meeting in the evening or the club did not have an archaic dress regulation or if it had not been an unusually hot day or if a nail had not punctured a tyre in our car or the stagnant water along the road did not stink to high heavens, then, surely you would not have become deliriously hot and I in turn, would not have decided to mobilize my resources to buy this new car. Now, if you come to think of it, you created with much difficulty, ten watercolours and graciously gifted them for a cause and, in turn, you are receiving a gift of an air-conditioned car.' Saying this, I symbolically presented the car keys to her with a flourish.

Mahema said, 'When I became breathless after the puncture, I wondered why God was punishing me so mercilessly. But really, the sequence of events you described just now, has only paved the way for the arrival of the new air-conditioned car, to lessen my sufferings in the years to come. I tell you, Mano, God's ways are often mysterious.'

I smiled, 'Come,' I said, 'I'll take you for a spin, even if you are not dressed for the occasion.'

Later, Mahema wrote to Sujatha and Michael about the car rapturously, calling it her 'ice cube' and her 'igloo'. I wrote that it was nothing but a mobile ice box to take 'Ice cream' around.

Just three days after the car arrived, there was an electric power shutdown at forenoon in the street where we lived. This was a sweltering Saturday in May. To make her feel cool, Rajan and I simply took Mahema out in her 'igloo' to New Woodlands for lunch and returned home only after the power supply to our street was restored.

A couple of months later, Mahema and I were invited by the British Council to a chamber music concert at the Park Sheraton Hotel—to be performed by a talented group from Great Britain. The music performance was preceded by cocktails and followed by a dinner. This was a formal affair, so I wore my well-tailored, dark grey Raymond suit. Mahema wore a peacock blue Kanjeevaram sari with a deep red pallu.

Our driver Rajan took Mahema and me to the mini-hall on the first floor of Park Sheraton, positioned Mahema's wheelchair, and returned to the car park. I did not want to go in for the cocktails, leaving Mahema all alone, so I skipped the drinks and sat with her. The director of the British Council, Sanderson, welcomed us and gave Mahema a fresh rosebud and moved away to welcome new arrivals. On seeing us sitting alone, a group of our women friends came over to chat with us. Mahema requested Rita Saldanha to fix the rose on my coat lapel.

I protested, 'Why should I wear a rose on my lapel when my rose is already sitting by my side.'

This amused the ladies no end and one of them said in a mock complaining tone, 'My husband doesn't say such nice things about me, Mahema.'

But Mahema seemed determined that I should wear the rose. So Rita obligingly pinned it on.

After the rich music and tasty dinner, it was time for us to leave. Rather than sending for Rajan and waiting ever so long for him to arrive, I decided to wheel down Mahema all by myself, without help from anyone.

'Don't worry, it is familiar terrain,' I assured her as I pushed the wheelchair along the corridors. I began taking it down a brief flight of steps. Standing behind as usual, I tilted the wheelchair so that the two small front caster wheels hung in the air. Then I began gently lowering the wheelchair, one step at a time. Suddenly, two waiters materialized and came rushing to 'help' me.

I shouted, 'No, no, no, no….. Please don't touch the wheelchair.'

Of course, like most unsolicited helpers, they did not listen to a word of what I told them. They simply grabbed the wheelchair and jerked it this way and that, causing me to stumble and fall awkwardly backwards at an angle. The wheelchair stood precariously balanced on two wheels, right in the middle of a flight of steps and Mahema sat dangerously suspended on it. Although I fell down, I did not let go of one of the wheelchair handles.

Within a matter of seconds, many dark thoughts crossed my mind. For two decades, I had been taking her up and down staircases, countless hundreds of times—including aircraft steps, without a single mishap. But now Mahema was all but poised for the next toss after the car accident—with what consequences I dared not think. Because of her quadriplegia, she would be totally incapable of softening her fall. For the rest of my life, everyone would blame me for taking her rashly down the steps, particularly when I was myself nearly blind.

Mahema did not scream nor did she crash down. The two men did not let go of the wheelchair. Fortunately they had not given it a forward tilt which would have tipped her out. By then, I bounced back and took control of the wheelchair.

One of the men told me, 'We are glad that we came at the right time to prevent madam from falling down, when you had yourself fallen down.'

My instinct was to shout, 'It was you two stupids who nearly caused the crash.'

But I had learnt that in situations like this, there was no use giving in to instincts. Besides, their intentions were noble. In any case they would never have figured out why I was getting angry with them and would have felt hurt. So I thanked them and managed to persuade them that leaving Mahema and me alone would be the best help they could render.

Now, without the waiters' help, I managed the task of lowering the wheelchair down the remaining steps easily. I manoeuvred it into the lift, came to the ground floor and proudly wheeled Mahema down the foyer to the main entrance and waited for the car to arrive amidst the many guests who were leaving the hotel, walking on either side of us.

'It's good to dress well once in awhile. With a rosebud, in the lapel of my excellent dark grey suit, I'm sure I look rather stylish.' I thought, full of self-satisfaction.

The air outside was warm and humid but the air-conditioned atmosphere within was cool and crisp. I felt warm in front and cool at the back. For some reason, however, my bottom alone felt colder than the rest of my back. I moved my hand casually, almost unthinkingly, towards my bottom and was shocked when my fingers came in direct contact with my underwear. During my clumsy fall on the steps, my trousers had completely split at the seam, fully exposing my underwear at the bottom! I realized that those guests—men and women—who had gone past from inside must have seen the split. Indeed, they could not have missed the whiteness of the underwear, illuminated by the chandelier, against the contrasting dark grey of the trousers. I had thought, only a minute earlier, that I was presenting a dashing picture of a stylish man. But now I knew that in reality, I must have looked rather silly, displaying a red rosebud in the front and lily-white underwear at the rear.

~

Suja came from Nigeria towards the end of 1992 to spend a couple of months with us. One day, she told me that Michael and she had an idea. 'I would like to honour Amma by celebrating her joyous survival for two decades. It would be a brief ceremony, sharing my thankfulness with some of our dear ones.'

I said, 'It's a wonderful idea. But Sujamma, we have so many many well-wishers. How could we select our invitees?'

So, she suggested that we invite those very dear ones known to all four of us—Michael, Suja, Mahe, and me.

Excepting for those who were out of town, all the invitees attended the event at the ballroom of Hotel Connemara, with its wooden floor and old world charm. Among the guests were writers, artists, musicians, diplomats, professionals, and doctors.

Suja gave a brief Bharatanatyam recital for which her guru Kameswaran had written the lyrics, composed the melody, and choreographed the dance, exclusively for Mahe and me, much to our surprise and delight of the guests.

The kuthu-vilakku that Mahe and I had lit on the day after our wedding stood gleaming on the podium. Suja narrated the incident relating to the lamp on our ninth wedding anniversary. In later years, the lamp had been lit on many special occasions. M. S. Subbulakshmi Amma now lit this lamp, which she had already lit once before at our art exhibition in early 1991.

When it was my turn to talk, I began in a humorous vein, calling myself Mahe's porter. Then among other things, I narrated briefly the evil intentions of quadriplegia. I said, 'Quadriplegia is really a monster, which excels in oppressing its victims. But I would say—and I am sure you would agree—that this monster could not suppress Mahema's zest for life.'

Our friends expressed their agreement with enthusiastic applause.

I then talked about the early years of our happy married life. We wanted a girl baby and Suja arrived obligingly. It was a period of learning, of rich experiences, of creativity, of humour, of fellowship with many dear ones. Then I talked about the past few years. This time, we gained a wonderful son in Michael. This too had been a period of learning, of richer experiences, of creativity, of humour galore, and of deeper fellowship with a wider circle of dear ones. This too has been a very happy period.

'So where is quadriplegia? Where is retinitis pigmentosa? But I knew that these two are relentless, unyielding enemies. A day might come when we would be defeated. But I declare that that day has not yet come...not yet.'

I received applause. Then I talked about Mahema as a young woman. I told the gathering that when Mahe was my bride of three and twenty, I liked her immensely for reasons aplenty. I admired her for her academic excellence, her talents, her innate goodness, her sense of humour, and for physical beauty. Now twenty-nine years later, at fifty-two, she is crippled and yoked. Turning towards where Mahe sat, I ended my speech saying: 'And yet, I say proudly and honestly that even as she is, I love my wife now more than ever before.' I was so charged with emotion that I had difficulty uttering the last few words. To my utter surprise, suddenly tears ran down my cheeks. The last time I had tears like this was in Bagayam, nineteen years ago and that was in complete privacy. I was to learn later from many guests that there was not a dry eye. That evening in the gracious hall, Mahe cried and hers were tears of joy. Her heart was full. As for me, I stood on the low dais uncertainly, listening to the waves of applause, until my friends Gabriel and Athma came to the podium to escort me back to my seat beside Mahema.

17

Sujatha called us from Nigeria frequently. She also wrote us evocative letters, which ran into tens of pages. For us, reading these epistles over and over again was sheer delight. I sprinkled my letters to the young couple with cartoons and light-hearted illustrations.

I told Mahema one day, 'Life now is thoroughly enjoyable and completely harmonious.'

But unfortunately, the enjoyment and harmony did not last long. Mahema's faithful night helper, Radha, who had worked in our house for seventeen years, retired. Around this time, the stay-in helper too had to leave suddenly, her marriage having been fixed. I could not get good replacements for either of them. A parade of women walked in and out of the house, which was, to say the least, very tiring and frustrating. Meanwhile Mahema's spasms were on the increase. Anxiety, I knew, aggravated spasms in paralysed persons and the unpredictable helper situation could be a source of stress. But then I also knew that Mahema excelled in the art of remaining calm in times of tension. She even enjoyed the hilariously comic aspect that some of the unsatisfactory helpers unwittingly contributed. I concluded that Mahema's spasms were not due to anxiety. I had read in medical books that an infection—any infection in any part of the body—could increase spasms in quadriplegics. The new untrained helpers were constant sources of infection. When Mahema contracted a severe cold and cough—from a helper who would not remember to turn her face when she sneezed or coughed—her spasms became so unbearable I had to admit her in a nursing home to aspirate her lungs. But whether the level of her infection went up or down her spasms kept increasing disproportionately.

Suddenly one day, when she was about to be transferred to her bed, Mahema screamed. I rushed into the bedroom and saw that she was seated at the very edge of the wheelchair. She would have fallen down when she had a violent spasm, had not the two helpers held her firmly. Her spasms had never been this severe. I moved her into bed as gently as I could. After a while, she began throwing up. Her diaphragm went into convulsions and she could not stop throwing up, though her stomach had become completely empty. Then she started sweating profusely above her shoulders. At one, in the middle of the night, she began to have severe palpitations with varying durations. During the palpitations, her heart beat 180–210 times a minute. Even with my limited vision, I could see the arteries at her temples throbbing. I did not need a stethoscope to count her heartbeat; I could feel it thumping if I touched her with my fingers anywhere near her heart. I was worried that she might have a brain haemorrhage and go into a coma or die. I telephoned the neighbourhood doctor, who first told me sleepily to give Mahema a spoon of Gelusil. I described Mahema's frightening palpitations. The doctor said that he could give her an injection, which would immediately slow down her heart.

I said, 'But, doctor, her palpitations are due to spasms. When the spasms stop, her heartbeat drops to the normal level. Under these circumstances, will not strong medication slow down the heart to a level where her brain might be starved for oxygen, making her go into a comatose state?'

The doctor replied, 'Mr Devadoss, I am not too familiar with the treatment of quadriplegics. I advise you to admit her in a nursing home.' and put down the phone.

I knew that rushing her to a nursing home or a hospital might not be a good solution. I remembered only too well, what had happened when she had been admitted in a nursing home a few months earlier. Though she had been admitted there mainly in order to have her lungs aspirated, a neurologist who walked in while she was seated in her wheelchair, tapped her knee with a rubber-tipped mallet, a simple but effective method of checking the reflex in a normal patient. For Mahema however, tapping the knee was a sure way to trigger uncontrolled, wrenching spasms and she was only too aware of this.

'No, no, no, doctor,' she had protested, 'Please don't. I'll get....'

Before she could complete the sentence, he had deftly hit her knee at the right spot, unleashing wave upon wave of spasms that made her sweat and suffer palpitations. Her friend, Rochelle, who was with her, had told the doctor politely but firmly to stop his investigations forthwith and leave Mahema alone. The physician observed that Mahema was trembling with fear and that she seemed to think his harmless mallet was an evil weapon with which he was going to attack her.

'I tell you, she has an irrational fear psychosis,' he diagnosed and walked out of the room. A couple of days later, I was surprised to find an entry of ₹150 on the nursing home's bill, for a neurological consultation!

In the normal course of events, regular doctors hardly ever came across quadriplegics, especially those like Mahema, who led normal, active lives. In such a situation, if the doctor also lacked a spark, he had no clue as to what to say to her, let alone how to deal with her special circumstances. I was naturally apprehensive about taking her to a nursing home. Besides, at that point of time Mahema was in a condition, where any jolt or even the slightest jerky movement of her body would trigger fresh waves of spasms. So it could be downright dangerous to move her from the bed to the wheelchair, to the stretcher, to the ambulance.... Therefore, I decided to wait till the morning in the hope that nothing terrible would happen, and then send for Dr Tommy, a spinal injury specialist who had become a concerned friend over the years.

In the meantime, Mahema continued to suffer uncomplainingly. For the first time after many, many years, I thought with anger and bitterness about the adolescents in the truck who had caused the accident.

Mahema survived. Early in the morning, Dr Tommy came rushing in, unshaven, on his scooter. He gave her Dantrium pills which had been imported. Very soon, her spasms subsided considerably. And she smiled.

'Dantrium,' said the doctor, 'gives relief, but does not cure the spastic condition. Besides, it can affect the liver function. We must find out why the spasms have increased and try to deal with them.'

An hour or so after Tommy left, the day helper noticed that the urine bottle was completely empty. I told her that this had happened because Mahema had thrown up everything she had eaten and had also sweated profusely. Now that she had drunk many glasses of water and had her breakfast, I said the urine would start flowing again. But unfortunately it did not. I managed to reach Dr Subramaniam, our thoughtful urologist, only in the evening. The doctor said that there had been a renal shutdown and her condition could be serious. He arrived at our house with all the equipment and solutions needed for an IV drip and managed to coax her kidneys to relent and start functioning again.

During the following months, Mahema was subjected to X-rays, ECGs and sonar, CT, and other scans, including the then newly introduced magnetic resonance imaging. Loaded with laboratory and scan reports, we consulted many experts. Their recommendations varied widely, ranging from the drastic to the exotic.

While pondering over Mahema's unhappy condition and grappling with the problems created by the unsatisfactory helper situation, I myself had an attack of malaria. So it came to pass that for a brief while, both of us shivered and trembled together, I with malaria and she with spasms. Just before I contracted malaria, I had been working on a detailed drawing of a temple gopuram, with a spreading rain tree by its side. I had more or less finished the gopuram and had just begun working on the tree. When I felt a little better, I decided to complete the drawing. I laid it on the easel, sat on my chair, adjusted the lamp, put on my +17.5 glasses and looked at the unfinished drawing. I was shocked to find out that I could hardly see the picture. The detailed drawing of the gopuram with hundreds of icons seemed a hazy, grey mass.

I had heard that a liberal dosage of chloroquine, normally administered for malaria, could affect the vision slightly. So, I had been cautious and had not taken chloroquine but took Croydon as recommended by the doctors. Despite this precaution, I seemed to have lost much of the little vision that I had. I had also found out that I could no longer read the book that I had been reading a week earlier. Mahema was sad and anxious. 'Maybe, your vision will improve when you are fully cured of malaria,' she said.

Suja's school friend, Srikala, who was now a doctor registered for her MS in ophthalmology, happened to visit my house that morning. She promised to make a search in the medical books for information relating to malarial parasite and vision. The following morning, she phoned to tell me that the malarial parasite likes to reside in the retinal blood vessels of the eyes since this area is relatively cool. The parasite caused the red blood corpuscles to burst. The debris of the blood cells blocks the blood supply through the fine capillaries, causing oxygen-starvation in the retinal cells. I knew that I already had constricted blood vessels in my retinae, a part of my syndrome. So, even at the best of times, my retinae were oxygen-starved. Blocking the already constricted vessels was not unlike parking big trucks in a haphazard manner in the narrow maze of lanes in George Town at Madras.

I felt low, especially because this serious setback could have been avoided. But, like Mahema, too harboured a hope that when I recovered fully from malaria, my vision would improve. The improvement was only marginal. How this sudden dip in my vision would affect my job, I wondered. If I was unable to pursue art, I would not only be robbed of a source of enjoyment, my income too would shrink like my vision and at a time when my expenses were mounting. Above all I might not be able to do more illustrations for the book.

One night, while Mahema lay asleep exhausted, after a spate of spasms, I sat at my desk in the bedroom, blankly staring at my unfinished drawing, not really seeing much of its details. With a heavy heart, I thought of the odds stacked so high against me. Perhaps the time had come for me to stop drawing. Perhaps it was better to ask for voluntary retirement. Perhaps the time had come to give up fighting and accept defeat. A sense of despair overwhelmed me. I began chanting spontaneously:

> My dreams, oh, my dreams,
> those highway bandits stole.
> And took away with them,
> a part of my soul.

I had not chanted these lines in twenty years. I had chanted them last in the mango grove of the Rehabilitation Centre in Bagayam when Mahema was staying there. Tears had run down my cheeks then. Now my eyes were as dry as my heart was. Without weeping, I repeated the refrain softly in the same melancholy, sing-song way I had done, two decades earlier. Mahema woke up hearing my voice. Was I telling her something? I was not. I was obviously talking to myself. But why did my voice have an altogether alien timbre? She listened carefully to the words and repeated them in her mind. The words pierced her heart.

Sobbing, she told me, 'Please don't say such things, Mano… Please don't…. I'll help you face your problem. I'll share the weight of your cross.'

Her weeping brought on new waves of spasms, which made her sob even more. I held down her flaying legs to minimize her spasms.

She said, 'You shouldn't worry about your job or your financial situation. I can always dispose of this property, it will bring us enough money for you to pursue all kinds of interests, like authoring non-illustrated books, for instance. You can learn Carnatic music.'

Later that night, after Mahema fell asleep again, I braced myself to face the difficulties ahead, strengthened by Mahema's resolve. I told myself firmly that there was a time for chanting old refrains and a time for facing new realities. I had recovered fully from malaria and the time for concrete action was on hand.

The following evening, I persuaded Turakhia Opticals to make me a pair of spectacles with a power +23. A week later, they supplied me with a pair having a power +23.5. The glasses were so thick that the helpers in the house called it the 'egg glass'. Dr Badrinath enlarged the iris of my left eye permanently by laser, to allow more light to enter my eye, which improved my near vision slightly. I began dilating my eye with drops so that I could see a little better in dim light. I realized with surprise that, for some inexplicable reason, my near vision improved considerably when I dilated my pupil with eye drops. But not my distant view. Dr Badrinath advised me to dilate my pupil whenever I required and as often as I wanted.

Using a combination of the laser treatment, dilation with drips and the use of my egg glasses, I began to draw again. I sent a letter to Badri and Vasanthimma with an illustration—the first drawing I did after the severe setback.

In the meantime, Dr Mohandas admitted Mahema to the Vijaya Hospital as his 'guest patient', at his expense and requested a whole set of experts in allied areas to try to come to some sort of consensus as to what to do to reduce her spasms.

Dr Jacob Abraham, Dr Mohandas, and Dr Parthasarathy independently suggested a safe hamstring operation for Mahema in which the tendons of the adductor thigh muscles would be severed on either side. After surgery, every time a spasm occurred, the muscles would involuntarily contract but the legs would not move, since the muscles and joints were isolated. This seemed to me too simple a solution for Mahema's grave problem. Besides, I was not sure whether the spasms in the legs triggered palpitations in the heart and convulsions of the diaphragm or whether these two conditions were independent of the leg spasms. It was hard to believe that mere prevention of leg movement would simply eliminate much of Mahema's suffering.

Subbulakshmi Amma and her husband Sadasivam Mama—who was in his nineties—had heard about all the troubles Mahema and I were going through. The saintly singer and her husband were deeply concerned and expressed a wish to know how the couple they had grown so fond of, were faring. Mahema and I visited their home one morning.

After listening to my tales of woe, Sadasivam Mama told me, 'You know, Mano, your difficulties remind me of the story of a man who went to a fortune teller....The fortune teller told the troubled man, "You'll lead a dog's life for two years." The man asked the fortune teller with hope and anticipation, "And after two years?" The fortune teller replied, "After two years, you'll get used to it."'

I would realize in later years that Sadasivam Mama's parable was prophetic. After the malarial setback, my vision not only had not improved, it continued to decline at a slow pace. Two years later, I was closer to blindness than I had been immediately after the malarial attack. But by then, I had got used to it and I did not mope or moan.

Mahema's operation was fixed for mid-January 1994. Suja decided to visit Madras to be of help to her mother. The hamstring surgery was performed on Mahema by Dr Ajith in the presence of Dr Abraham. The extraordinary kindness of the doctors, Sujatha's presence, the ambience of Tamil Nadu Hospital, the bouquets of flowers, the fellowship she shared with her visitors, the spectacular winter sunsets....all these made Mahema's stay in the hospital, located way out in the countryside, an altogether enjoyable experience. But what was really heartening was that the operation was successful beyond my expectations. Mahema's spasms stopped almost completely. To be sure, Dr Abraham warned Mahema that though pieces of the muscles at the tendons had been removed on either side, her thigh muscles would eventually rejoin the tendons and that this could happen in two or three or four years. The spasms might then start all over again. Besides this, she could develop spasms in her arms anytime. But Mahema and I had learnt not to worry about probable, gloomy events of the future. We would take pre-emptive actions, if such actions were possible, and cross bridges as they came to us. In the meanwhile, Mahema would enjoy the sunshine while it lasted.

It took three years for the spasms to creep back slowly into Mahema's physiological system. However, with regular physiotherapy and improved medication, the spasms were no longer allowed to go totally out of control.

During this period, I took up drawings that were particularly challenging, evolving new techniques to compensate for the loss of vision. My colour perception had deteriorated so much that I could hardly see tonal differences. In spite of this, I began working on a pen-and-ink portrait of M. S. Subbulakshmi, in colour. I used only four tones of brown ink: pale brown (for the skin), light reddish brown (for the lips, her sari and her jewels), light yellowish brown (for her ornaments and the border of her sari), Van Dyke brown (for her hair, iris, and eyebrows) and all four inks for the background. People perceived it as a full-fledged colour picture.

M. S. Subbulakshmi Amma and Sadasivam Mama came home to see the portrait and they loved it. My friend and patron Chacko was enamoured by the portrait and was keen on buying it. I wanted the money to go to Sankara Nethralaya. Chacko received the artwork from me and gave the cheque to M. S. Amma who in turn handed over the cheque to Dr Badrinath.

While Mahe felt happy that the artwork would help some visually challenged people, she was also sad that we did not own the portrait. She said that it was a dazzling piece of work. Many friends thought about it the same way. Let me give just one example:

In 1996, I made a presentation at the venerable Madras Club about my art and my other interests, which was immensely enjoyed by the club members. In his concluding remarks, S. Muthiah said, '...it makes me very sad...I think Mano's best picture ever is of Subbulakshmi, which is not here for all of us to see.... It is a wonderful picture of Subbulakshmi. She is a lovely woman and Mano has made her lovelier....'

As for me, I was happy that only three years earlier I had even briefly considered giving up art. But now, what with the support of Mahe, doctors and friends and what with my own innovative ideas, I had managed to create the colour ink portrait, notwithstanding my poorer eyesight and poorer colour perception. And I could not have done it two years later, even with a +23 power glass.

After the severe setbacks of 1993, by taking a multiplicity of corrective actions, both Mahe and I bounced back to a good extent to lead a very creative enjoyable life again, with the hope that this period would last out for sometime.

I think it was November 1995. I went to Madurai from Madras by train, on yet another sketching expedition. Rajan took me to the reserved, air conditioned, second class carriage of Pandian Express. I saw in the list pasted near the door the names of Mrs Nancy Roche, Dr and Mrs Carmodi, along with mine, in the compartment for four. I assumed that they were Westerners. Rajan guided me into the compartment and left. No sooner did I enter, the old, white woman sitting on my side declared, 'The lower berth is mine.'

I could vaguely perceive that she had already spread a blanket on the long seat. I smiled and said to her, 'I am sorry, lady, the railways have allotted the lower berth to me.'

She answered belligerently, 'It is mine and get lost.'

Had she requested me politely, I would have really given up the berth, even though I was fifty-eight and visually impaired. But her nasty stance was a bit annoying. I told her sarcastically, 'Don't you know that India is not a colonial country any more? So, you can't take what is mine.'

She replied angrily, 'Has Independence given you the right to treat white people rudely? I am in my seventies. I won't be able to climb up. Where can I sleep?'

I said smiling, 'You can spread the blanket on the floor and sleep there.'

She said bitterly, 'It's a pity that I can no longer tell the people in my country that all the men I met in India were gentlemen.'

I laughed and said, 'What you tell your people is no concern of mine.'

Saying this I sat down, pushing the blanket.

From the way she talked, I thought that she was an Irish woman. The old couple who sat on the opposite side and she began talking vehemently in some language which I thought could be Gaelic (it was). Just then the ticket examiner entered.

The lady got up at once and complained to him, 'Sir, this man is grabbing my lower berth.' He asked me curtly to show my ticket. He asked the old woman politely to give hers too. He then told the woman, 'Can't you read English, lady? In the ticket under the title 'berth' yours says UB which obviously is upper berth. His says LB which is lower berth.' He examined the tickets of the Carmodis swiftly and left.

Nancy Roche sat in stunned silence. She then told me apologetically that the travel agent had assured her that the lower berth was hers. He had explained that there always was an ambiguity in the numbering as it was block printed at the lower level. He had claimed that he knew that this Devadoss fellow was a grabber, and so she should assert her rights. 'I am very sorry I was rude to you. Please forgive me,' she said.

I stood up, bowed slightly and said, 'Now that you have graciously apologized, I offer my lower berth to you. I request you to kindly give me the upper berth.'

There was a brief moment of silence. Then she got up and gave me a hug and said, 'Thank you.'

We had a lively conversation. They were from the Republic of Ireland. I tried to locate my shoulder bag to pull out my harmonica.

Suddenly, Dr Carmodi asked me, 'You have a serious setback in your eyesight, don't you? Do you suffer from retinitis pigmentosa?'

I was impressed. I briefly explained my situation. I told him that the illumination level in the carriage was not sufficient for me to see things clearly. But in soft daylight I could still see reasonably well. He asked how old I was and I said I was fifty-eight.

Nancy impulsively took my hand and said, 'You are not young and you have vision problem. And yet you are taking the upper berth for my sake. I would proudly tell my people that I had the good fortune of getting to know a perfect gentleman. But the man from the travel agency is no gentleman,' she said and laughed.

Now I pulled out my harmonica and, to their delight, played 'When Irish Eyes are Smiling'. I told them that though I had not been to Ireland, I had seen stunning scenes of their beautiful country, all in three dimensions, thanks to a View-Master and discs on Ireland that my father had acquired while I was in middle school.

Nancy said, 'Why don't you come to Ireland and be my guest? Ours is a small country. I can take you around in my car.'

I told her that I could not and briefly explained to them about Mahema's situation. Dr Carmodi, a nephrologist, expressed his concern and the doctor even advised me about kidney management.

Nancy pulled out a couple of hundred rupee notes and requested me to buy picture postcards of Madras heritage buildings. There I was creating designer greeting cards of Madras heritage buildings and here was an Irish lady asking me to buy picture postcards for her. I promised to send her a set of cards as a gift.

In Madurai she gave me a goodbye hug with tears in her eyes.

After I returned to Madras, I sent a set of our cards, gift-wrapped, with a brief note on the genesis of our greeting card project. In her thank you note she expressed her utter astonishment and joy. We then began exchanging letters regularly. In one letter she even said that meeting me in the train was the best thing that had happened to her during her visit to India.

18

In early 1973, Mahe lay on a JIPMER Hospital bed, for many months with her head clamped down, her body limp, her mind alert and her spirit robust. Suja was six then. When our daughter visited Pondicherry, she would lie down next to Mahe. My wife would tell her stories that she had concocted, especially for her.

Later in the mid-1970s, friends introduced Mahema to Usha Aroor of Orient Longman. Usha agreed to publish a collection of the stories as a supplementary reader for middle school students. So, Mahema began working diligently on the book, titled *The Magic Garden*. I was delighted that Mahe was creatively engaged in this enjoyable venture. My gifted friend Jayaraj did the illustrations for the book, which was published in 1981. Usha was very pleased with the outcome. Indeed, over the years, the book saw many reprints. The project brought a modest annual income for Mahe. The book brought yet another valuable gift for us. Usha and her husband became our lifelong friends.

One year, Mahema went to many neighbouring schools, met the principals and headmasters, showed them her book and requested them to use it as a supplementary reader during the following academic year. Many agreed. Some even invited her to give informal speeches to middle school students, which she did obligingly. Why, she even gained a few fans. The following academic year, Usha was surprised to find a steep increase in the sale of Mahe's book and was pleased to present Mahema a royalty cheque for a higher amount. All India Radio, Madras, invited Mahe to read a couple of stories from *The Magic Garden* for the children's programme in English. The director was very pleased. So were many children who listened to Mahe's readings.

It was Usha Aroor who introduced us to Gita Krishnankutty in 1995. Gita was a person highly skilled in editing manuscripts. She readily agreed to work on my manuscript, all free. This was an enjoyable, long-drawn process. I finished the text in 1996. Gita, in turn, introduced Mahema and me to Padmanabhan (Paddu), managing director of East West Books. I handed over to him a compilation of the entire typed text with the illustrations in the right places, as an A4 spiral book. After studying the book, Paddu made a proposal: he wanted me to take care of the printing expenses. As East West would not incur publication expenses, he would offer a royalty of 60 per cent instead of the conventional 15 per cent. Moreover, he offered to supply me any number of copies free of charge. Above all, he gave me complete intellectual and artistic freedom.

Later, Mahe and I visited our friends, Suresh Krishna (chairman, Sundaram Fasteners) and Usha in their residence and explained Paddu's proposal to them. Unhesitatingly, Suresh said that Sundaram Fasteners would financially support this worthy project. One of my sources of joy was that I had included an illustration of the stately house at Madurai in which he grew up. But I kept it as a surprise for him till the eve of the launch.

Jaspar Utley, the dynamic director of the British Council—who had read a few chapters and seen some of the artwork—told me, 'Mano, the British Council would be happy to launch *Green Well Years*, that is, if you are interested.'

I said, 'I'd be delighted.'

Needless to say, the launch in April 1997, in which Mahe was actively involved, was a beautiful and moving event, with gales of laughter. Later, I wrote to Rathi Jaffer of the British Council that I would always cherish the memory of the evening.

Even before the release of the book, articles, and reviews began appearing in the press and continued for some more time. In general, the book enjoyed excellent to rave reviews. Pushpa Chari wrote a moving piece in *Madras Musings*, quoting from Milton. In a fairly long article in *The Hindu*, Kausalya Santhanam wrote: 'He is that rare author, who is in the fortunate position of being able to illustrate his own book. And what magnificent illustrations they are....' Arun Katiyar described my book in *India Today* as a touching rites of passage novel written by an artist on the brink of blindness. Prema Nandakumar, an erudite scholar, wrote a deeply insightful review in *Deccan Herald*. My favourite line is: 'For Manohar, life for all its trials has been worth living, if only to prepare such a meaningful gift for Indian literature in English.' I could go on but these few examples would suffice. I did not even get to read all the reviews and articles about the book. Friends telephoned to tell me that they read a nice piece about my book in this or that magazine. Why, even after ten years, in an article in *The Hindu*, S. Muthiah, the legendary chronicler of Madras, wrote that people were captivated by *Green Well Years*.

A stream of highly appreciative letters came to me, sent by strangers, care of the publisher. I answered them all. Then in mid-August 1997, I received a letter from yet another stranger, one Chitra Thulasiraj. This interesting letter began thus: 'I am halfway through your book *Green Well Years*, exactly at the point where you three heroes were totally vanquished by Thotha Vathal...' She went on to write that she bought the book after reading the review in *The Hindu*, and purchased more copies to give away as gifts. She was fascinated by my sketches and by the fact that, by reliving my growing up years, I had captured the history and the beauty of Madurai. On behalf of the citizens of Madurai, she thanked me for making them feel proud of their city.

After writing her letter on 30 July 1997, Chitra had second

thoughts about sending it to me. Fortunately, her husband, Thulasi, encouraged her to mail it, which she did a week later on 6 August 1997. Then I could not find her address in the handwritten letter. Fortunately again, she had written that she and her husband worked for Aravind Eye Hospital. So, I could answer her, care of the hospital.

When I received her letter, I could never ever have guessed that her letter would be a watershed event—the very beginning of the blossoming of a precious, beautiful, bond of friendship between the close-knit 'Aravind Family' and mine. Over the years, I have come to admire the family and to love all the four generations of the Aravind family. I feel blessed that this extraordinary family holds Mahe and me in great affection and high esteem. They treat me as their own family member.

Had Thulasi not encouraged his wife to mail her letter to me or had she not written that she worked for Aravind Eye Hospital, I could not have written to her. In turn, the wonderful, loving, enriching fellowship between the Aravind family and mine might well not have flowered the way it has.... And that would have been a very great misfortune—a misfortune I would have been blissfully unaware of. Happily, the misfortune has been averted by two slender threads.

In my reply, I wrote that there was to be a Madurai launch of the book in late September at the Study Centre for Indian Literature in English and Translation (SCILET) at American College, and I warmly invited her family to attend the event.

A major part of my book covers the period between 1947 and 1953, when I was in middle and high school. My school—affectionately called 'Shayschool'—and my interactions with my schoolmates and teachers, often set in a larger sociological backdrop, are an integral part of this book. My friendship with the highly talented Fernando brothers has an important place in the book. Indeed, had I studied in some other school, I could not have written such a book. As an expression of my thankfulness to the school, I decided to gift the entire royalty of the book to my alma mater. It had taken me fourteen years to publish the book. During this period, I made countless visits to Madurai from Madras.

If I added to the money that I had spent on my Madurai visits, all the other expenses I had incurred due to the book project, the total amount would far exceed the royalty that I received. And yet Mahe and I decided to give away the royalty. The money that I had spent on the project had been spread out over many years, hence I had not felt the pinch. The gift to my alma mater was one more step in our pursuit of the art of giving, despite our challenges. Besides, all my visits to Madurai were sources of sheer joy and as Mahe said in a launch, 'It was a labour of love.'

In September 1997, I took Mahe and a helper to Madurai. At fifty-seven, Mahe enjoyed the train journey like a child, because after the accident, such journeys had become rare events for her.

I had expressed to my school my wish to institute three endowments, for art, general excellence, and for stage related skills, in the names of three teachers. But I had also given the school complete freedom to make changes in the endowments in any manner they wished. To our utter surprise, my school arranged a well-planned beautiful event where some teachers and students of my school years, present day teachers, administrators, and a large body of students participated. One speaker mentioned from the Tamil Bible, 'Ask and it shall be given to you. Knock and it shall be opened unto you,' and observed, 'Now here is a Christian who is giving without asking, and this to a Brahmin school.'

The school managed the endowments wisely. One year my school students won the first prize in a state level Art competition organized by *The Hindu*. In another year the school won the first prize in a national level competition of collage art, organized by the Indian Postal Department. These are just two examples. M. S. Meenakshisundaram, the dynamic secretary of the board, told me a few years later that my gift to the school triggered an idea. The management approached former students who had become eminent citizens, for similar gifts, and had built up an impressive corpus fund.

Let me go back to September 1997. My school function was

on the 25th evening and the book launch was held in my college at SCILET on the very next evening. I felt blessed that two of my alma maters honoured me on two consecutive evenings. The college function actually went far beyond a book launch. It was truly a celebration—a celebration of Madurai, of victory over debilitating physical challenges, and of the artwork and writing of one of the college's 'beloved' (their word) alumni. There was much bonhomie and laughter and salutations by the principal, my professors, and old students. In his speech, the principal Dr Peter Jayapandian, telling the audience about the time he and I spent together at Oberlin College in 1969, said, 'We were wandering about like jolly good fellows'. Later, he said how he and I would invite people for 'Indian Dinners'.

I intervened and said, 'He says modestly "people". We invited girls mostly.' The audience laughed along with Peter. Peter continued to say that, during our Oberlin days he heard me talk about Mahema with affection...that with her help I learnt car driving and oil painting... and that she also helped me with my writings. When Mahe came to Oberlin in 1970, he found her to be a very unassuming beautiful person. He then turned and looked at her and said, 'Even now she looks very beautiful.'

I interrupted him and said, 'If you say my wife is very beautiful, I am going to punch your nose.' Peter and the audience burst out laughing. In how many colleges, other than American College in Madurai, I wondered, could a chief guest in a programme tell the principal, 'I am going to punch your nose!' This high level of prevailing informality is yet another reason why I so love my alma mater. Professors Paul L. Love, Nair, Premila, and many others in the college became dear friends.

Happily it was at the book launch that I met Chitra and Thulasi of Aravind Eye Hospital. Our very first meeting was fortunately recorded in a nice photograph taken by SCILET. During our brief stay at Madurai, invitations poured in for breakfast, lunch, tea, and dinner. I became a bit apprehensive as to whether Mahe's quadriplegic body would take it all.... It did. Actually she enjoyed every minute she spent at Madurai.

At the Taj, atop Pasumalai (Cow Hill), my college friend, Ramu, and his wife hosted a lunch for us. I placed the wheelchair facing the large bay window so that Mahe could enjoy the panoramic view of Madurai with the brooding Yaanai Malai (Elephant Hill) as the backdrop. I took a seat facing her, but without blocking the view for her. I felt ever so happy, looking at Mahe's face radiant with joy.

We returned to Madras with a treasury of happy memories, so I told our two monsters, Quadriplegia and Retinitis, 'You have not defeated us...not yet.'

I received yet another warm letter, now to my house address, from one Professor Shyamala A. Narayan (a respected literary critic, author of *Indian English Literature 1980-2000*, and two books commissioned by the Sahitya Akademi). She wrote that M.Vijayalakshmi, the Sahitya Akademi Librarian, spoke highly of the book, so she bought a copy of *Green Well Years* from a book store in Delhi with some difficulty, and loved the book. She had gently chided East West Books for not entering my book for the Commonwealth Writers' Prize. She has been in charge of the 'Annual Bibliography—India' published in the *Journal of Commonwealth Literature*. For the 1998 issue, she wrote that the two best novels of 1997 were *The God of Small Things* by Arundhati Roy, and *Green Well Years* by Manohar Devadoss. In the comparative review, her preference for my book was obvious. Later, she published a scholarly paper, 'A Study in Contrast' of Arundhati Roy's novel and mine.

I might have missed an award or two, but what I gained was the lifelong friendship of Shyamala's family. Her daughter, Lakshmi, a professor of economics at Harvard, and her husband, Vinay, a talented violin player, have become our dear friends too. The couple named their daughter 'Mahima'.

In between the Madras and Madurai launches of the book, I had retired from Oldham and joined a new, small venture as its technical director. The retirement age at Oldham was fifty-eight. But the company requested me to stay on year after year, while encouraging many others to opt for voluntary retirement. I would happily tell Mahe, 'There was a time when I feared that, because of my retinitis, I might lose my job. Quite the contrary is happening. I had to persuade the company to relieve me at sixty-one.'

Earlier I had shared the text and the artwork of my book with N. Ram of *The Hindu*. His suggestion was that, after publishing *Green Well Years*, I should continue to create more artwork on Madurai, totalling at least fifty. I should write brief insightful texts with personal touches, if possible, for each drawing. He said, 'If you come out with such a book in A4 format, then there is even a possibility that it could become a classic.'

Mahe agreed. I began diligently working on this project.

Later, a very fortunate thing happened. One early morning I had a dream. In that dream, I was going in an Aravind car to the western outskirts of Madurai. I could see everything in the rural scene very clearly—the blades of coconut fronds, tiles on the roof of a house, the distant Western Ghats, and more, in the early morning sun. Soon I woke up into the real world. I wrote a letter to Chitra and Thulasi, describing my dream, and even included a whimsical colour drawing.

I wrote, 'Even at this stage, I can still vaguely see such scenes at dawn and dusk.' They took this up very seriously. Every time I went to Madurai, Chitra took me—sometimes with Thulasi—out into the countryside before dawn, each day in a different direction. In the soft morning light, I began sketching and photographing, and listened carefully to Chitra's detailed description of many beautiful views. Later in Madras, I would work on a colour drawing as a salutation piece in my letter to Chitra and Thulasi and also for some dear ones. This would be my 'dress rehearsal' for the black-and-white artwork for the proposed book. Chitra also helped me in sketching many imposing monuments within Madurai.

In 1999, on our thirty-sixth wedding anniversary, I plonked a heavy gift-wrapped packet on Mahe's wheelchair table. I tore the packet open. She saw a pair of not very attractive, slightly rusted dumb-bells, 10 kilograms each. Mahema looked a bit bewildered, but soon smiled and said, 'You are going to strengthen your biceps for my sake, aren't you?'

Two months earlier, while transferring Mahe from the car to the wheelchair, I had a back catch with excruciating pain. It took a week of massaging and medication for the pain to slowly fade away. Earlier on, I did have, now and then, minor backaches, while transferring Mahe, but never like this one. Something had to be done. I was sixty-two then and not growing younger.

In the mornings, I began doing the dumb-bells, while listening to *BBC* for world news, *NDTV* for Indian news and *Sun News* for local news in Tamil. Later, Suja gifted me a new pair of plastic coated 12.5-kilogram dumb-bells. I gradually increased the number of pumpings to around 600, with gaps after every twenty. Soon my biceps became somewhat like those of boxers. Mahe would look at my arms and declare that I was her 'he-man'. Truly, after the dumb-bells, the good thing was that I never even had a suggestion of a back catch while transferring her. One day, in 2007, I laughingly told Mahe, 'In 1997, when I was sixty-one, I felt that you weighed heavy like a sack of potatoes. Now at seventy-one, thanks to the dumb-bells, I feel that you weigh light like a basket of flowers.'

~

Let me go back to our wedding anniversary in 1999.

Our friends Ramu and Bunty came to Madras to spend a couple of days with us. That evening, I gifted Mahe with an artistically crafted thin portfolio titled, *Mahe and I*, where I presented our story, mostly through copies of selected illustrations in my letters to her, with some artistic photographs taken by me, accompanied by brief texts which were read aloud by Bunty. Mahe's eyes glistened with tears of joy.

Bunty said, 'Mano, this is sooo beautiful. I suggest that you enlarge this portfolio with more illustrations and appropriate texts and publish it as another book.'

Ramu heartily agreed.

And I said, 'Why not?'

At this stage, I was fully involved in the new venture, called Compact Power Sources. It came to pass that in addition I worked simultaneously on three books—the Madurai book in black and white, a biographical novel on Mahe without pictures, *A Poem to Courage*, and a colourful portfolio on Mahe as a documentary, *Dreams, Seasons and Promises*.

I had joined the new venture in September 1997, the very next day after I retired from Oldham. We were ready for production within eight months, starting from scratch. Our products required test certificates and approvals by various agencies like BIS, CMRI, DGMS, RDSO, ISO 9000, and more. Our products were much appreciated. We received all the needed documents well in time. However, unfortunately, in 2001, the company faced certain unanticipated problems. Fortunately though, a large and dynamic Hyderabad-based company, Hyderabad Batteries, offered attractive terms for a takeover. Our company moved lock, stock, and barrel to Hyderabad in 2002. However, I continued with the technical consultancy for the company for a while.

In the meantime, I could breeze through the books on Mahema, partly because she was fully involved in the making of these.

Eunice Crook, director of the British Council (Madras), readily agreed to have the launch of my two books towards the end of February 2002. Let me now narrate an incident that happened about a week before the launch. This needs a brief description of a problem associated with catheterization.

Those who are paralysed at the waist level and above do not have bladder control. Urine would dribble out. To avoid this, continuous indwelling catheterization is required. The catheter is inserted and a small balloon (15 millilitres) is inflated with water inside the bladder to prevent the catheter from slipping out. Unfortunately, the catheter often causes irritation inside the bladder and is a source of urinary infection. Sometimes, tissues in the inner wall of the bladder would detach themselves as flakes. The stream of urine flowing into the catheter would often take the tissues to the pores, which in turn would block the urine from flowing into the catheter. As more urine flows into the bladder from the kidneys, pressure would build up within, causing extreme discomfort to the patient. Sometimes, the pressure would push the tissues into the catheter and free the passage, giving immediate relief to the person.

A week or so before the launch, Mahema's catheter had a block in the wee hours of the night. She did not want to disturb me, so she waited with discomfort, hoping that the block would clear itself. It did not. So, she woke me up at about 4.45 a.m. To give her quick relief, I placed a big kidney dish between her legs and cut the catheter near the outer end. Immediately, the balloon collapsed and the catheter came out at once. Urine squirted out in a rush to fill the kidney dish, giving Mahema immediate relief. Because of my visual problem, another person was also needed to change the catheter. The night helper, did not know the procedure. So, I placed a rolled towel (used for such purposes) to prevent the urine from spreading out on the bed sheet. A large rubber sheet below the bed sheet protected the mattress from getting wet. To avoid Mahe getting a cold by the urine wetting her gown, I had to remove the gown and not cover her with a sheet either. I told her that I would wake up Rajan, our driver at 5.45 a.m. to take the car and bring Josephine. Then she and I would insert a sterile catheter and all would be well. After resetting the alarm I went to bed.

At about 5.15 a.m., the house doorbell rang. Who would ring the bell at this time? The night helper opened the door and began screaming. I thought, 'Oh God, what now.' But then the tenor of her voice did not display a sense of horror. She soon shouted, 'Sujamma has come!' Suja decided to participate in the book launch by the British Council and the International Women's Association (IWA). She had decided to give us an utter surprise. I rushed to the drawing room. She dropped her suitcase, gave me a quick hug and before I could stop her, rushed into the bedroom to give her mother a hug. She switched on the light and saw Mahe lying there without her gown.

'What the heck is happening?' she asked but soon saw that the catheter was missing. Mahema was quickly covered with a bedsheet. We had a hearty laugh.

Soon a new catheter was fixed, Mahe was given a bath, the bedsheet, the towel, and the wet gown were washed separately and all was well. Mahe later told me that this was yet another rare coincidence where something tedious, boring and painful had a joyful, hilarious ending. I pointed out to her that the urine blocks kept happening, but this was the first time it had such a wonderful ending.

~

In February 2002, Eunice Crook held the launch at the sprawling lawn of her residence, partly because it could hold more people than the auditorium at the Council. At the launch, welcoming the gathering, Eunice spoke about the books and why she was happy with the launch. But first and foremost she said, 'We are here to celebrate the achievements of two astonishing people.... When Mahema called me up to say that she wanted to see me, I knew that I was up against an irresistible force. Not because she evoked sympathy. Never that. It was the sheer power of her personality....'

S. Muthiah, the one-man army battling to preserve the heritage of Madras, launched the book. He said (I quote): 'Mano and Mahema.... Mahema and Mano are probably the most admirable people that I have met in my life. I admire them for many reasons...importantly, I admire them because they have not allowed adversities to squelch their talents....' Later he said, *A Poem to Courage* is a very very moving, poignantly told story. It is still told through the eyes of Sundar but it's always Mano masquerading as Sundar.'

He further said, 'I am hoping that one day all these will be put together in a book as an omnibus volume which will deserve the blitz in the publicity world.'

Our friends P. C. Ram, the voice of Madras, and Phil Crook with his impeccable British accent, read passages from both the books. The audience was alternately moved and delighted. Then Suja spoke. Laced with humour, she described how Mahe and I managed to do so many things in a chaotic household that normal human beings would find difficult to manage. She thanked Eunice for so beautifully arranging the launch and for bringing to Madras culturally enriching programmes from the UK. Then the launch ended with cocktails and snacks.

Very soon, we made a presentation of the books for the members of the IWA at the residence of the American Consul General. The large number of women who attended gave us a standing ovation. I was beginning to get used to standing ovations.

A couple of months later, The Duchess Club invited us to make a presentation at Savera Hotel. Then it was for the girls of Stella Maris College. Their emotional response was overwhelming. Then a sensitive TV journalist, Anuradha, made a presentation of the two books and ourselves. Many professors and former students of Asia House at Oberlin, among others, purchased the books. We felt blessed that we could reconnect with some of the Asia Housers of our time at Oberlin.

My train friend Nancy Roche, wrote that *A Poem to Courage* was the most moving book that she had ever read and that *Dreams...* was like a journey through a magical land. Mahe and I continued to exchange letters with her. Her handwriting was becoming shaky. Then we received a letter written on a piece of brown paper cut off from a paper bag. We could hardly decipher her handwriting, but we could sense that it was full of love. Mahe responded immediately. Later, I sent Nancy two letters. We did not receive any reply from her.

Divya is a film and television star (her screen name is Abirami). Around this time, a movie named *Virumandi* was being shot, in which she acted opposite the very famous, highly talented movie hero Kamal Haasan. She happened to read *A Poem to Courage* which made her alternately cry and laugh. This heroine of the movie, Divya (as Abirami) was determined to meet the heroine of the real world, Mahema (as Kavitha), and her hero, me. A journalist saw a photo essay opportunity and brought Divya to our house. We found her to be a sensitive, unpretentious, lively girl. She was tall, slim, and very beautiful. She told us that she became a film star in her teens. Now she was in her early twenties. She said that after completing her movie commitments, she had decided to leave the cinema world and go to the US and do her university studies there. She did precisely that. But since then, she came to love us and has become our dear friend.

Lakshmi was a splendid character actress of yesteryear. Later she created a successful TV programme in Tamil, entitled *Not a Fiction but the Truth*. She presented us in one episode. The response was so gratifying to her that she did another episode on us, now shot mostly at our house. We were invited by many other channels for other programmes too.

The years from 1996–2006 became yet another golden period in our lives. I turned sixty in 1996 and seventy in 2006. During this period I had completed three books and was working on the fourth one. Mahe and I were pleased with a wide circle of extraordinarily affectionate and supportive friends. Among those who bestowed their love upon us were many living legends.

I was invited by many institutions to make PowerPoint presentations. The responses were always enthusiastic. Let me give just one example. I made a presentation about our challenges and our creative endeavours for the Lions Club at Hotel Connemara. At the end of my presentation, our friend, Seshathrinathan walked to the microphone and informed the members that as a token of his appreciation of our endeavours, he would print the forthcoming book on Madurai to my satisfaction, all completely free, at his press.

That was not all. A beautiful, young woman came to us after the other members of the club who had surrounded us moved away. With a twinkle in her eye, she made a unilateral declaration to me, to the effect that she would have liked to marry me, but what with I having a wonderful wife and she a wonderful husband, that could not be. I was a bit taken aback. The encounter with this young woman reminded me of my very first encounter with Mahe thirty-three years ago, but under very different circumstances. Later, I came to realize that the young woman Anuradha and Mahema shared the same date of birth too. Mahe was highly amused by Anu's declaration and promptly invited her home. She promised to visit us soon and kept her promise. We learnt that she was the daughter of the late K. V. Narayanaswamy, a legendary Carnatic musician of yesteryear. Anu had experienced some difficult periods in her life but was blessed with an understanding husband (Suresh) and parents-in-law. She was an extremely informal, exuberant person. She loved the dish 'Thulasania' (which was my own recipe) so much that she said she would visit us again, on the condition that I would serve her the same dish.

Mahe and I had planned to attend a South India Heritage performance at the TAG Centre. But Mahema had a setback, so she requested Anu to escort me. During the breakfast at TAG, many people came to talk with her and I heard the word 'Sahana' again and again. I learnt she was the heroine in a high class TV serial, *Sahana*, based on South Indian classical music, which was inspired by the highly acclaimed movie *Sindu Bhairavi*. Since then, Mahe and I began watching *Sahana*. I liked her singing. She was a Carnatic singer who had given recitals internationally and had cut many CDs as well. Anu and Suresh have continued to remain our friends.

During this period, the British Council, the British Deputy High Commission, the Goethe-Institut, the German, American, Japanese, and other consulate generals brought to Madras from their respective countries, cultural programmes of excellence—especially music recitals and plays. Mahema and I were invited not only to the programmes, but also invariably invited with a smaller group of people for a dinner honouring the visiting artists. We made it a point to interact with the honoured guests, who sometimes were touched by our keen interest and gave us gifts!

Our friends in the Foreign Service too who organized the events, appreciated our regular attendance, our punctuality and our fellowship despite our double challenges. So they often went out of the way to make things a bit easy for us. Let me give just one example.

In 2005, Zubin Mehta came to Madras with about eighty Bavarian State Orchestra members to perform at the Music Academy. Mahe and

I were invited with a gold sticker by the German Consul General, who allotted us two seats in any one of the first four rows. For various reasons, the invitees were asked to park their cars in a neighbouring school compound and walk into the premises of the academy. As Mahema and I were physically and visually challenged, we were given special exemption for parking the car within the academy parking lot. Not only that, we would need more time to move in a crowd to settle down. So we were allowed to enter the hall first and the doors were flung open to all only after we had settled down. We were deeply touched. For us it was the wonderful beginning of an even more wonderful evening.

In early 2002, Sheila, a Santhomite, offered to help me with my manuscripts by typing them in her home computer. By her own initiative, she created an email address for us. (Later, mahemano14@ gmail.com). We became very good family friends. The entire text for *My Madurai* and later for my other books and much else, were all typed by her in her home computer. She and her family continue to be yet another happy blessing for us.

The Madurai launch of the two books was organized by SCILET at American College on the evening of 17 August 2002. Mahe and I, along with Josephine, spent four days in Madurai, packed with activities. As in 1997, now in 2002, countless invitations came to us for breakfast, lunch, tea, and dinner. Often the wheels of Mahe's chair rolled on long stretches of rough terrain. Frequently she had to be taken up and down flights of steps, including a rather long flight of rough-hewn steps on a rocky slope of Pasumalai. She had to sit up for long hours. Fortunately, she was in good health and we had prepared her well before going to Madurai. Her body endured it all, while her heart overflowed with joy.

On the 16th evening, she delivered a speech in Tamil at the Aravind Eye Hospital to a gathering of nursing staff and middle-level management personnel, about 500 plus in all, most of them women.

Mahe first described why the first nine years of her life with me were extraordinarily happy ones for her and how all our early dreams had come true, even surpassing our fond hopes. Now we dared to entertain brave new dreams. Then the accident happened. She briefly narrated all the ill-effects of her condition. After ten months of hospitalization, she returned to the very house where she grew up and led her married life, now to a vastly different kind of future. To add to our problems, around this time, her husband began losing his vision. It is not easy for a woman in a wheelchair to be rolled by a man with declining eyesight.

When she was in college, she came across a one-stanza poem with just four lines, which she liked. At that time she could not have guessed that the verse would have such relevance in her later life. She narrated this poem in English first and then took up each line in Tamil and explained its significance in her life.

> Believe in yourself—to falter is to fail.
> Believe in mankind—to question is to quail
> Believe in God—to doubt is to deny
> Believe in your dreams—to lose them is to die.

She believed in herself. Instead of moaning and weeping about what had been taken away from her, she decided to put to good use what had not been taken away. For example, she believed that, by using her shoulder muscle with a well-designed splint, she could learn to write. She had to work very hard but succeed she did, in being able to write legibly. She believed in others. Her husband stood steadfast like a strong rock by her side. Her mother-in-law looked after her with devotion. The doctors went beyond the call of duty in medical care and the nurses attended to all her needs day and night. Later, many dear ones kept her morale high. Her faith in God gave her peace of mind and the strength to face trials and tribulations.

Even after the accident she dared to have many new dreams. For instance she dreamed of providing a very happy home for her daughter, which became a complete reality. Life was so enjoyable for each member of the family. Using her shoulder muscles, she went one step ahead and managed to create original watercolours and gave the sale proceeds to charity. She gave a few more examples.

She then talked eloquently about Dr G. Venkataswamy and how each line of this poem aptly epitomized his vision to achieve his noble mission. She ended her speech saying that her prayers for those who worked for this great institution were that they would work for the cause with diligence, supporting one another, and that their dreams, with God's grace, would come true. The response was profoundly enthusiastic. One girl walked to the stage and read a poem about Mahe that she had written then and there. Other girls came to the stage to say many extraordinarily kind things about Mahe. Later on, Pavithra, the grand-niece of Dr G. V., a college student then, wrote a sensitive, insightful article, 'A Lesson in Grace' in the website of Charity Focus.

The Madurai launch of the books by SCILET at American College became truly a celebration. Professor Nair welcomed the gathering. He uses words chosen carefully and sparingly, and is known for his understatements. And yet, among other things, he said: 'We are here not just to launch these two books....We are celebrating the fabric of love and affection that binds this glorious couple together.... Manohar's writings distract me and sometimes inspire me. They are my consolations, sometimes they are even my salvation.'

I gave a donation cheque for an amount that was a bit more than the royalty for the two books I had received till then and hoped to give more as the sales of the books picked up. The money went for an endowment. I said that I was aware that the amount was not very large, but it was an expression of my affection for my alma mater and SCILET.

Five persons read passages from the books. Readings by Dr Paul L. Love, the father of SCILET and Angeline, an MA student, rivalled the performances by any professional stage persona. Professor Vasanthan, at the end, said, 'You may be going blind, Mr Devadoss, but you have taught us all how to see.' The programme ended with Mahe's brief, beautiful speech and a standing ovation.

In the train, on the way back to Madras, Mahe told me, 'I have had many, many happy periods in my life. The time we spent now in Madurai is certainly one among them.' I smiled because this poem to courage was truly a woman for all seasons. I smiled also because the words came from the heart of my wife, despite her being a quadriplegic for three decades. I observed, 'I do not know what we have done to deserve this outflow of love and affection from Aravind, American College, our dear friends, and relatives.'

She replied, 'The answer is simple, Mano, it is all because of God's grace.'

19

By 1975, I had lost vision in my right eye. Now in 2002, I was finding it increasingly difficult to draw with the fine 0.1mm nib of a Rotring pen, even with the +23 power glass. I knew that if the power went above +30, I would have to keep my face so close to the easel that my nose would virtually touch the paper. One day I asked Dr Badrinath whether it would be possible for me to get a pair of bifocal spectacles with a power between +26 and +29 for near and +15 for distant vision. Sankara Nethralaya made a worldwide search and found out that an Australian company could custom-build a bifocal pair with any power up to +27.

Sankara Nethralaya sent the necessary measurements and my choice of +27 and +15 bifocal power. Badri gifted the Australian spectacles to me. I found out that it was spectacular. The plastic lens had a high refractive index and also had a high level of clarity. Besides, it was far lighter than the +23 pair with glass lenses.

Now in 2002, I could again see fine, very pale brown ink lines on paper, as I could in 1995. This was yet another small victory in my losing war against retinitis pigmentosa. Should I not do something now that I could not have done without the new gift? Yes. I decided to create a colour pen-and-ink portrait of Mahema, similar to the one I did of M. S. Subbulakshmi Amma in 1995.

Way back in 1972, when Mahe was thirty-one, a few months before the accident, I had taken three photographic portraits of Mahe, her face side-lit with her slightly pouting, well-defined lips being highlighted. I took blow-ups of the photographs—light, medium, and dark prints and pored over them. Then with Mahe's help, I diluted the brown ink to the right level to draw her face, then added a few drops of red ink into the pale brown ink for the lips and so on. Mahe was pleased and touched that I took so much trouble over this project. So she called it her dear husband's 'magnificent obsession'. As soon as I finished the artwork, Mahe and I went to Sankara Nethralaya and showed it to Badri and Vasanthimma. They said it was stunning.

In early 2003, much to everyone's joy, our first grandson Aniketan arrived. When Mahema was born in 1940, she was brought from the hospital to the house where we lived. In 1966 when our daughter Suja was born, she too was brought into the same house. Now in 2003, it was Suja's baby Aniketan's turn. The house was acquiring a family aura, Aniketan representing the fourth generation to live there.

Mahema was so impressed by the interior of the Natakasala in Thirumalai Nayak Mahal in Madurai that she strongly felt that I should capture its grandeur in ink for the book. Actually, I wanted to do an artwork of the hall a few years earlier. Even then, the level of illumination inside was insufficient for my poor eye. Now my eyesight had declined further. So, I felt diffident, but Mahe was persuasive.

'Please try to do it, Mano,' she said, 'if you succeed—I am sure you would—then this piece of artwork would make your book that much richer.'

Chitra agreed with Mahe. She took me twice to the Mahal and patiently explained all the details which were, for me, a reminder of what I had seen earlier. She also arranged a series of photographs covering various aspects of the hall. Now, I understood the intricate complexity three-dimensionally. Using my knowledge on perspective, I began working on the artwork. Night after night I worked till two in the morning and completed the drawing in January 2004.

Approaching blindness had not yet beaten me. I smiled.

In 1964, when we began our annual Christmas card project, it was like a tiny potted plant. Each year it grew and was transplanted as our greeting card project. By 2004, it had grown into a large tree, and was growing bigger each year. We began using my Madurai drawings too for the cards—four to six of them each season. Aravind at Madurai also printed our cards to supply to the Madurai clientele, which saved us the transportation cost.

One day Mahe told me, 'Soon after the accident, I had a sad thought, along with many other sad ones, that our situation was likely to scuttle our pursuit of the art of giving. Because of the greeting card project, now I rejoice that we have been able to give more than I had ever hoped to.'

I told her that through the greeting card project alone this season, she had been able to give more than my annual take-home pay before my retirement from Oldham. We were also giving away the royalty from the sale of my books.

In the early summer of 2005, the bougainvillea climber near the western gate of our house had grown quite tall. It had such an abundance of white paper like flowers, which covered nearly half of the neighbouring frangipani tree, that the bougainvillea looked like a cascading bridal veil. Not to be outdone, the frangipani tree came out with a profusion of flame-like blossoms, hiding its own green leaves. The western entrance to our house looked more beautiful than ever before.

1 May 2005, was a landmark day, even a red-letter day for Mahe. Why? Our road accident happened on the 11,810th day of Mahe's life on 30 December 1972. Now, on this day, 2005, she had completed the next 11,810th day of her life. In other words, on this day, she had spent exactly half of her life as a quadriplegic—a prisoner in her own body. And yet, what a triumphant life she had led. She did not allow her setbacks and difficulties to dampen her spirit. She had not allowed our financial burden to choke our desire to give.

On 1 May 2005, exactly on the 11,810th day after the accident, early in the morning, we woke up, hearing the patter of rain and the whistle of wind, unusual for this time of the year. I thought that perhaps the windy, rainy morning was an appropriate metaphor for the day. Amazingly, a far more lyrical metaphor was in store.

We soon found out that the wind had broken a large part of the frangipani tree, which in turn had brought down a big chunk of the bougainvillea. A thicket of tangled, fallen branches lay sprawled across the street, completely blocking the cul-de-sac.

On our ninth wedding anniversary, in 1972, a billowing curtain had pushed down our wedding lamp and had broken it, but the flames continued to burn. Three days later, a lorry had pushed our car off the road, which had broken Mahe's spinal cord, but not her spirit. Now, 11,810 days later, the wind had broken a part of our tree and the climber. The tree and the climber still lived. The street in front of the gate looked beautiful with a profusion of flowers from the fallen branches.

I picked up a stalk of frangipani, which had many fully opened red flowers with yellow centres, some partially opened ones, a profusion of buds and a cluster of leaves. I studied the stalk with care and found it very beautiful. I plucked the petals of one flower with pleasing curvatures and flattened them on a white paper. I was struck by the strong resemblance, in terms of colour and shape, between the petals from the fallen frangipani and the five flames of the kuthu-vilakku that had fallen 11,813 days earlier.

Having fully understood the beautiful structure of the stem, I created a watercolour of the frangipani.

So it came to pass that the very first artwork of a frangipani stem with flame-like flowers that I was destined to create was on the special day in which Mahe had completed exactly half her life as a quadriplegic, with grace and dignity. How Mahema managed to get all the fallen branches cleared on this May Day, which was also a Sunday, when the workers of Madras celebrated the triumph of labour with their eyes glued to television sets, is quite another story.

Lynn Connor, wife of the British Deputy High Commissioner in

Madras, was very keen that I should create an artwork of Cottingley, their official residence—a stately colonial building. I was hesitant to do it. With my narrow cone of vision and low acuity, I could vaguely see at close range, only a very small fraction of this sprawling, large bungalow. How would I be able to comprehend it fully? But she was very persuasive and I agreed to try.

One very early morning, while it was still dark, our dear friend Joan took Mahe and me in her car to Cottingley. By the time we reached the place, morning had just broken. Joan wheeled Mahe in her chair hither and thither in the vast compound till Mahe decided on the right spot from where the edifice should be captured on paper. Mahe gave me a detailed description of various aspects, which I tried to see.

We had to go to Cottingley on another day around the same time. I gave a strip of paper to Joan and requested her to fold it in approximately the right proportion, following the structure of the building. Then we went close to the building. I ran my fingers on the walls, the lower windows and the like. Joan gave a very detailed description while I did this. She took many photographs—general views and close-ups in her digital camera. Now, I had 'seen' Cottingley reasonably well in my mind's eye.

That afternoon, I decided to make a pencil sketch of the building before my memory began to fade. I fixed the vanishing points for it on either side. I completed the drawing of the building using my deep knowledge on perspective. When Mahe saw the drawing on the easel, she exclaimed, 'O Mano, how did you ever manage to draw Cottingley this well?'

A couple of days later, Joan sent me a set of prints on A4 paper. Jayanth outlined some of them in black ink for me to see the details better. With all the necessary information in my head I began the artwork and finished it without too much of a hassle.

Lynn was delighted. 'Mahema,' she said laughingly, 'you must thank me for this fine piece. I bullied Mano into doing it.'

With his eyes twinkling, her husband, Mike observed, 'I am glad to know, Mano, that I am not the only one she bullies.' We all had a hearty laugh.

My daughter Sujatha told me that the Pudu Mandapam built by that talented king, Thirumalai Nayak, three-and-a-half centuries ago, was a very special entity of Madurai, and as such I must include an ink drawing of it. Even as a schoolboy, I looked admiringly at the imposing structure with its massive granite pillars, with a multiplicity of high relief statuary, with integral stone lions sitting on top of each pillar, their backs supporting the running beam. When I was in high school, I once tried to draw a view with my fountain pen in my notebook, with not very satisfactory results. Now, my eyesight had declined to a level that I could hardly see the lions atop the pillars in the dimly lit upper region.

I agreed with Suja that I should include a drawing of the Pudu Mandapam. Chitra, Mike, Julian, Jayaraj, and Jayanth helped me in different ways to clearly understand the structure and the activities in the hall. So I took up the artwork of the complex view, the very last one I did for the first edition of the book on Madurai. I was filled with a sense of pride and humility. I had been looking at the hall with an artist's eye from my boyhood. Ironically, I 'saw' the pillars in their full glory only after I was nearly seventy and nearly blind.

Later Mahema observed, 'It seems to me, Mano, that the Natakasala and the Pudu Mandapam are truly a boon for the pen-and-ink artists. You have so spectacularly captured them on paper. The beauty of your book is that, while the striking drawings are all in black and white, the accompanying texts are often quite colourful.'

In mid-2006, I wrote a thank you note to my dear friends Vara and Bala at Madurai. I did a watercolour of a small bunch of roses as the salutation piece. In the brief note, by mistake, I had jumped a line. Instead of writing the second line below the first, I inadvertently wrote it above, on account of my vision problem. So I discarded this sheet and started working on a fresh one. Mahe asked her assistant to retrieve the discarded sheet from the wastepaper basket, flatten it and cut off the written part.

I wondered why Mahe was doing this. She replied that, while I had made so many freehand watercolours of roses for others, she did not have a single one. So, she was salvaging this piece for herself.

I was touched by her boundless enthusiasm for my artwork—even the light-hearted ones. I told her that the bunch of roses I painted for her would have to be the best one of them all. Almost immediately, I did a bunch with care on a proper watercolour board—two big roses representing Mahe and me, two smaller fresher ones representing Michael and Suja, an opening bud representing Aniketan, and an unopened tiny bud covered by green sepals representing the child whom Suja was expecting then. I mounted the picture in a beautiful frame and presented it to Mahe—a total surprise for her—on her sixty-sixth birthday. She was overjoyed and hung it opposite her bed so that she could see it for its simple beauty and the thought that went behind it.

I shall write later about yet another beautiful outcome relating to this artwork, which featured in an exhibition to raise money for the blind.

I was pleased that for the season 2006–07, Mahe managed to sell, directly from our house, more than 26,000 greeting cards for charity, the largest number till then. This was mainly because year after year, more and more companies proactively patronized our cards. Again, each year unfailingly, *The Hindu, Indian Express, Madras Musings, Eves Touch, Madras Plus, Mylapore Times*, and others wrote enthusiastic and interesting articles about our project, with reproductions of the artwork in the cards. So, year after year, more and more people came home to buy the cards.

Many happy events happened to us on account of this project. Let me give just one example: We received a telephonic order for the Chepauk Palace cards. When we asked the name of the caller, the reply was, 'I am the Nawab of Arcot.' An engaging verbal exchange ensued, at the end of which he warmly invited us to tea. Our friend Zubie took us to the Amir Mahal. The Nawab and the Begum, a fragile beauty, were gracious hosts. Our greeting card project brought us an exclusive invitation by the Nawab to his palace.

Each year, the month of December would be a very hectic and enjoyable one for us. We would attend many carol services and have dinner parties in our house with plenty of carol singing. We would attend carefully chosen Carnatic music recitals and would enjoy many dinner invitations.

Mahe would send off our Christmas cards, along with our Christmas letter (300 plus) to our dear ones around the world, well before the end of November. We would receive a stream of cards, many with Christmas letters. Mahe would take the stamps from the envelopes to give away to stamp collectors. A majority of institutional orders for our greeting cards came in November, but there were also many spillovers into December. Besides, hordes of people would visit our house in December to purchase varying numbers of our cards. Mahe had to attend to all those.

It would soon be time for her to pull out the Christmas decorations and get them installed. She used the Christmas cards that we received as a part of the decoration. Then it would be time to bring into the house our large potted Christmas tree and decorate it. On the 24th, Mahe would be very busy packing and sending Christmas goodies to all our neighbours. We always attended the midnight Christmas service. A helper and I would roll her wheelchair down Santhome High Road to our church and then back home. For years she withstood all these.

Unfortunately, in December 2006, she could not take it. She became very tired frequently. We even skipped many carol services and music recitals. But she would not make any compromise on her charity work. For the midnight service as usual she had to sit on her wheelchair from 9.30 in the night till 2 in the early morning. She was so exhausted this time that she could not sit up for the special Christmas breakfast. I hoped that she would bounce back in January. She did...but only partially. In January 2007, I realized that Mahe bounced back only because her activities were far less now.

February 2007 was a very happy month for our family because

our second grandson Ethan arrived, and came from the hospital into the same house.

In March 2007, were Mahe to take up activities at the same level as she had in December 2006, she might well have found it even harder to cope.

However, she was very happy that the launch of my book *Multiple Facets of My Madurai* was to be held in April by the Madras Book Club at Hotel Connemara. She was totally involved in all the preparations for the launch. At the launch, guests started arriving in such large numbers that the hotel had to bring sixty extra chairs. Even after this, about seventy people had to stand. The American Consul General, David Hopper, gave up his seat to an old lady and stood at the end of the hall throughout the programme, winning the hearts of many.

Our friend N. Ram, who first suggested that I come out with this book, was the chief guest. Other guests who spoke, sat on the podium but I did not. Neither did I give a speech as I thought that the book would speak for itself. However, Mahe gave a very brief talk. The sum and substance of what she said was this: when she asked our four-year-old grandson, Ketan, where his father, Michael, was born, his reply was 'America'. When she asked the same question about Michael's mother, Pat, his reply was the same. How about Ketan's mother, Suja? She was born in 'India' was his reply. How about Suja's mother, Mahema? 'India' was the answer. Where was Suja's father, Mano, born? His ebullient response was 'Madurai'. Mahema ended her speech by observing that her grandson's final statement, in a sense, conveys my special feeling for Madurai.

Among those who read excerpts from my book was the British Deputy High Commissioner, Mike Connor, who read a passage about Madura Mills, started by two Britons in the late nineteenth century. Before reading the text he declared, 'I am a proud owner of "a Mano".' He referred to my artwork of Cottingley, of course. It was for Mahe and me yet another evening, the memories of which we would cherish.

Our friend Anuradha, the television journalist, made a sensitive television presentation of the book, the launch and those associated with it. S. R. Madhu wrote an insightful review in the *Indian Express*. I was delighted to find that *The Hindu* had devoted a full page for its review. There were other launches and reviews too.

Happily, all the copies got sold within two months. So I had to hurriedly plan the reprinting of the book. Bangera, a Madurai-based industrialist, who was an enthusiast of the book, readily agreed to sponsor the second edition. SCILET of American College, Aravind Eye Hospital, and Suri of the Madurai Readers' Club were all keen on launching the book at Madurai. Three launches were planned in August 2007 on consecutive days.

By June, Mahema's stamina waned noticeably. When we went out to attend one programme or another, she would often return home completely exhausted. So, we were in a quandary as to whether she should go to Madurai with me. What happens if she becomes very ill in Madurai? We talked about it and with sadness decided that she should not go.

All the three launches in Madurai went off extraordinarily well. Mahema was missed by countless many. But I think I missed her the most. Thulasi thoughtfully took a video of the Aravind launch for Mahe to see and hear the event back in Madras. Mahema and I listened to the CD on our ordinary CD player. She was very happy about all the speeches by different people. She said that she was touched to hear Dr Usha talk about me as 'this jewel of Madurai', and again, 'For Mano art is his life. For us his life is art'.

Mahema said, 'Raja Govindasamy's talk expressed his great love for your two books on Madurai, for Madurai itself and for the English language.'

I would like to add two brief quotes from two other speakers, which had humorous elements. Professor Vasanthan, in his long talk observed at one stage, 'Mahema, as you know, is a beauty...Mano is not .... He is a very strong man.' My interjection, asking him, 'Beauty and the beast?' was greeted with much laughter.

Bangera, who graciously sponsored the second edition, said in his speech that this book links the past, the present, and the future of Madurai. He ended his speech with these words: 'From where he got his art. And they say behind every successful man there is a woman...in his case it's his wife', evoking a burst of laughter.

In September, one night, as usual, Mahe read to me while I drew. After an hour, she began to slur. Then she began reading the same line again and again, without realizing the mistake. My heart ached to see the decline in her mental state.

In early October, I asked Mahe whether she would be able to stand the strain of working on the demanding greeting card project for the coming 2007–08 season. She observed that I too was finding it increasingly difficult to create stunning ink drawings. I said that for now we could at least use the drawings that I had already created. After a brief discussion she said, 'Let us do it for the coming season alone, Mano,' and added with sadness, 'let this forty-third season be the last one.'

She sent a formal, common letter to her journalist friends. She began the letter saying that she was writing it both with joy and sorrow. She was joyful because her friends in the print media gave unstinted support to the project close to her heart. She was sad because, after careful deliberation, she and I decided that the six cards of the 2007–08 season would be the very last ones for our greeting card project. She also explained in this letter why we took this difficult decision.

The response to Mahema's note by the press, in terms of the articles published, was heartening. Let me give just one example: *Indian Express* chose for its article entitled, 'Those Greeting Cards to be History'. Just these six words, I felt, said ever so much. The sensitively written, factually accurate, long article had included the artwork from three cards, out of the six we had designed for this season, along with a photograph of Mahe in her wheelchair and me standing behind her. This photograph in the paper triggered in my mind a counterpoint for Bangera's last words in his speech, a few months earlier. 'Behind every successful woman is a man. In Mahema's case, it is her husband.'

R. T. Chari is a highly successful industrialist, who manufactures world-class heavy-duty electric transmission equipment, making it possible for the government to completely avoid importing these at a high cost. He is also a generous philanthropist. Above all, he has fashioned a very innovative programme to spread awareness of the richness of South Indian heritage. He invites highly talented musicians, artists, writers, dancers, dramatists, architects, historians, and many more to make PowerPoint presentations, which are educative and highly entertaining. He invited me with Mahema to make a presentation on the making of an artist/author, culminating in the Madurai book.

Our programme, held in November 2007, was well attended. Chari's friend Madhu, an excellent journalist and former UN official, introduced Mahe and me. And as it often happened, the hall was full and many had to stand. Throughout our presentation, there was uproarious laughter. I was told later that there were tears aplenty too. Laughter and tears seem to have become the hallmark of my presentations. I was so apprehensive as to whether Mahe would be able to do her part that I requested our friend Nirmala to sit with us as a standby for Mahe. Happily, Mahema managed...just so. The programme ended with Madhu's concluding remarks. I was quite surprised to hear his very last words. I quote: 'I think most of us would be willing to give up our achievements to be able to draw like Manohar Devadoss.' I was even more surprised to hear the audience applaud approvingly. This happy event also took on a special, sad significance in my mind, as this was destined to be the last occasion where Mahe and I would share a podium.

Whenever she went out, Mahe wore a tastefully chosen sari of simple elegance. She had to be rolled like a rolling pin on the bed to tie it. Fortunately, Josephine tied the sari for Mahe ever so neatly that now and then journalists wrote about how well Mahema presented herself in public. But she never wore expensive saris, the highest priced one she wore being for Suja's wedding, which cost a mere ₹3,500.

Around the time of her birthday in 2007, I offered to gift her with a sari costing around ₹10,000. She reluctantly agreed only when Suja persuaded her and offered to share the expense. At Sundari Silk House, Mahe thoroughly enjoyed looking at more than 100 saris before we together chose a peach-coloured Kanjeevaram silk shot with purple costing ₹8,500. All three of us also liked an excellent cotton sari costing ₹3,000, with a real jarigai border and an exquisitely designed pallu. Mahe decided that one sari would be for Christmas and the other for our wedding anniversary.

Most of the corporate enthusiasts of our greeting cards, as usual, acquired the cards in November 2007. A very large number of people came home to get the cards. Mahema, in her state then, could not have coped dealing with the stream of visitors. So I played a very supportive role. Despite this she had two brief blackouts.

Fortunately, Suja's family spent this Christmas season with us. Suja took care of the Christmas decorations and Michael, the Christmas tree. Mahe was keen on attending the Christmas watch night service of 2007. In order to be prepared for the arduously long midnight service, she stayed in bed all through the 24th evening, until she got ready to go to the church. She wore the beautiful cotton sari with jarigai for the first time. Instead of rolling the wheelchair down the road, we went in our car. We were well ahead of time. The interior of the church was all aglow with light from the multiplicity of chandeliers and lamps. I took a few steps back to look at my wife.

Fortunately, the illumination level was perfect for my imperfect eye. Surprisingly, I could see her reasonably well. At sixty-seven, she looked rather nice in the beautiful sari. She saw that I was looking at her admiringly and she smiled. She looked even nicer when she smiled. This was the last time I was to see my wife this well. Fortunately, the image of her smiling face has been etched in my mind.

Now as usual, I pushed a pew inwards, so that the wheelchair could be located in a way it would not block the aisle. She slept lightly like a bird till the service began. Amazingly, she not only enjoyed the beautiful, joyful, triumphant Christmas service but also the socializing with her many dear church friends in the garden after the service. We returned home at 2.15... And she had withstood it all.

I was glad that Mahe was determined to attend this midnight service. It was at this Christmas special service that she took her very last holy communion.

On our forty-fourth wedding anniversary, Mahe decided not to wear the anniversary sari. She wanted to tie it for the first time for some very special event. But she wore a pair of beautiful silver golusus (anklets). She had been delighted when our helpers jointly gifted her the pair on this day. Suja had requested our friend Krishnan, an eminent photographer of Madras, to take some family pictures. The portrait of Mahema was so well taken that it even resembled an oil painting. This picture was destined to appear in the papers after two months.

The New Year began joyfully for us because on 1 January 2008, we had a wonderful reunion with Norm and Ann Craig. Norm Craig was a much admired chemistry professor at Oberlin and I had been his student. Mahe, Suja, and I came to love the Craig family and they came to love ours too. The Oberlin Alumni Association had organized a visit to India, especially to Madras and Madurai, for a small group. Norm and Ann decided to join the group. Among other things, they would have the great joy of meeting Mahe after thirty-five years, Suja and me after twenty-five years. Fortunately, Suja's family was with us then.... And what a marvellous reunion it was.

After returning to Oberlin, Norm wrote a detailed insightful account of his Indian visit with Ann, to share with many. In this portfolio, he described with great affection, his visit to our home. Let me reproduce just the last two lines from this section: 'It had been a wonderful evening with old friends in an attractive Indian home. We had been truly blessed by this warm welcome in the Devadoss home.'

Ever since we returned to Madras from the US, our Oberlin friends continued to visit us, frequently stayed with us, often for long stretches. We thoroughly enjoyed those reunions. The visit of Norm and Ann had a special but sad significance. They were the last two Oberlin friends to meet Mahe.

Even in January 2008, people kept visiting our house for the greeting cards. So we tallied the figures only in early February. We were delighted to find that from her bed and wheelchair, even while she was not too well, with my support, she had managed to supply more than 33,000 cards, all from our house.

'Not at all a bad end,' she quipped.

After mid-February 2008, she signed many charity cheques. The total amount was far higher than ever before.

In *Madras Musings* of 16 February, our friend Sriram published a long review of my book *Multiple Facets of My Madurai*, in which he wrote, 'It is difficult to judge as to which is better in this book—the drawings or the accompanying copy. They actually form a perfect combination, rather like Manohar and Mahema, complementing and strengthening the other.'

When Mahe read this review to me, she felt happy. So, on the 22nd, she wrote a very brief thank you letter to him. Her handwriting was a bit unsteady, yet decipherable. This was to be the very last time she would sign her name.

Dr Prema Padmanabhan, medical director of Sankara Nethralaya, is a brilliant eye surgeon. This petite beauty has the voice of a nightingale. It is a delight to hear her speeches in English or in Tamil and to hear her recite in Sanskrit. It was Dr Prema who had, years earlier performed the cataract surgery in Mahe's eyes in a most conducive environment, with Suja watching the proceedings. Much later, she wrote an article on Mahe and me in the January 2008 issue of a journal, a copy of which Mahe received from a friend towards the end of February. Mahe was elated and moved when she read the piece. Let me quote a few lines from the article:

How rare it is to come across someone who bears his cross with joy. Sometimes fate strikes a hammer blow with malignant force, as it did on a lovely couple, whom I have had the good fortune of knowing. 'She has my eyes', he would say. 'He has my limbs', would be her rejoinder, capturing the ardhanari (half male-half female) concept in their total oneness. I was conscious of my dual responsibility when I operated on her eyes. 'Remember, doctor,' she said just before I commenced my surgery, 'your surgery will have to restore vision for both of us!'....they have made of their lives a work of art, filling the canvas of each day with the rich colours of love, laughter, and joy.

Ranji (Dr Mani) and Appukka who had taken a decision to meet us whenever they came to Madras from the US, visited us on the last day of February, which cheered Mahe and me greatly. Then Dr Kannan, who was briefly my colleague at Oldham, visited us with a bag full of Malaysian fruits, which Mahe loved. To make my wife happy in February, I often prepared dishes of my own recipes, which were her favourites.

Mahema was quite aware of her physical condition rapidly going downhill. And yet, because of the many good things that happened, emotionally, February had been an exceptionally happy month for her. This was most fortunate because she lived only for the first two days in March. She passed away in the small hours of the following morning, well before sunrise.

On 2 March 2008, Mahema felt so exhausted that she stayed in bed all day long and sat up only at seven in the evening. She requested her helpers to give her a bath. A helper asked, 'Why do you want to take a bath this late, when you are so tired?'

Mahe's tongue-in-cheek reply was, 'I must bathe because my man expects me to be clean. Besides he would like me to appear fresh and nice, even if he cannot see me!'

I was glad, that she retained her sense of humour even when she was down.

At that point of time, I was working on a drawing of the Madras University clock tower. After making herself presentable, she sat close to me and began reading *The Hindu* for me. She did not slur but her voice was weak. I asked her whether she would like to lie down. Uncharacteristically, she at once said, 'Yes, Mano.' I transferred her into the bed as gently as I could and resumed my artwork, listening to an audiobook through earphones.

As always, I worked on my drawing till two in the night and then began the procedure of turning Mahe in bed, with the help of an assistant. Mahema wanted to know the progress in my artwork, as she had not sat with me in the evening. So I cranked her bed a bit, switched on all the lights and held the paper in a way she could clearly see it. She studied it carefully and said in a feeble voice that she was happy with the progress. She then said that she felt very uncomfortable an hour or so after the previous turning and asked me whether I could turn her sooner the next time. So, I set the digital alarm clock at 3.33 a.m. and slept immediately. At around 3.20 a.m., I woke up hearing Mahe's voice. She was saying 'Baa.... baa.... baa...' (ba as in bat and not ball), in a long-drawn-out way. I smiled and asked her whether she was trying to become an aatukutty (little lamb). She did not reply but continued the chant, each time a little softer than before, till she fell completely silent. I thought that she had gone into deep sleep. When I woke up to turn her, I realized that she had gone into eternal sleep ever so gently.

I was deeply touched to realize that just an hour or so before her passing, she had taken sufficient interest in knowing the progress of my art work. Mahe was quietly religious. It occurred to me that in a symbolic way, she went to her Lord like a little lamb saying 'baa... baa...baa...' She was lovable till her very last moment.

Our tenants, Stanley and Carolyn, came within a few minutes to help me take a series of necessary steps, to make phone calls and to be of moral support. Actually, Stanley took care of much of the funeral details. Josephine lovingly tied the peach-coloured sari with purple shot for Mahe. This was the very first time Mahe was to wear this sari... This was also to be the very last sari that she wore. The helpers fixed the silver golusus they had gifted her. One helper placed a Jordanian wooden cross in Mahe's hand in such a way that the cross faced Mahe's face. This reminded me of the line, 'Hold Thou Thy cross before my closing eyes', in the hymn, 'Abide with Me,' sung traditionally at funerals.

Our friends began arriving and many dear ones stayed on. Deepa, Chitra, and Thulasi from Aravind flew into Madras from Madurai to attend the funeral. Thoughtfully they brought a small basket of fresh, strung jasmine. I remembered the small basket of jasmine that Verna's parents had brought for Mahe to Oberlin for a happy occasion in 1972. Our helpers twisted three strands together and I garlanded Mahe with it...this for the very last time. We placed the rest of the flowers in Mahe's hair.

My wife had donated her eyes to Sankara Nethralaya, thus pursuing the art of giving, even after her passing. Dr Prema Padmanabhan, whose glowing article Mahe read only a few days earlier—was the one to remove her eyes. Prema closed Mahe's eyes with such perfection that nobody, nobody would have known the difference. Indeed, many said that her face was radiantly beautiful or that she was like a bommai (doll) or like a sleeping beauty in the coffin. I had to accept other people's words because I could not see my wife.

N. Ram chose the photographic portrait of Mahe to appear in *The Hindu* along with an article, the following day.

In mid-February, Aparna, a journalist of *The Week*, had come from Kerala to Madras to interview us. In late February she had telephoned Mahe to inform us that her article, 'A Poem to Love' would appear in the 2 March issue of the magazine. The article reached us when Mahe was in her coffin.

Our daughter's family reached Madras on the evening of 3 March. I had hardly slept for an hour the previous night. I did not eat anything. However, our helpers kept giving me buttermilk, tea, milkshake, and the like to sustain me physically. I was sustained emotionally by the overwhelming love that I received from our dear ones.

On the night of 3 March, I was exhausted physically, mentally, and emotionally. So, that night I had a deep, dreamless sleep, until

the alarm rang at 3.33 a.m. On the previous night, I had stopped
but had not switched off the alarm. So, it rang now. I woke up and
went to Mahe's bed to turn her. She was not there. Only then the
reality struck me hard. Mahe was sleeping in the drawing room. I
had a wrenching feeling. I dragged myself into the drawing room. I
was surprised to see some people—including our aunt Savithri, in
her early nineties—sitting there on vigil in candlelight.

Soon after daybreak on 4 March, our house was full of people
with an overabundance of flowers like never before. Later, at the
church, I was surprised and pleased to find that our friend Rita
Saldanha, the super soprano of Madras, a Roman Catholic, sitting
prominently with the choir in this, our Protestant Church. The brief
service was moving. Almost all those who paid their final respects
to Mahe hugged me, and most of them, men and women cried.
Geeta Doctor, a strong woman, cried so much that my shirt at the
shoulder became wet. She said, 'I find it so hard to bear the pain.
How do you bear it, Mano?'

I in turn shed so many tears that I made her sari wet with mine.
My wife was interred in a beautiful spot in the cemetery, under the
shade of tall trees, with a row of flowering bushes very nearby.

Quadriplegia is a devastating condition. And yet for the thirty-five
years since the accident, Mahe had lived a life full of dignity, grace,
and beauty. Now Mahe was no more. My consolation was that she
passed away with the same dignity and grace. She looked serenely
beautiful in her coffin, surrounded by her loved ones. She took her
final journey in style, in a beautiful sari with her favourite Madurai
jasmine around her neck and her hair and with a Jordanian cross in
her hand. Fortunately our friends VGP Rajadas (Suja's friend Joan's
husband) and Chelliah managed to get a nice spot at the cemetery
for Mahe's final resting place. It was a beautiful end.

~

In a house of bereavement, the family would be in deep sorrow and
many dear ones would attend to the details of the funeral. Here, I

was the only family member, until Suja, Michael, and the children arrived in the evening. Many details were taken care of in a beautiful way. Unfortunately, however, some peripheral persons took certain actions, based on their own beliefs and prejudices, which were totally unacceptable to me. They did not even care to inform me of what they had done, which I could not see. One person took a unilateral wrong decision, which was hurting to me and many others. But then, the negative aspects had been more than adequately compensated by the countless, poignantly beautiful happenings.

After returning from the cemetery, I took a high-quality photocopy of my semi-finished drawing of the university clock tower in order to keep a frozen image of the drawing as Mahe had seen it before her eternal sleep. In the early afternoon, I sat at my desk, placed the original incomplete drawing and began working on it.

That night, when I went to bed, I was acutely aware that Mahe's bed lay empty. I knew that I would miss her greatly. I would miss her proactive support of whatever I did and the innovative ways in which she expressed her gratefulness for the way I cared for her. I would miss her tinkling laughter. Above all, I would miss her unabated love for me. Should I allow myself to be enveloped by sadness each night? My mind said 'no' and my heart said that I should 'rejoice'. Why rejoice? Well, because she lived for thirty-five years after the accident. Dr Tommy, an expert in this field, told me that he did not know of any person, directly or indirectly, other than Mahe, who survived as a quadriplegic for thirty-five years. That was a record in itself, he said. And, during those long years, she did not suffer from a single bedsore. That, I am sure, would be an additional record. Besides, Mahe did not merely survive…she in fact, thrived. Above all, in general, she was an extremely happy quadriplegic.

A thought had come to my mind, even before Mahe passed away. If a mythical angel (like Abu Ben Adam's angel) prepared a list of living persons who led happy lives as quadriplegics for more than three decades, I would suspect that the list would not be long! What is more, I would not have been surprised at all if Mahe's name (like

Abu's) found itself at the very top of the list.

I told myself with utter honesty that never did I ever feel, not even once, that she was a burden. She was quite aware of this aspect, which contributed to her happiness.

When her noble heart stopped, I knew that an ennobling era had ended for me. But then, I had a vast treasury of gem-like, precious memories of events spanning over forty-five years, to be cherished. I told myself that the happy memories of thirty-five years after the accident far outnumbered those of the nine years before her spinal injury. I took a decision that, during the months to come each night, when I went to bed I would remember in great detail one rich happy event or another and would fall asleep in a happy frame of mind.

20

Many friends kept visiting me. V. K. Ramachandran chose to visit me from Kolkata a week after Mahe's passing, to spend quality time with me. I received countless phone calls from around the world. Letters and emails kept pouring in. Let me give a few lines from just two emails: Reverend David and Reverend Padma Gallup wrote: 'We suspect that in heaven, the angels will be taking lessons from Mahema....' Al Dieffenbach, the star dean of Oberlin College during our time there, wrote: 'I don't need to tell you how special a woman she was. I recall having my doubts when you first approached us at the Deanery, about hiring your gentle wife to ride herd in a dormitory full of American undergraduates at the height of the campus sexual revolution. My concerns evaporated, of course, as soon as I met Mahema. She managed to cross the cultural divide without surrendering the grace and dignity of her own background. I know that scores of Oberlin students benefited enormously from her presence in their lives—and a considerable number of staff and faculty members as well.'

Over the years, Mahe had often told me that if she went before me, as she hoped she would, I should lead an active and as happy a life as possible after she was gone. My answer would invariably be that I would try to.

On our thirty-seventh wedding anniversary, I told my wife, 'Mahe, if you go before me, I'd like to institute an endowment or two, honouring you, so that the art of giving would continue in your name even after you were gone.'

Mahe replied, 'Oh, Mano, that's a beautiful thought. I am glad you chose to share this thought with me on this special day. I would like the endowments to go to Sankara Nethralaya and Aravind, so that some visually challenged poor could be benefited.'

Now, after she passed away. So I spoke to Badri and Vasanthimma at Sankara and with my friends, especially Chitra and Thulasi, at Aravind. They graciously agreed. Srivatsa of Wheels India, who had been a star patron of our greeting card charity project, heard about the endowment. He gave a liberal personal cheque for the Sankara endowment. In July 2008, my fifth book, the Tamil edition of *Green Well Years*, published by Kannathasan Publications, was launched at Madurai by Aravind. This enlightened institution combined the formal inauguration of Govel Trust, Mahema Devadoss Endowment along with the launch. Gandhi Kannathasan and Dr Krishna made the first two contributions.

I transferred a major part of the amount from a fixed deposit which had matured, into the two endowment funds. I decided to sell a small property to enhance the corpora of the two endowments.

I began creating large-format watercolours to build a portfolio of at least thirty paintings, which would help increase the funds further. My colour perception had become weaker, my acuity poorer and the cone of vision narrower. I could only vaguely comprehend gradation of colours and could not perceive gradual blend of colours. And as months passed by, my eyesight would worsen. And yet I chose the medium of watercolour. Why? Fortunately, Suja had gifted me with a box of thirty-six Staedtler watercolour pencils, and Satya a set of eighteen watercolour pens of the same German brand. Without those, I could not have created watercolours.

Aesthetically sensitive friends, who happened to see my semi-finished paintings on the easel, were spontaneously enthusiastic about what they saw. Two or three friends, (Swarup among them) even reserved for themselves whichever painting they happened to see.

I was glad that, by devising my own methods and adopting my own style, I was able to circumvent the problems imposed upon me by the limitations of my eyesight, to create watercolours to my satisfaction. I was glad again that I could 'see' my artwork in colours through the combination of my physiological eye and my mind's eye. I was happy yet again that I was creatively occupied, which in time would help some visually challenged poor.

Six months after Mahe's passing, two incidents that happened linked the past with the future in a poetically beautiful way and enriched my life.

My dear friend Devika brought her friend Shobha home on 19 September 2008. Shobha and her husband Viswanath established a publishing house, Karadi Tales, for children. With Shobha's initiative, Karadi Tales and a Dutch publisher jointly came out with a tactile book of Eric Carl's classic *The Very Hungry Caterpillar* for visually challenged children, for the first time ever in the world. The book was successfully published in six languages of affluent nations, both in print and in Braille. Tamil Nadu is an ideal place for producing, at competitive cost, this labour-intensive book that demands super craftsmanship and a philosophy of service-mindedness.

As Shobha talked with bubbling enthusiasm, I began 'seeing' the imaginatively crafted tactile pictures, partly with my fingers and partly with my eye. The book had been created mainly for children with limited or no eyesight. The book also offered a visual feast for children who have eyesight.

Shobha was organizing a launch of the English version at Madras on 4 October 2008. She requested me to be the chief guest for the event. Why me, when Madras is teeming with so many eminent people? Her reply was simple. She wanted me to participate because I was an artist, a writer, a scientist, and was visually challenged. I felt so honoured.

Suja and her sons happened to come to Madras the following morning on 20 September 2008. On the way home from Madras airport, she and her sons stopped at the Quibble Island Cemetery to have moments of serene peace where Mahe had been interred. They saw beautiful butterflies aplenty, fluttering around the blossoms in the bushes that were just next to where Mahe sleeps. There were also many caterpillars, eating away the leaves of the bushes. Suja brought home just one caterpillar with a big bunch of leaves. I was struck very happily by this remarkably rare coincidence. Only the previous morning, Shobha brought a tactile book, *The Very Hungry Caterpillar*. Now this morning, Suja brought home a very hungry caterpillar, which was busily eating away the leaves and what was special was that this caterpillar was from where Mahe rests. Suja placed these inside a plastic box, so that her sons could watch the amazing metamorphosis. And indeed they did. On Gandhi Jayanti, our butterfly had its own jayanthi. Yes, a beautiful butterfly emerged from the pupa on 2 October 2008. When the lid of the box was opened, it immediately flew towards the light outside, into the open sky.

This was allegorical. Mahe, in her pupa of the wheelchair had been, it seemed to me, like the butterfly, released, so that her beautiful spirit could fly free.

I was struck again by yet another rare coincidence that connected two thoughts of mine at two different junctures. When Mahe was in her coffin with a Jordanian cross in March 2008, I remembered the line, 'Hold Thou Thy cross before my closing eyes' of the hymn, 'Abide with me'. Now six months later, the butterfly that flew into the sky made me think of the very next line in the poem, 'Shine through the gloom and point me to the skies'.

At the book launch on 4 October, I briefly explained to the gathering how two months before our wedding, Mahe implied that I was a teddy bear. Since then, I had remained her teddy bear. Now, it was quite appropriate for a teddy bear to launch a book published by Karadi Tales.

Shobha being an imaginative, sensitive woman, chose not a

celebrity, but a blind little girl to receive the first copy from me. This girl, in turn, became totally involved in the book, by 'seeing' the tactile pictures and reading the text with her fingers.

Suja kept bringing caterpillar after caterpillar from Mahe's bushes. All the butterflies that emerged had the same colours and pattern. Our friend Ranvir Shah wrote a charming article in a journal effectively capturing 'the magic of the simple ephemeral moment' of the butterfly emerging from a box after the metamorphosis and flying away towards the sky.

I decided to capture on paper a butterfly that would closely resemble the shape, colours and design of the butterfly from Mahe's resting place. A new butterfly had emerged from a pupa in a box. Two helpers held it flat on a white paper set on my easel. I illuminated it from above and from underneath. The pleasing colours of the wings softly glowed with iridescence. I was thankful that with the help of a +27 power glass, I had been granted the grace, even in late 2008, to be able to see at close range the beauty of the little creature with my inadequate eye. So, I managed to create a colour drawing of this butterfly with a high level of accuracy.

Our friend, Athena, an eminent sculptor, wrote to me that in Greek culture, the soul of a departed person is represented by a butterfly and as such, my idea of symbolizing Mahe's beautiful spirit as an iridescent butterfly was quite apt.

Mahe had gone, but her spirit remained with me. A wonderful thought came to my mind. Way back in 1963, in a letter to my fiancée Mahe, I had drawn a happy doll resting her hand gently on the arm of a teddy bear, which in turn was looking at the doll with great expectation. Now in 2008, I did a large-format (16 inch x 12 inch) watercolour of the same teddy bear without the doll. Instead I featured a butterfly...not any butterfly...but 'The' butterfly lightly sitting upon the same arm of the teddy bear, which looks at the lepidopterologist with an expression of surprise mingled with joy. When I completed the artwork I was jubilant. I added this piece to the collection of my paintings that I was getting ready for the art exhibition, to enhance the funds of the endowments.

Another happy idea came to my mind. In 2007, at the Madurai launch of *Multiple Facets of My Madurai*, when my friend Professor Vasanthan in his speech said that Mahe was a beauty and that I was a strong person, I had interjected, 'Beauty and the Beast?', evoking much laughter. So, for the artwork, I chose the most appropriate title, 'Beauty and the Beast'.

Now let me make a very brief flash forward. On October 2010, Prakrithi Foundation sponsored my art exhibition with the title 'Mahema and the Butterfly'. The much-admired aesthetician of Madras, Kiran Rao, procured 'Beauty and the Beast'. This in turn enhanced one endowment a bit.

In October 1963, my fiancée had told me with subdued laughter that two months from then, she would be taking a big teddy bear to bed with her. At that time, could she have guessed that her hilariously witty response to my drab question would bring about some humorous, beautiful and poignant events which would culminate, forty-seven years later, in helping some visually challenged poor? I felt ever so happy that in the movie *To Kill a Mockingbird*, the child heroine happened to have a teddy bear in her bed. If she had not, then a range of simple yet wonderful events in my little world might well not have happened.

I organized remembrances of Mahema for different small groups, for instance, one for her very special church friends and another for a group of our dear ones from Aravind, Madurai. But the very best celebration of Mahe was organized by Suja and Michael. The house was beautifully decorated with lamps and candles galore and flowers aplenty. Suja's childhood friend Mahalakshmi had now become an eminent dancer. She gave a Bharatanatyam performance for the song 'Chinnan-chiru Kiliyea', which became Mahe's lifelong favourite ever since I sang this song for her at Belur for the first time.

N. Ram spoke eloquently, quoting extensively from my book, *Dreams, Seasons and Promises*. The only other person that Michael and Suja had requested to speak on the occasion was the insightful journalist, Geeta Doctor. Instead of a speech, she recited a poem that she had composed, entitled, 'For Mahema—A Remembrance of Jasmines'.

We were all moved, I especially, as I have many cherished memories of Mahema and her jasmines. Here are a few excerpts from the poem:

> She wore it around her hair
> The last thing when she was dressed and ready
> A bracelet of bright pearls
> from the jasmine fields of Madurai.
> Wound in a tight circle, neatly pinned about her head.
> She always left a faint trace behind her.
> A remembrance of jasmines in the air.
>
> And as Manohar hoisted her up,
> To remind her to laugh at herself:
> A Sack of Potatoes as he called her.
> With a sprig of jasmines stuck in her hair.
>
> She watched the seasons spin by
> as swiftly as the wheels turning on her wheelchair.
> And marked each December with a set of cards,
> delicately dipped in black and white.
> Each stone, brick, glass window-pane, cloud, tamarind tree,
> a hint of rain meticulously wrought by husband and wife
> working in tandem.
> Her eyes, his hands,
> both hearts lost in the re-creation of the past.
> A jasmine for remembrance etched in ink.
>
> And that's how she lay in her casket
> When they brought her into the church.
> Calm and composed, her hands crossed
> For the last time, her face serene
> her spirit released at last, running once more

as she had done through the fields
of her childhood, fingers plaiting the fat creamy blossoms
that she could never place
in a circle of bright buds about her dark hair.

And that's what we have come to celebrate:

'For Mahema—A Remembrance of Jasmines'
Geeta Doctor
13 August 2008

Let me now make a brief fast-forward:

Later, Geeta came out with a collection of her poems. A selection from this book was read out in different forums by skilled readers. Many felt that her poem for Mahema and her jasmines was the most poignant one. Dr M. S. Swaminathan said that this celebration was one among the most beautiful moving events that he had ever attended.

In 2008–09, Dr Geetha Ravi, a dedicated professor of English Literature at Fatima College in Madurai, initiated a multipronged project to help visually challenged college students, especially those who did English Literature. She came to know me through this project. We had an instant rapport and she became my lifelong friend. For the academic year 2009–10, she envisaged an imaginative assignment for the twelve MA Literature students. The twelve girls were requested to study, and not merely read, my four books—two on Madurai and two on Mahe. An audio-visual documentary on me, based on the four books, was to be produced. Two professionals from Dhan Foundation were to take care of the shooting and to teach the students to handle the digital movie camera.

Now a word about Dhan Foundation: Dhan was the brainchild of Vasimala, a visionary who successfully created the foundation to enhance awareness of various strata of the society on water conservation, preservation of heritage, pollution control, promotion of cultural activities, and the like. The foundation used some of my artwork in a project. Since then a strong bond of friendship blossomed between Vasi, his colleagues, and myself.

I visited Madurai in March 2010. Geetha Ravi, the twelve girls, and two professionals from Dhan spent two days with me from early morning, till late evening, visiting many of my favourite haunts, seeing, shooting, interviewing, eating, chatting, and laughing. At the end of the session, some students told me that they saw Madurai in an altogether new light now and others enthusiastically agreed.

A few days later, the indulgent professor and her adoring wards with the two professionals came to Madras. Again they spent two days with me. Now the girls interviewed me, about Mahe, saw the watercolours that I was getting ready for the art exhibition, danced to my harmonica playing and enjoyed my recipes. Some girls told me that the four days they had spent on this project were the happiest ones ever in their lives. Others readily assented. Laughingly, I told them that they were still young and I was sure that in the years to come they would all enjoy countless happier events...especially in their wedded lives.

The total duration of the video that had been taken exceeded 150 minutes, while it was to be edited down to about thirty minutes. After their annual examination and summer vacation, the students were to participate with Dhan in the editing process. After July, Geetha and others kept informing me about the progress in editing.

Mridula (Mimi), the granddaughter of T. S. Krishna, grew up in the T. S. K. Bungalow. I had included my pen-and-ink artwork of the stately house both in *Green Well Years* and *Multiple Facets of My Madurai*. Understandably, Mimi loved the house, all the more because she was born there. She requested me to make a watercolour of it for her. I had a good relook of the house. Soon I completed the work and was very happy with the outcome. I telephoned and emailed Mimi. For some reason she did not respond.

By August 2010, I had my own set of watercolours for the exhibition. One evening, our dear friend Ranvir invited Suja and me for a dinner at a fine restaurant. During the course of the dinner, he said, to my utter surprise and delight, that Prakriti Foundation instituted by him would be happy to hold the art exhibition in toto, with my participation. A couple of weeks or so later he visited me to discuss the details of all aspects relating to the art exhibition.

In the meanwhile, I had prepared a brief portfolio titled, *Mahema and the Butterfly* for my two grandchildren. This was a compilation of simple and charming, seemingly unconnected but strangely intertwined events over decades, relating the fragile yet resilient beauty that is the butterfly to the vulnerable yet serenely gracious beauty that was Mahema.

During the course of our conversation, I showed Ranvir the portfolio. Ranvir being Ranvir, studied it with all the artwork of colourful butterflies and colour portraits of Mahema, with utter concentration. He then turned to me and said, 'Uncle, this is a beautiful piece worthy of publication. Prakriti would be happy to print and release the portfolio along with the inaugural of the art exhibition.' Indeed, he titled the art exhibition, *Mahema and the Butterfly*. With Ranvir's and my participation, the portfolio turned out to be 'an exquisite piece' as one friend described it. The exhibition was held on the third week of October 2010. By then, I had completed three more watercolours.

A few days before the exhibition, my friend and patron Suresh Krishna and his wife visited me. As the son of T. S Krishna, he too grew up in the T. S. K. Bungalow, as Mimi did a generation later. He decided to gift the watercolour of this house to his niece and requested me not to breathe a word to her about it.

Suja, from Delhi, and Chitra and Thulasi from Madurai, came to Madras to attend the inaugural. There was excellent media coverage. Enthusiastic articles appeared, with reproductions of the watercolours and with titles like 'An Ode to Love', and 'An Ode to Mahema' and 'Wings of Hope'. One reproduction in a paper was that of the T. S. K. Bungalow. Most of the paintings got sold on the inaugural itself. Cheques written favouring either Sankara or Aravind were handed over to a representative of Prakriti. Thulasi acquired five paintings on behalf of the Aravind family members.

When Mimi came to know that the T. S. K. artwork had been

sold, she became very upset. When she telephoned me, I could not tell her that she would be the recipient, because Suresh wanted the gift to be a total surprise for her. When she did receive the painting, she was overjoyed. She was in fact so overjoyed that she made a second contribution to Aravind for the painting. So it came to pass, that on account of her gracious gesture, this particular painting brought a distinctly higher amount for the endowment, compared with the other paintings.

SCILET at American College celebrated its silver jubilee on 2 December 2010. The novelist Nayantara Sahgal was the chief guest and I, the guest of honour. So, I reached Madurai on the first evening. On my way from the airport to the Aravind guest house, my cell phone rang. Geetha excitedly told me, 'Mano, here is a piece of good news for you. The documentary is ready. Fatima College, with the participation of Dhan, is organizing a beautiful function on the sixth of this month to release the video. Some eminent citizens of Madurai would be there. I would be sending you the tickets and....'

I interrupted her saying, 'Don't send any tickets, please.'

With a perplexed tone, she asked me, 'But, why not, Mano?'

I laughingly told her, 'You don't have to because I have just arrived in Madurai.'

She had to hurriedly go to the guest house to collect my return ticket to change it suitably.

At the American College function, I gave Nayantara Sahgal inscribed copies of my five books on behalf of SCILET, and received her latest book from her. The programme went off smoothly. At an informal lunch, she sat next to me and helped me by serving the dishes. A few weeks later, I received an email from her appreciating my books.

Fortunately, I was kept quite busy between the third and fifth. Among other things, there were interactive sessions and PowerPoint presentations, at different institutions.

Geetha had titled the audio-visual as 'The Third Eye', which I liked. The twelve students, the stars of the evening were clad in beautiful, identical churidhar sets, a gift from Geetha. The college had expected 100 students, faculty and guests. Happily, more than 200 were there. The principal of Fatima College, Vasimalai of Dhan, Professor Venkataraman, the eminent historian of Madurai, and others spoke evocatively. Then the audio-visual was projected. Surprisingly, it began with my voice, humming the tune of 'Green Sleeves'. The narrative, with bell-like clarity was by Geetha, with frequent, interactive, spontaneous, unrehearsed, on the spot comments by me and others. The video ends with a haunting melody accompanying the pleasing visuals. At the end of the show there was prolonged applause. The twelve heroines of the evening were in high heavens. I was told that the visuals had been artistically taken. During the days that followed, excellent articles appeared in the media, both in English and in Tamil. Not surprisingly, I returned to Madras a very happy man, with a wide range of memories—especially those pertaining to 'The Third Eye', to be cherished.

Now let me take you, the reader, very briefly back to October 2008. After the launch of the tactile book, *The Very Hungry Caterpillar*, I wrote an appreciative letter to Shobha. After reading my letter, Shobha became interested in knowing more about my years with Mahe. She procured both of my books on Mahe. After reading them, she became even more interested in the way we met our challenges, while keeping our creative candles burning bright.

Karadi Tales has an imprint named Charka Audio Books, which narrated stories of great people like Mahatma Gandhi and J. R. D. Tata, in an imaginative way. Happily, she and Vishwanath decided to capture aspects of two ordinary people, Mahe and me, in a musical audiobook. I was jubilant when I learnt that the highly talented, deeply knowledgeable pianist, Anil Srinivasan, would be the music director of the musical audio book. Manasi, a poetess, took chunks of passages from my two books on Mahe and where necessary, wrote the script. The narration is by Jehangir in his resonant voice. Sharanya, the gifted poetess, spoke for Mahe and Kaushik, Shobha's son, for me.

The audiobook starts and ends with the same song, sung hauntingly by Vedanth. Excellent singers and instrumentalists made their own contributions to enrich the book.

The launch of the musical audiobook, held in August 2012, was well attended. I was told that there were 220 seats. At least fifty people, including the German consul general and his wife, had to stand. My ink portrait of Mahema, festooned with a garland of her favourite jasmine, hung prominently. Below the portrait stood our kuthu-vilakku. Five women lit the five wicks of the lamp. Anil Srinivasan played live snippets from the book. Shobha played a brief audio-visual piece. In her speech, Shobha, the brain behind this project, said that she wanted to create this audiobook because she felt that the lives of everyday heroes in our society should be celebrated.

Gopalkrishna Gandhi began his speech saying, 'The greatest gifts that can be given to anyone is the gift of a friend, and I cannot thank Madura and Ramachandran enough for giving me the gift of the friendship of Mahe and Mano.' N. Ram, in his speech, narrated humorous anecdotes culled from his long and deep friendship with Mahe and me. In response to his talk, I recalled an incident that happened in early 1986. Mahe and I visited a couple who lived in an apartment in the second floor of a building without a lift. Just when we were at the base of the staircase, a tall, handsome, strong, young man arrived at the scene. He too was visiting the couple. He and I bodily carried Mahema through flights of narrow stairs to the apartment. Of course, the young man was none other than N. Ram. And this was the very first time that we met him. This unconventional first meeting blossomed into a lifelong friendship.

V. Sriram told the audience that he moved into Madras from Calcutta in the early 1990s. He saw in the printed media, enthusiastic articles about our heritage greeting cards. When he visited our house to procure the cards, he was utterly taken aback to find that the woman with an exuberant voice over the phone was a wheelchair bound quadriplegic. He had a long, lively conversation with her. He happily told the people in the jam-packed hall that he simply fell in love with her. And he is a few months younger than our daughter Suja! Throughout the programme, there were gales of laughter. A journalist reporting the launch wrote, '....laughter is a defining feature of the Devadoss's marriage.'

I told the audience that Anil's musical arrangement in the book was haunting. The accomplished pianist's response was that the music was not as haunting as the story in the audiobook. Later, I heard that there were tears aplenty too.

During the following years, many good events and some not so good have continued to happen.

A course requirement of the Government College of Fine Arts of Egmore in Madras is that the student should submit a thesis in a book format on an artist's artwork. Nithya Raju, in 2007, wrote a 150-page piece on me and my ink drawings titled, 'Creative Wonders in Black and White' which was much appreciated. A course requirement for the MA Literature students of Lady Doak College at Madurai were that they should prepare an in depth report of a book or two of a literary figure. Bharathi Srinivasan, in 2010, chose *Green Well Years* and *A Poem to Courage*. Her eighty-page project report entitled, 'The Triumph of Human Spirit and Love over Adversity' was awarded the best project of the year.

Besides, I received invitations galore from schools, colleges, confederations, clubs, societies, festivals, institutions, and private companies to give speeches, make PowerPoint presentations and have interactive sessions. I also received awards for lifetime achievements for distinguished service and many more.

My dear friend Joan offered to write about just a few of them in her own style. I feel happy that an epilogue by Joan is included in this book.

So, I decided to end the book with the concluding, poignant words by Manasi in Jehangir's voice, in the musical audio book, *Quiet Courage* launched in August 2012.

The house that Manohar and Mahema lived in has now been renamed 'Mahema', with Mahema's own signature

inscribed on the nameplate. Manohar still lives there....
Manohar often visits Madurai and finds much joy in his
boyhood haunts.... He remembers his promise to Mahema
and lives life as fully and joyously as possible. But with
his every breath there is Mahema. His conversations are
sprinkled with references to the woman he married, loved
and cared for.

On the western entrance of their sprawling house, there
is a frangipani tree in full bloom over which a flowering
bougainvillea cascades like a bridal veil. The frangipani
flowers fall abundantly from the tree. Manohar is struck
by how closely the petals resemble the shape and colour
of the lamp flame. The five petals of the flower spread
out gloriously like the five flames of the brass lamp. For
Manohar, the flower and lamp together, represent his
Mahema, broken yet beautiful, fragile yet strong, accepting
yet defiant and perennially glorious.

EPILOGUE

I've had the privilege of working and interacting closely with Mano for over thirty years. In this span of time, I've learnt to lean heavily on what I call his 'inner eye'. You can be all spiritual about it and call it the third eye, or you can just apply science to it and reason that, in the absence of external vision, he has finely honed the skill of being able to 'see' something without seeing it physically.

Very often, I've recounted to him some problem or situation that I happen to find myself in, and he's always unerringly put his finger on the crux of it—and there you have the solution. Conversely, when he recounts a story, (and few can do that better than him) you can literally see it happening in marvellous technicolour in front of you, replete with sound and light effects.

So, as I set out to describe some of the events that have happened in the latter half of his life, I know that it won't matter if I have not been physically present at all of them, because I've 'seen' them through his eyes. And seeing something with his vision is often better than seeing it yourself, because of the many subtexts and layers of detail that he perceives with his inner vision and from the hidden inflexions in voices and meanings that he hears. And so the overall picture that emerges is nuanced and loaded with subtle strokes and shades, much like the trees or buildings that he used to lovingly sketch.

Among the happy occasions that we have been together, laughing, chatting, reminiscing, Mano's birthdays always stand out vividly. Right from the time Mahema used to plan and execute surprises for his birthday, and make me an accomplice in the proceedings, to the present years, we all enjoy cooking up a surprise for his birthday, sometimes literally so. As on the occasion when she (Mahema) put together a scrapbook for him, thoughtfully chronicling his years as the foremost battery technologist, and the birthday which coincided with the year he retired from Standard Batteries.

After her passing too, her gentle spirit hovers over her beautiful home, rewarding us with happy moments galore. One such happy memory is of the time Suja arranged a group of friends to turn up for a surprise party at the Santhome House. My niece Preethi baked a very 'arty' cake, the idea for which was given by my daughter Deepika. The cake was shaped like an artist's palette. Each splotch of colour on the palette represented a different aspect of his unique life—his passion for chemistry, art, writing, music, cooking, inspirational speaking—all in 3D, edible models. And on it we wrote, 'Happy birthday to the Man(o) of many hues'. Many of Ketan's friends and their parents who were present, felt that the cake was an excellent concept. We eventually let the children choose which model they wanted to eat, and we cut up and gave them that piece.

Mano's seventy-ninth birthday was again spent in the company of youngsters, this time from a school called HLC International, run by the Mahesh family. The children, as part of a project, were asked to go to different places to meet up with service-minded people, interact with them for about six hours each for two days, and to prepare a presentation based on their observations. About twelve students of class 7 and 8 came on the 10th and 11th of September, accompanied by three teachers. They were not told that the tenth was Mano's birthday. However, on both days, they were served homemade cake and biscuits, courtesy Sheila, Mano's friend and long-term associate.

On 22 September, the students were asked to showcase their

findings. Mano and the other persons interviewed were the guests of honour. The children, to highlight Mano's unique story, presented a skit, which touched him immensely. Two girls played Mahema's part, one before and one after the accident. A wheelchair-bound girl fittingly played the part of the quadriplegic Mahema. They also showed some clippings. As in the case of the skits, the clippings featuring Mano were the most endearing and also the longest. All the guests received unique and handmade gifts from the children. Mano received a glass painting of butterflies, his favourite theme in recent times, and also his portrait.

A very special event that happened at the time was that Chitra, Vara, and Kannamma, the three sisters of the Aravind Eye Hospital family, unanimously decided to donate ₹9.38 lakhs, realized from the sale of a common property, to the Mahema Devadoss Endowment fund at Aravind. What a fabulous birthday gift! Mano, in writing and telling his close circle of friends about it, declared that Mahe must be smiling so much in heaven that her lips and cheeks must be surely aching. And we all were only too happy to acquiesce.

His eightieth birthday was celebrated in Madurai, fittingly so—and, with the Madurai Aravind Eye Hospital family, with whom he shares a special bond. It was a happy coincidence that he happened to be in Madurai on the day. There was a note of palpable excitement in Chitra's (wife of Thulasiraj, ED, Aravind Eye Hospital) voice that morning when she asked Mano to keep the evening free. This she did because she knows that Mano's calendar is always chock-full whenever he visits Madurai. So, Mano was all dressed up and waiting, thinking that they were about to take him for dinner, and that, probably, some family members might join in.

What he was totally unprepared for was that all the family members, from the youngest upwards, were all present to give him a rousing reception. They had even thoughtfully assembled some of his close friends from Madurai, including his cousin Prema, and Pramila from SCILET. Both of the last-mentioned spoke on the occasion, with interesting vignettes from their long association with him, each narrative spiced up with some photographs displayed on the background monitor. Sanil, one of the Aravind officers, sang a specially composed song for the occasion. The karaoke track had been put together only the previous night, and very few of those present had heard it before. That made it sweeter and more moving. The song was called, 'Un Ninaivil Vazhgiren'. It translates to, 'I live with your memories'.

Mano had put together ₹35,000, which came from sundry book sales and donations from friends, for the Mahema Devadoss endowment fund. Thulasiraj and his brothers topped up the amount, to make it a total of a little over ₹1,00,000 on this special and memorable day.

Shortly before Mano's birthday in 2013, he received a very moving birthday gift. I still remember the note of excitement in his voice when he called to tell me the glad news. 'Joan, Badri (Dr Badrinath) called me up two days ago. And you know how he started off? He said, "Mano, I'm going to give you a punishment". The punishment was, I'd been selected to receive the very first M. S. Subbulakshmi Award for my service to the hospital!'

I was thrilled and overjoyed too, on hearing the glad news— because, receiving the first award in the name of the legend was an honour in itself. We fixed up for me to take him to the venue. I'd taken some trouble to dress up, and, as we alighted at Nethralaya, a cameraman took a very beautiful picture of the two of us. A lot of people complimented me on my sari, and Mano rued the fact that he couldn't see it.

As was usual, quite a few people came forward to greet Mano. One was Dr Prema Padmanabhan, eminent corneal surgeon. She laughingly pinched his cheeks, as if he was a small child.

His Excellency, the then Governor of Tamil Nadu, Dr K. Rosaiah, was the chief guest on the occasion of Nethralaya's Founder's Day. The other recipient of the award was Mrs Kausalya Appukutty.

Dr Badrinath, in his customary thoughtful way, had arranged for Mano to present a print of Mano's pen-and-ink drawing of

M. S. Subbulakshmi, to Dr K. Rosaiah. The exquisite lines of the black and white portrait highlighted the strength and beauty of the singer–philanthropist's face beautifully.

Suja, in an ethereal white dress, joined Mano on stage to receive the award, making it a complete picture. That happened on 9 September 2013, just a day short of Mano's seventy-seventh birthday. The award was, in his words, 'a splendid birthday gift'. For one thing, he discovered for himself that he was not as smart as he thought he was. When Ketan, his grandson, as a child of four, asked him how his sandwiches were always cut in neat geometrical shapes, and how he managed to cut meat into identical cubes, and yet not cut himself, Mano replied that he did not do so because he was smart.

Yet, on his seventy-seventh birthday, he slashed his finger while cutting a strawboard. His doctor-cousin, who came over to help him deal with the injury, teasingly asked whether he had decided to deviate from the time-honoured custom of cutting a cake and had, instead, cut his finger. She also gave him a birthday hug and kiss. Ah, he thought to himself, everything has its compensations. While telling me about this incident, he also added, with a nudge and a wink, 'unfortunately, all my injuries heal pretty fast, so I couldn't even show it off to more women and get more hugs and kisses!'

While we're on the subject of kisses, here's one more such incident: Mano was pleasantly surprised to receive a visit one day from a group of seventh standard schoolgirls from Rosary Matriculation School, which incidentally, shares a common compound wall with him. These girls rang the doorbell and asked for his autograph, because, they said, the English teacher was teaching his 'lesson', and they really loved it. It was news to Mano that an excerpt from his book had even been included in the Government-prescribed supplementary textbook for the year. Nevertheless, he was profoundly moved and thrilled to hear that they had taken the trouble to write, not only about him, but about his beloved Mahema and the tremendous odds that they valiantly battled against. The book was *Multiple Facets of*

My Madurai, and the lesson in question was 'Yaanaimalai'. One of the questions at the end of the piece, reproduced with drawings, went like this, 'Notice the language used. What makes it beautiful?'

Small groups of students in this age group did visit him for quite some time after that. One afternoon, two girls came and had a lively discussion with him. When leaving, one of them gave him a kiss on his cheek and said, 'I love you, thatha.' This apparently encouraged the other, less outgoing one, to do the same. Mano was pleasantly surprised to see small children of that age being so forthcoming. He, on the other hand, is generous with the hugs. They're his way of connecting to the outside world. Go any day, any time to meet him, and you can be sure of being enveloped in a warm hug. We, his friends, wouldn't have him any other way.

Another thing we wouldn't want to ever change is that deep baritone voice saying, 'Manohar Devadoss', when he answers the phone. What I didn't know was that he is also adept at wolf-whistling. How I came to know was when he attended the college day celebrations of American College, Madurai, his alma mater, as the guest of honour. He was excited when someone told him that they had put up an illuminated blow-up of that impressive picture of himself pushing Mahema in her wheelchair. As he walked up to the dais, he was even more overcome to hear wolf-whistles and cheers from among the 3,000-strong audience.

When he stood up to address them, he started by saying that he could also wolf-whistle. He demonstrated this over the mike, much to the joy of the young audience. He then went on to state that he had, in all his life, whistled at only two women—his wife, and the bursar of the college, Professor Monica, who happened to be then standing next to him. How he happened to do this, egged on by Professor Monica and Professor Justin, is another story in itself. Many of the professors who met him later told him that this was the first time in all their college day celebrations that a special guest wolf-whistled from the podium.

Mano's was quite an unconventional speech in many ways. He

spoke of his childhood in Madurai, stressing on his stint at American College from 1953 to 1957. He claimed that many of his batchmates had been very unhappy when Lady Doak College opened its gates, because, the lady students who would have joined American College went there. However, this did not affect Mano because American College still admitted lady students in physics and chemistry—and he was majoring in chemistry. Some of his lady classmates were beauties, according to Mano especially a girl called Bhavani. He used to amuse himself during lectures by discreetly sketching her face in his notebook. A lecturer once caught him at it and, instead of admonishing him, went to the extent of praising him for his artistic skills. Such was the liberal atmosphere that prevailed then.

Many of the buildings of the college, claimed Mano, were the most beautiful ones among all college campuses in Tamil Nadu that he'd ever seen. In fact, he's immortalized a few of them in his drawings, especially the College chapel. It was also at SCILET, an institution run by the same college, that he first met Thulasiraj and Chitra of Aravind Eye Hospital, with whom he forged a lifelong friendship. Mano also dwelt briefly on Mahema's handicap, their life after the accident, his own setback, and on how humour, laced with creativity, keeps him going. He ended to wild applause.

Joe D'Cruz, the chief guest, who spoke after him, praised him lavishly. Later, M. D. Christober, the college principal, called him and said that many of the students had conveyed their gratitude to him for having invited such a noble and inspiring guest. Well, we're not surprised!

Madurai, as I've already mentioned earlier, holds a very special place in Mano's heart. He grabs any opportunity to go there. So, when Aravind Eye Hospital released the Tamil edition of a book on the extraordinary life of the late Dr G. V., founder of the hospital, Mano was invited to be the chief guest. He was most happy to be there on the occasion. Speaking in chaste Tamil, Mano mentioned that it was ironic that the book entitled *A Journey Towards Light* was being released by a person (himself) who was journeying towards darkness. Nevertheless, he added, his heart was ever-shining.

Incidentally, on account of this visit, he met Mr Kumaraswamy, who helped with the translation. The seed for the present book was sown then, because it was the Nagalakshmi–Kumaraswamy couple who suggested that Mano should begin work on a non-fictional narrative of his own life story.

It was raining heavily in Chennai when Mano boarded the flight to Madurai to take part in twin programmes—one, a heritage walk, based on his book *Green Well Years*, organized by the Dhan Foundation, and the other, an art event organized by Aravind Eye Hospital. The heritage walk, which started at 7 a.m., went on till 9 a.m., and spanned some of the simple landmarks featured in *Green Well Years*, noteworthy among them being the Madurai junction, the Regal Talkies, his alma maters Sethupathi School and American College, and the Collector's Office, where he worked as a clerk for three months. He enlivened the walk by playing the harmonica and his whistling, much to the delight of the heritage enthusiasts who had gathered for the walk. He returned to Chennai amidst pouring rain, landing just an hour before the airport was closed down completely. A providential escape, indeed, because the entire city was brought to its knees in a matter of hours. Heritage or high rise building—they all stood inundated.

I doubt if anyone has sketched the heritage buildings of Chennai as passionately as Mano. Hence, when the Madras Week celebrations were underway, it came as no surprise that he was invited, along with a host of other Chennai buffs, to address an audience of Chennaiites. He found himself chatting with the Nawab of Arcot, and the Kumararani of Chettinad, Meena Muthiah. He remarked that it was not every day that he, a commoner, got to rub shoulders with royalty and that too, with a rani on one side and a nawab on the other. And, he added, it spoke enormously for the religious unity of Madras, that a Hindu, (the rani) a Christian, (Mano) and a Muslim (the nawab) should share the same dais. Later, the Nawab of Arcot paraphrased Mano's remarks in his speech, to enthusiastic applause.

Another such incident, featuring a royal, happened in early

2014. The phone rang, and the voice at the other end said, 'Babaji from Thanjavur speaking.' Mano asked if he was, indeed, speaking to the Prince of Thanjavur. The answer was in the affirmative. Mano then asked what he, a man from Pandianadu, had done to merit such an honour as a call from the Prince of Thanjavur. The prince laughingly replied that culture and heritage had no barriers. He had been fascinated by his reading of *From an Artist's Perspective*, ever since it was presented to him at the National Conference of Architects, held at Chennai. This, apparently, was not his first encounter with the books of Mano. On an earlier occasion, Dr Badrinath presented a copy of *Multiple Facets of My Madurai* to the Prince of Thanjavur, and spoke glowingly about Mano. The purpose of the present call was to invite Mano to make a PowerPoint presentation about his art and books, with special reference to Madurai.

Mano stayed briefly at the palace, along with his architect friend Balaji. After a delicious tea in the palace grounds, Mano left early for the venue with the prince. He entered the hallowed precincts of the famed Brihadeeswara Temple at about 6.15 p.m. For the two preceding years, he had hardly been able to see anything in the outside world. But, in the soft red-gold glow of the setting sun, he saw, briefly, but clearly, the silhouette of the vimanam of the temple. He felt truly blessed because of the time at which he entered the compound. If he had gone there even ten minutes earlier, the harsh light would have obscured everything. Ten minutes later, and darkness would have dimmed his sight. So the timing seemed to have been divinely ordained.

As always, the presentation went off well. When he boarded the train, he felt happy and light-hearted, though his suitcase was heavy with gifts.

To say that Mano continues to be busier than ever, ten years after Mahema's passing, would not be an exaggeration. Writing, sketching, music lessons, awards, speeches, PowerPoint presentations, social gatherings.... His calendar is crammed with appointments. In the midst of all these, he finds time to whip up tasty meals for friends like me. Precious interludes in the mad cacophony of life, these are moments to cherish and look forward when we unwind and laugh and talk nonstop about the whims and vagaries of our fellow human beings. We dwell happily on the blessings that we have received; we skim briefly over the brickbats that may have been flung at us.

So, each time that I've visited him, I've ended up adding more and more material to what was supposed to be a tiny epilogue, till Mano and I mutually decided that we had to draw a line somewhere. The stories that we have not been able fit in here would fill another book. As Suja rightly observed in her speech at the launch of *From an Artist's Perspective,* 'with Mano, you can be sure that another book is on the way. So, anyone who has missed this book release due to unavoidable circumstances can come for the next one.' Prophetic words, these, for here we are with his next labour of love.

I'm sure that you felt inspired by this chronicle from the heart, On behalf of all us, I thank you, dear Mano, for giving us the privilege of listening to a few notes from the rich cadence of your life. Let the music play on for many more years.

Joan Rajadas

ACKNOWLEDGEMENTS

In 2001, I handed over manuscripts of my second and third books to Padmanabhan, my publisher at East West Books, Madras. The second book, *Dreams, Seasons and Promises* is a colourful portfolio, a documentary essentially covering the period between 1963 and 1975. The third book, *A Poem to Courage*, is a biographical novel, describing the aftermath of our car accident with some flashbacks and fast-forwards, covering the period between 1972 and 1992. The book describes how my wife, Mahema, and I managed to lead happy, creative and giving lives, despite her quadriplegia and my failing eyesight. The book is also laced with ironic humour.

Padmanabhan (Paddu) liked both the books, but wondered as to why I wrote *A Poem to Courage* as fiction, when much of what I had written about in the book were true events. The true story would have greater value and appeal.

I weakly defended myself, observing that I wrote this book as a sequel to my first autobiographical novel, *Green Well Years* on growing up in Madurai. The two books are virtually a study in contrast, yet there were commonalities. I used the same name 'Sundar' for myself in both the books.

S. Muthiah, the much-admired citizen of Madras, during the

course of an address to a gathering in 2002, expressed his wish to see an omnibus volume of our real story.

A Poem to Courage ends with an event in 1992. Since then, despite the multitude of problems that kept visiting us, Mahema and I led extraordinarily happy lives. Our creative candles were all aglow, even brighter than before. An increasing number of wonderful people became our lifelong beloved friends. The love and support that we received from them cheered and sustained us. Many interesting incidents kept happening, and there was no dearth of good humour.

So, as Muthu observed, an omnibus volume, now covering the entire period, including the period after Mahema's passing, is well worth recording. Many, many dear ones—especially the Nagalakshmi Kumarasamy couple, who do marriage counselling—strongly felt that such a book would be fascinating and highly inspirational.

So, I worked diligently on the manuscript and completed it in two years. I was satisfied. But, when I had to write negatively about some people and events, I camouflaged the identities, while preserving the contents unaltered.

I sent the first draft to the Nagalakshmi Kumarasamy couple. They felt that if a movie of our story were made, it might win the Academy Awards! As I worked on the manuscript, many many happy submerged memories of wonderful, even fascinating events, came back into sharp focus repeatedly in my mind. These were in themselves, my awards and rewards.

The Ministry of Home Affairs officially announced on 25 January 2020 that I have been one among those selected for the Padma Shri Award. This made me very happy. When David Davidar, the publisher of Aleph Book Company, took the decision to fast-track the publication of this book, I became happier.

I thank the Nagalakshmi Kumarasamy couple for persuading me to write this book. I thank Raghini Badhrinarayanan, Professor Geetha Ravi, and Professor Shyamala Narayan for proofreading and editing the manuscript. I am thankful to Joan Rajadas for ever so closely working with me on this project. I thank Sheila D' Souza for repeatedly typing the text. I also thank Chitra Thulasiraj for all the support I received from her. I specially thank M. Gowri for meticulously making the additions, changes, and corrections in the final script.

Manohar Devadoss
Chennai
August 2020